INVISIBLE HAWKEYES

INVISIBLE
HAWKEYES

*African Americans
at the University of Iowa during
the Long Civil Rights Era*

* * *

EDITED BY

LENA M. HILL AND MICHAEL D. HILL

* * *

UNIVERSITY OF IOWA PRESS, IOWA CITY

University of Iowa Press, Iowa City 52242
Copyright © 2016 by the University of Iowa Press
www.uiowapress.org
Printed in the United States of America

Design by April Leidig

The University of Iowa Press is a member of Green Press Initiative
and is committed to preserving natural resources.

Printed on acid-free paper

Library of Congress Cataloging-in-Publication Data
is on file at the Library of Congress.

ISBN: 978-1-60938-441-8 (pbk)
ISBN: 978-1-60938-442-5 (ebk)

This book is dedicated to
Jewel Prestage and
Chuck Swanson

CONTENTS

Acknowledgments ix

INTRODUCTION
Hidden Names and Complex Fates:
Black Students Who Integrated the University of Iowa
Lena M. Hill

1

CHAPTER ONE
"Excellent Work and Superior Traits of Personality":
Composing an Integrated Music Department
Brian Hallstoos

17

TESTIMONIAL ONE
I Never Thought of Myself as an Outsider
Dianna Penny

45

CHAPTER TWO
The Fine Art of Representing Black Heritage:
Elizabeth Catlett and Iowa, 1938–1940
Kathleen A. Edwards

51

TESTIMONIAL TWO
A Different Kind of Beauty Contest
Dora Martin Berry

67

CHAPTER THREE
Staging Authentic African American Character:
Regionalism, Race, and UI Theater
Lena M. Hill

75

TESTIMONIAL THREE
Iowa Was One More Step toward My Future
Lois Eichaker
103

CHAPTER FOUR
Obscured Traditions:
Blacks at the Iowa Writers' Workshop, 1940–1965
Michael D. Hill
107

TESTIMONIAL FOUR
Going the Distance
Theodore "Ted" Wheeler
135

CHAPTER FIVE
"Tireless Partners and Skilled Competitors":
Seeing UI's Black Male Athletes, 1934–1960
Richard M. Breaux
141

TESTIMONIAL FIVE
The Two-Edged Sword
Don Tucker
169

CONCLUSION
An Indivisible Legacy:
Iowa and the Conscience of Democracy
Michael D. Hill
175

About the Contributors 187

Notes 189

Index 215

ACKNOWLEDGMENTS

This book reflects the rewards of collaboration. At base, it strives to restore black students to their rightful place in the University of Iowa's legacy. This restoration required insights from rigorous research and lived experience. Thus, we sought both scholarly chapters and firsthand testimonials. For accomplishing the forceful exhibition that follows, we are grateful to Dora Martin Berry, Richard Breaux, Kathy Edwards, Lois Eichaker, Brian Hallstoos, Dianna Penny, Don Tucker, and Ted Wheeler. Your contributions made this book a reality, and we appreciate your inspiring efforts.

This project grew out of the 2011 residency at UI, "Iowa and *Invisible Man*: Making Blackness Visible." We are grateful to the many partners who supported that week of events: Hancher, the office of the provost, the University of Iowa libraries, the Obermann Center for Advanced Studies, the chief diversity office, the Iowa House Hotel, the program in African American studies, the English department, the Center for Teaching, the African American Council, Humanities Iowa, the history department, and the American studies department. We thank Christopher McElroen for proposing the very idea of the residency. The University of Iowa Press encouraged us to transform this week of remarkable programs into more permanent meditations. For their enduring belief in this book, we are grateful to Elisabeth Chretien, Catherine Cocks, Allison Means, and Susan Hill Newton. Numerous libraries and archives enabled the research at the heart of this collection. In particular, we recognize the University of Iowa special collections and university archives and the Library of Congress. We greatly appreciate the research support granted by Dean Chaden Djalali and Provost Barry Butler, as well as the scholarly community and delightful workspace provided by the Obermann Center Fellows-In-Residence program. John Callahan and the Ralph Ellison Trust have been encouraging throughout the completion of this volume.

This book commenced and concluded serendipitously. In the summer of 2013, we enjoyed two long, meandering conversations with Jewel Prestage. Professor Prestage offered a luminous view of the black experience at UI, and her guidance, advice, and wisdom directed us down the road of discovery that led to this collection. She passed before its publication; nonetheless, this book could not have been written without her. We are similarly indebted to Chuck Swanson. His inimitable, smart, and gracious support provided the first foundation for this project, and Chuck's unyielding determination to tell the UI story fully and artistically encouraged our work. We are humbled by his friendship and inspired by his creativity. Lastly, Caitlyn and Michael Carl ceded time so that Mommy and Daddy could do this vital work. We hope that the fruits of our labors will justify your sacrifices.

INTRODUCTION

LENA M. HILL

. . .

HIDDEN NAMES AND COMPLEX FATES

Black Students Who Integrated the University of Iowa

. . .

The decision to launch the 2012 world premiere stage adaptation of Ralph Ellison's *Invisible Man* with a residency at the University of Iowa (UI) may have surprised the casual observer. But for Chuck Swanson, the director of UI's Hancher multidisciplinary performing arts presenter, and Christopher McElroen, the producer and director of the play, the partnership made perfect sense. The university's artistic and athletic performance programs boast a rich if unheralded history of frontline action in the struggle for civil rights, and both Fanny and Ralph Ellison traveled paths that brought them to Iowa City. In fall 1934, Fanny enrolled as a junior in the Department of Speech and Dramatic Art. Although she later described Iowa as a school "full of prejudice" where "things were awkward for all Negro students," as a young woman she persevered and graduated in 1936.[1] Ralph never attended UI, but his 1959 visit culminated with a job offer to become the Iowa Writers' Workshop's first African American faculty member. He declined, in no small part because of Fanny's ambivalent memories,[2] yet he maintained warm relations with workshop notables such as Vance Bourjaily. The dual role Iowa played in the Ellisons' lives — both as a site of educational opportunity and testament to professional accomplishment and as a place embodying the persistence of midcentury racial inequality — offers an instructive example of the complicated role that large white public universities played in aiding the nation's faltering steps toward becoming a pluralistic society.

Like the Ellisons' little-discussed ties to the University of Iowa, the names and complex sojourns of the black students who integrated its arts departments and athletic programs during the difficult years of the civil rights movement too often remain hidden or ambiguous. UI changed between the 1930s and the 1960s. Prodded by the deanship of Carl Seashore and the progressiveness of departmental leaders such as Edward C. Mabie, Philip Greeley Clapp, Grant Wood, and Paul Engle, as well as coaches such as George Bresnahan and Francis Cretzmeyer, the school's reputation as a training ground for racially diverse creative artists and athletes grew. This book uncovers the details of this story. As these white male professors and coaches refined the infrastructure that allowed Iowa to assume a leading role in theater, music, studio art, creative writing, and athletics, their efforts unfolded in the context of an increasing African American enrollment at the university.[3] The parallel development of UI arts departments and sports programs alongside the growing numbers of black students discloses an underexplored subplot in the university's history. By analyzing this relationship, *Invisible Hawkeyes: African Americans at the University of Iowa during the Long Civil Rights Era* not only reinforces Iowa's leadership in educating creative artists and athletes but also illustrates how local cases of black faces in white spaces anticipated and echoed national scenes of interracial striving and accomplishment.

Notwithstanding resonances with nationwide trends, the reality of integration looked different at UI than it appeared across the most vehemently Jim Crow southern and midwestern states. The State University of Iowa, as the University of Iowa was known at the time, admitted a black law student as early as 1878[4]; thus, unlike the University of Missouri or the University of Oklahoma, it never became a target of the National Association for the Advancement of Colored People (NAACP) Legal Defense Fund's assault on segregation.[5] Although this legacy of openness distinguished UI from schools that forcibly integrated, it did not protect the university from the challenges posed by a multiracial student body. By examining the quieter collisions between Iowa's polite midwestern progressivism and African American students' determined ambition, *Invisible Hawkeyes* focuses attention beyond the James Merediths of the world.[6] We enlarge the frame to insist on the importance of pondering a more complete picture that emerges outside the realm of big midwestern cities such as Detroit, Saint Louis, and Chicago or the colleges and universities that denied blacks admission. By looking at UI and a smaller college town like Iowa City, we unearth how fraught moments of interracial collaboration, meritocratic advancement, and institutional insensitivity

FIG. 1. Fanny Ellison in her graduation gown, University of Iowa, July 1936. Photograph from the Ralph Ellison Papers (PR 13 CN 2010: 045 Container 1 Folder 10), US Library of Congress, Prints and Photographs Division. Courtesy of the Ralph and Fanny Ellison Charitable Trust.

FIG. 2. Ralph Ellison (*second from right*) at the University of Iowa, c. 1960. Photograph by George T. Henry, courtesy of Bettina Bourjaily. Used with permission from the Ralph and Fanny Ellison Charitable Trust.

deepen our understanding of the painful conversion of the United States into a diverse republic committed to racial equality. In contemplating the experiences of black students in arts programs and athletics between the 1930s and the 1960s, we note that far from being marginal to the progress of white institutions of higher learning, race sits at the center of their evolution into flagship examples of peaceful yet painful racial integration and exceptional training. The reality of Fanny's time at Iowa considered together with Ralph's trenchant commentary on African Americans' importance to achieving US democratic ideals make the Ellisons apt guides for framing UI's special contribution to resolving the country's racial drama.

The unique role that artistic and athletic performance occupied in acclimating the midwestern white campus to interacting with African Americans is not surprising considering broader national currents. The civil rights movement used Mahalia Jackson's voice, Sidney Poitier's sophistication, and Harry Belafonte's magnetism to advance the work of creating a participatory democracy. Similarly, the presence of accomplished black students performing in musical concerts, participating in visual art exhibitions, acting on stage, publishing literature, and competing on sports fields forced white students, instructors, and administrators to confront their undeniable intellect and talent. In contradistinction to the work completed in traditional academic units, these students' contributions to the university community burst beyond the walls of their individual units and primary spheres of experience to reach a much larger audience both on campus and in the city and nation beyond its boundaries. Thus, they also enhanced Iowa's emerging status as a forward-thinking artistic and athletic powerhouse. Indeed, their presence alongside the native sons and daughters enrolled at Iowa challenged stereotypes that dismissed the university as flat, naive, and bereft of aesthetic urbanity as coastal Americans imagined the flyover region it called home. To do justice to this story, we expand our frame to the years leading up to the 1940 founding of the NAACP Legal Defense and Educational Fund and concluding with the 1968 assassination of Martin Luther King Jr., thereby spotlighting the most intense years of the desegregation struggle. This integrative impulse that we highlight, together with the famed work ethic and cultural style that made the Midwest an avatar of the American spirit, sought to lead the way to the nation's attainment of the founding ideals it proudly trumpeted yet rarely realized.

This leadership was no easy task. Philip G. Hubbard — the university's first tenured black American professor — designated the years before 1960

UI's "pre-human rights era."[7] Hubbard argues that from the 1850s well into the 1950s, "the presence of African Americans in the [UI] community was accepted only to the extent defined by the least tolerant member of the majority." Fleshing out his position, he opined, "The University felt no responsibility to encourage incorporation of the 'visitors' into its life. . . . It was this 'benign neglect'. . . that permitted discriminatory practices with no basis in formal policy."[8] Hubbard's fifty-year UI tenure granted him good vantages from which to see the school's racial revelations. What is more, the period he surveyed presented a changing landscape.

In the 1930s, Iowa sought to assert its modernity by supplementing its regionalist reputation with national and international preoccupations. These assertions took the form of a curricular focus on European theorists, a university organization that embraced emerging fields such as communication studies, and an educational philosophy that viewed creative work as rigorous and degree worthy. *Invisible Hawkeyes* contemplates how the modernization of Iowa looks when the black presence at UI is viewed as a part of the university's desire to be an urbane, progressive institution. Hubbard rightly points out that Iowa's attitude toward its black students at the mid-twentieth century vacillated between tolerant indifference and cautious support. He notes that his advisors in the engineering department prove that before such formal programs as affirmative action and Opportunity at Iowa, "rigorous academic administrators were able to select and evaluate students without" manifesting racial prejudice.[9] Likewise, the varied experiences of black students who studied as undergraduates and graduates in the university's arts departments and participated in its athletic programs unveil the hidden levers that maintained Iowa's pioneering place in American race relations. The significance of their story does not, however, end in Iowa City. To discover the full implications of their legacy, we must retrace the roads that led toward and away from the State University of Iowa.

Iowa and "the Jug": The Pipeline to Historically Black Colleges and Universities

In his 1963 essay "The World and the Jug," Ralph Ellison accuses the white liberal critic Irving Howe of misunderstanding the reality of African American experiences within racially segregated spaces. Howe, Ellison asserts, sees "segregation as an opaque steel jug with the Negroes inside waiting for some black messiah to come along and blow the cork." Begging to differ, Ellison explains, "If we are in a jug it is transparent, not opaque, and one is allowed not only to see outside but to read what is going on out there, and to make identification as to values and human quality."[10] Ellison's metaphor fittingly captures the relationship between historically black colleges and universities (HBCUs) and the wider world of higher education. Most HBCUs were founded after the American Civil War as land-grant institutions to address the reality of a segregated South that denied blacks access to white state colleges and universities. The Morrill Act of 1890 expanded the original 1862 act to insist that states either "provide separate institutions for Blacks or access to state public White colleges and universities." The revised law also demanded "a just and equitable division of funds to be received under this act between one college for white students and one institution for colored students."[11] As a result of these cases, by 1902 the original eighteen black land-grant institutions had grown to eighty-five schools established expressly to educate African Americans.

As the nation marched toward midcentury integration, the vast majority of African American students continued to attend predominantly black institutions of higher learning. A number of factors, however, kept them highly attuned to the innovative, forward-looking progress at majority white colleges and universities. For starters, HBCUs' ongoing struggle to maintain their accreditation inspired both faculty members and students to seek additional opportunities to work toward graduate degrees. Most black students took advantage of scholarships supporting African Americans who pursued advanced coursework out of state. Notwithstanding landmark cases such as *Pearson et al. v. Murray* in 1935 and *Lloyd Gaines v. S. W. Canada and the University of Missouri* in 1938, two cases that sought to push segregated states toward admitting black students, most southern and border states continued to flout federal law by providing the meager out-of-state scholarships that had become a common solution to satisfying the legal demands of separate but equal.[12] The difficulty posed by the inadequate support on which students were forced to depend as they traveled away from home failed to deter them from enrolling in out-of-state colleges and universities. In 1943, only twelve HBCUs in the South offered graduate work leading to a master's degree, and no black institutions offered doctoral degrees before 1954, so African American students had little choice but to pursue advanced degree work at out-of-state majority white institutions.[13]

Black students' ambitious gazes through the institutional jug of the HBCU led directly to their growing numbers in UI arts departments and athletic programs. As the first and final chapters of *Invisible Hawkeyes* highlight, the legal reality of the Jim Crow South initiated the creation of an enduring pipeline to Iowa. In Brian Hallstoos's examination of the impact that such laws and practices had in Oklahoma and Texas in particular — two of the earliest states to establish a pipeline between their HBCUs and the University of Iowa music department — he explores the consequences of these segregationist laws. Indeed, their impact stretched far beyond the story of Iowa since by 1937, a number of states embraced the practice of supplementing out-of-state graduate work for minority candidates instead of opening their doors to black students. In addition to Oklahoma, Maryland, Missouri, Tennessee, Virginia, and West Virginia all supported African Americans' quest to attain professional schooling beyond their state borders.[14] By the 1960s, UI formalized its relationship with HBCUs through partnerships with Rust College in Mississippi and LeMoyne College in Tennessee. These alliances stemmed from Iowa's acceptance of federal funds under a provision of the Higher Education Act of 1965 and solidified the university's emergence as an active recruiter of black students.

Of course, both the state of Iowa and the university had attracted African Americans long before the civil rights era. Although Iowa never officially sanctioned slavery, a few early settlers brought black slaves with them to the new territory. The state was home to a small population of African Americans before the Civil War, but as coal mining grew during the 1880s, so did the numbers of black Iowans. During this time, one large coal-mining town, Buxton, boasted a population of more than 5,000, and a majority of these Iowans were black. By 1900, census figures placed the population of Iowa at 840,739, and 12,693 of these residents were listed as "Negro." The small numbers of African Americans in Iowa made it a generally quiet site when it came to race relations. Although the university did not admit black students when it opened in 1847, an 1867 Iowa Supreme Court decision made it illegal to exclude students based on their race. This decision cleared the way for Alexander G. Clark to become the first African American to graduate from the University of Iowa in 1879. By the 1930s, the black population of Iowa had grown to 14,426, and most of these citizens lived in Des Moines, Sioux City, Waterloo, and Davenport.[15]

Still, UI became a destination of choice for black students coming from outside of Iowa as early as the 1930s, and the school's rapidly growing performing arts departments proved a significant stimulus for African Americans' increasing interest. Fanny Ellison came to Iowa City in part because word of Iowa's bustling drama scene reached the Depression-era arts organizations in Chicago. By the late 1930s and early 1940s, Thomas Pawley, Elizabeth Catlett, Oscar Anderson Fuller, and Arthur Lamb were creating what would become a well-trodden path between HBCUs and UI. This pipeline flowed both ways as these students often returned to HBCUs to begin their teaching careers. Even as they "were discouraged by their major professors from returning to the south" — mentors who effectually counseled them against working at HBCUs — African Americans who received their master's and PhD degrees felt a "commitment to the education of African American students, and [to] historically Black institutions."[16] Their convictions directly reflected a desire to promote expanded access to the democratic possibilities of the United States. In the words of Hubbard, black graduates of UI advanced degree programs contributed significantly to "staffing the historically black colleges and universities."[17]

Their return to HBCUs in teaching capacities also reflected the midwestern work ethic that their UI instructors instilled in all their students regardless of race. Building on the sturdy foundation of the deep commitment to student development instilled at HBCUs, UI professors such as Clapp and Engle — men who enjoyed long careers as professors even as they continued to produce impressive creative work — served as models for the African American students they instructed. Most black graduates of UI's performing arts programs, as well as many male athletes, boasted distinguished careers as artists and sportsmen. Their legacy also included bold instructional efforts in the classroom and on athletic fields. Although many of these students enjoyed star status at the pinnacle of their careers, their heartland training reminded them to pair their singular talent with a humble dedication to hard work. Graduates such as Elizabeth Catlett and Margaret Walker demonstrate that artistic success and celebrity status almost never inspired entitlement mentalities in UI African American graduates. Instead, these students completed their programs and accepted the sobering, if rewarding, responsibility of educating the race's next generation. What is more, the irony of black excellence in the Jim Crow era facilitated their participation in the civil rights struggle as teachers. Like their peers who became doctors, lawyers, and nurses, performing artists and athletes were pressed into service as racial ambassadors. Their teaching also assumed the responsibilities of freedom fighting.

Ultimately, the mastery they boasted across diverse fields infused the HBCUs they joined after their graduation with new dynamism and accomplishment. As HBCUs filled their faculties with UI graduates, their ability to hire performing artists and athletes who enjoyed national and international reputations enhanced more than just their course offerings and team records. These hires gave black institutions prestige with state legislatures, national accrediting bodies, and global intellectual and sports communities. In turn, these schools' impressive profiles burnished their mission of educating the future. Thus, while the high-profile accounts of the Little Rock Nine and the Greensboro sit-ins risk suggesting that a black presence in a white space begins and ends the ordeal of integration, African American students at the University of Iowa demonstrate the ongoing processes within an integrating community. The interracial collaborations in its arts departments and athletic programs became a mirror of the convergences and divergences that attend the emergence of a pluralistic community. In many ways, these exchanges offer both a prelude to and an echo of the race relations sweeping across the nation in neighborhoods as well as on televisions and movie screens. The Iowa story explores the challenges of black presence in white environments that fully flower in the post–civil rights era. In unearthing this history, we recover the extraordinary impact African American graduates of UI made on the world beyond Iowa City.

"A Very Stern Discipline": Performing Black Excellence at UI

In the interview that Ellison eventually published as "A Very Stern Discipline" (1967), his advice to African Americans striving to be creative writers might easily be extended to black students of any creative art form. After admiringly quoting from a 1965 speech in which President Lyndon B. Johnson declared, "Your art is not a political weapon, yet much of what you do is profoundly political," Ellison offered valuable guidance to rising black artists.[18] He admonishes them to remember that they are "entering into a very stern discipline" that requires rigorous study; moreover, Ellison counsels minority artists to eschew merely "*talking* about" their art "or carrying picket signs, or sitting-in as a substitute activity." Finally, he cautions talented African Americans to "avoid the notion that" artists "require no education."[19] Although Ellison considered education in broad terms that stretch well beyond traditional academic institutions, he firmly advocated a commitment to learning more about US society as necessary to proving that "the integration of American society on the level of the imagination" remains a foundational task for black creative artists who seek to "help shape the values of large segments of a society which otherwise would not admit his existence, much less his right to participate or to judge."[20]

The black students who enrolled in Iowa's arts departments and competed athletically both anticipated and fulfilled Ellison's eloquent advice. They relished the stern disciplines they entered and considered achieving excellence the only option. Geneva Southall, a music student who received her doctorate from Iowa in 1966, drily observed that black students responded to racist indignities by being "so damn good that" the naysayers in their departments and across the campus "couldn't ignore them."[21] In other words, they let their performance speak on their behalf. Just as artists such as Paul Robeson and Marian Anderson famously triumphed over stereotypes of black inferiority, African American arts students and athletes demonstrated their exceptional talent at UI in terms that garnered attention and respect. In this way, their accomplishments echoed black celebrities between the 1930s and the 1960s who tended to be either performing artists or athletes. Their well-publicized performances in white spaces smoothed the way toward broader conceptions of a multiracial democracy. In addition to Robeson and Anderson, the fame of such celebrities as Cab Calloway, Lena Horne, Joe Louis, Jackie Robinson, and Althea Gibson justify this book's focus as a means of providing insight into the struggle surrounding integration. *Invisible Hawkeyes* recovers and commemorates African American arts students' and athletes' Iowa experiences to trumpet how stories of achievement in the midwestern university paved the way to the 1964 Civil Rights Act alongside famous black Americans *and* the marchers, freedom riders, and other activists who passionately fought for racial equality. These students, however, fought with what Jewel Prestage called "intellectual power"[22] and rigorously developed talent. They clearly understood their trailblazing position, but as Ellison urges, they sought opportunities at UI spurred first by their desire to excel in their disciplines.

The untold narratives of their training divulge the inspiring reality of relationships between black students and white instructors. The professors and coaches who invited, accepted, and even courted African American students played a significant role in developing the artistic and athletic gifts they brought to the UI community. Many black students discovered new opportunities for advancement at a college that boasted cutting-edge tools and resources not available at the high schools and HBCUs that provided their initial training ground. When Thomas Pawley arrived on Iowa's campus in 1937, he was astounded by the new theater building that featured all the bells and whistles necessary to establish the vanguard position of UI's Department of Speech and Dramatic Art.[23] But more important than the building was the theatrical philosophy advanced by Edward C. Mabie. His notion of experimental theater with an emphasis on regionalism and cultural specificity found voice in the works of the influential group of black students who matriculated through the program from the 1930s to the mid-1950s, the period of Mabie's tenure as chair of the department. Although Pawley did not view Mabie as a mentor, his aesthetic sensibility and pedagogical philosophy bore the marks of his Iowa degree branded by Mabie's theory of theater.

The relationship between the guidance of the professors and the excellent work produced by African American students tells a more intimate story of the consequences of midwestern integration on the campuses of white public universities. For instance, when Elizabeth Catlett reflects on Grant Wood's mentorship or when Leon Hicks alludes to Mauricio Lasansky's advice, they suggest that their sustained encounters with white male instructors led to artistic approaches that they otherwise may not have considered or might have lacked the confidence to pursue. Although Ralph Ellison describes a similar interracial tutorial when he credits T. S. Eliot with opening his eyes to the ways he could draw on black folk materials in his fictional explorations of black identity, Ellison's enlightenment occurred in the context of private reading. Catlett and Hicks, however, enjoyed daily, systematic interactions with master teachers. Consequently, their work benefited from a more rigorous exposure to the creative convictions of professors at the forefront of their fields. Yet even as their work matured under the influence of their teachers, these students' special knowledge of black culture made a top-down approach to their training impossible. In fact, the unique nature of the mentorships between black students and their white instructors highlights one more important aspect of the interracial microdramas unfolding on the UI stage.

After all, discussions of US segregation typically cast African Americans as rebelling against exclusionary practices that bar admission to white institutional fortresses hoarding rich resources of excellence. While the fundamentals of such reasoning ring true, accepting the totality of such an argument

necessitates naively interpreting integration as blacks gaining admission to
a valuable sanctum that exists solely within white spaces. *Invisible Hawkeyes*
complicates and thereby rectifies this story by filling its glaring gaps. As Professor James Washington poignantly declares, "The doctrine of integration
argued that African Americans needed to become as close to perfect copies of
white people as possible. This required the emasculation of their culture and
history. In order to do this, one had to infantilize African American history by
placing black people on a lower scale of historical development."[24] That this
was rarely the case at the State University of Iowa bears pondering. In contrast
to the prevailing narrative, black students and white instructors acknowledged
that relationships built upon reciprocity rather than dictation would be necessary to develop African American talent. As news of this attitude spread
beyond the heartland, black performing arts students and athletes enrolled
at UI in growing numbers. Although Iowa City could not promise its black
visitors a broad-minded environment beyond the campus, its classrooms and
sports venues provided settings and a cast of characters that facilitated black
student development in terms of mutual respect.

The consequences of these collaborative relations between black students
and white instructors reverberated through the careers of African American graduates in ways that influenced the nation. As a matter of fact, several
black UI graduates went on to play influential roles in the world of cultural
choreography. For instance, graduate of the Iowa Writers' Workshop Herbert
Nipson landed a position with *Ebony* that led to a career at the magazine's helm
for nearly forty years. Through his work with Johnson's flagship publication,
Nipson reached millions of readers, and as the head editor in charge of layout,
his aesthetic proclivities assumed a dominant role in marketing the magazine
to the public. Nipson's career demonstrates how skills acquired within white
higher education spaces were transferred and translated into highly influential
black enterprises. While the high-profile nature of Nipson's work spotlights
the transition of his UI training to a sphere of black cultural influence, his
position resonates with that of other black Iowa graduates. *Invisible Hawkeyes*
dwells on these remarkable experiences to uncover what they can tell us about
the subtler negotiations that a multicultural democracy demands. Through
chapters that touch on music, sculpture and printmaking, drama, creative
writing, and athletics, this book casts UI's hosting of black students between
the 1930s and the 1960s as a deeper reflection on the work that attends interracial cooperation. By considering the university's midwestern location and
its unique concerns with race and performance, this volume explores why

Iowa's mid-twentieth-century racial realities make it a weather vane for democracy. It seeks to excavate the experiences of a diverse group of students and, in the process, to make blackness visible. Its structure plays a key role in accomplishing this objective.

. . .

After this introduction, *Invisible Hawkeyes* unfolds in five chapters and a conclusion, with five testimonials from black alumni who attended UI from roughly 1935 to 1968 interspersed between chapters. This blend of historical analysis and memoir reflects a desire to think expansively about race, region, and American democracy. By braiding in observations from students who represent changing eras and different areas of study, we hope to refine our explorations of how encounters between black students and UI's arts and athletics programs relate to the national drama of pursuing integration. The contributors to this project facilitate such refinement. While the scholarly chapters provide vital research that draws on archival material, the testimonials offer intimate, firsthand perspectives of life at UI during a critical moment of US history and recover voices too often absent from the acknowledged record.

In chapter 1, Brian Hallstoos analyzes how the university's music department, led by Philip G. Clapp, became an early destination for the nation's most promising black music students. By chronicling the fascinating legal history surrounding segregation in higher education in Oklahoma and Texas, Hallstoos explains how an early pipeline formed between UI and two HBCUs. With this history, he uncovers Iowa's paradoxical attitude toward race relations: the university welcomed African American students into individual departments yet failed to protect them from the bigotry they faced both on and off campus.

Despite this maddening institutional inconsistency, Dianna Penny, the author of the first testimonial, spiritedly and convivially participated in numerous university musical groups when she commenced her undergraduate studies as a student in the fine arts department. Penny entered UI the same year that her family moved to Iowa City so that her father could take a position as pastor of a local church. This confluence of events uniquely colors her wide exposure to and participation in the arts. For Penny, Iowa City was a place of adventure as well as home.

Kathleen Edwards's chapter 2 deepens this focus on the visual arts training at UI. Studying Elizabeth Catlett, the first recipient of a master of fine arts degree at Iowa, Edwards in her sustained look at the renowned sculptor, painter, and printmaker verifies UI's early contributions to global cultural developments. Edwards presents a helpful history of Catlett's undergraduate training at Howard University before offering a meticulous examination of Catlett's Iowa course of study. Edwards reveals how Catlett's UI accomplishments provided a crucial foundation for her successful career as a visual artist representing minority experience.

Drama major Dora Martin Berry's testimonial recounts her journey from Houston, Texas, to her election as the first black Miss State University of Iowa. Berry describes her improbable accomplishment as evidence of the authentic goodwill showered upon her by black and white students alike. Notwithstanding the university's failure to acknowledge her accomplishment, Berry maintains that no one can deny the progressive campus environment that made her election possible.

Lena Hill's chapter 3 spotlights other black students pursuing degrees in the Department of Speech and Dramatic Art. Specifically focusing on Fanny Ellison and Thomas Pawley, Hill considers how Professor Edward C. Mabie's early commitment to regionalism and the experimental theater appealed to African American students invested in exploring black culture on the US stage. For black drama students from the 1930s to the mid-1950s, Iowa provided an essential training ground that prepared them to assume leading roles in HBCUs as well as the larger world of theater, film, and television.

Lois Eichaker's testimonial details her experiences as a second-generation UI legacy and student in the College of Arts and Sciences. Although health challenges forced Eichaker to divide her undergraduate studies among three universities, she comes to view UI as home.

In stark contrast, the subjects of Michael Hill's chapter 4 never develop an intimate relationship with Iowa. Studying Herbert Nipson, Michael Harper, and Margaret Walker, Hill in his chapter probes how the Iowa Writers' Workshop proved both a nurturing and an exclusionary environment for early African American graduate students. Hill ponders how the program's practice of admitting one black student at a time denied black workshoppers' ability to create meaningful community within their program. This tradition forced Nipson, Harper, and Walker to refine their artistic identities without the support of devoted instructional guidance. Ironically, the independence this reality fostered led these lonely workshoppers to success: they all produced work that attained a position at the forefront of civil rights struggles.

Track athlete Ted Wheeler's testimonial epitomizes the reality of how the midwestern black UI experience becomes freighted with international significance. Wheeler discusses how competition at Iowa helped him reach the Olympics and pursue a stellar coaching career. Even before this accomplishment, he explains how running track at UI fundamentally shaped his character.

Richard Breaux's chapter 5 on black male athletes expands on many of the themes and experiences Wheeler recounts. Breaux broadly surveys the tensions produced by the simultaneous adulation and adversity black male athletes experienced. His meticulous account of the difficulties arising from segregated housing, discriminatory practices of downtown businesses, and insulting treatment during out-of-state team travel discloses the contradictory reality African American male athletes endured in UI's integrated athletic program.

In the final testimonial, Don Tucker remembers his exhilarating days as a football player and wrestler at UI. He credits his undergraduate experiences, both on the field and in the classroom, with giving him the life knowledge and skills necessary for the successful career in government service he went on to enjoy.

Tucker's experiences of interacting broadly with diverse groups throughout his college years dovetail with James Alan McPherson's embrace of UI and Iowa City as a place where pneuma — one's soul and creative spirit — finds space to reign. In his conclusion to the book, Michael Hill considers how the stories of black students captured in the collection, together with McPherson's reflections, provide a necessary though often ignored history behind how Iowa became a launching pad for the twenty-first-century presidential candidacy of Barack Obama. The preparatory work that occurs between the 1930s and the 1960s makes visible how African American college students at the University of Iowa helped guide the nation toward a true understanding of democratic pluralism. Thus, *Invisible Hawkeyes* concludes with a long overdue bow. By weaving together the threads of black students' stories, we proclaim the potency of their original message of hope and change, and we thank them for undertaking this project even when very few onlookers recognized or applauded their accomplishment. In the end, we embrace the literary project Ralph Ellison's invisible protagonist completes underground: we celebrate the appearance of unvarnished US history. After all, the story of invisible Hawkeyes is not simply the story of a university; it is the story of a nation.

"EXCELLENT WORK AND SUPERIOR TRAITS OF PERSONALITY"

Composing an Integrated Music Department

In April 1942 Albert Walter Dent, the president of Dillard University in New Orleans, wrote to the director of the University of Iowa's Department of Music, Dr. Philip Greeley Clapp, inquiring about graduate student Oscar Anderson Fuller. President Dent sought a director of music and had heard that Fuller, who less than three months later would become the first African American to earn a PhD in music, "would be a good person for the position." He explained to Clapp his desire to develop music appreciation among his university's students and other African Americans in the area. Far from limiting his inquiry to Fuller's musical qualifications, Dent clarified that his real concern regarded the thirty-seven-year-old Fuller's ability to interact interracially. "The director," wrote Dent, "should be a person who is not so conscious of being a Negro that he is uncomfortable with white people."[1]

In his lengthy response to Dent, Clapp extolled Fuller's skills as a composer, leader, and pianist and his grasp of music application and theory. Based on his student's academics and personality, Clapp predicted that Fuller would attract students to the chorus and orchestra, enthusiastically develop their skills, and produce "a superior group of performers." He commended Fuller's doctoral thesis, an original oratorio based on a poem by James Weldon Johnson. The distinguished mentor clearly viewed Fuller as one of his most talented students.

Yet Clapp understood that Dent's interest in Fuller's fitness for the position at Dillard had less to do with music than issues of race. "You may be sure that I understand the racial and personality problems which you discuss," wrote the aging white director from the North to the young African American president in the legally segregated South. "I am happy to say that I believe Mr. Fuller is exactly the person you are looking for in this respect as well as musically." Clapp devoted the final five hundred–plus words of his letter to describing his community's own brand of segregation and how Fuller and his spouse possessed traits that enabled them to thrive under such conditions. While acknowledging regional differences in opportunities for African Americans, such as the total exclusion of black students from southern state schools, Clapp implied that the Fullers' skill at handling race relations in Iowa prepared them to handle them in Louisiana. Praising Fuller by damning his school, Clapp wrote:

> The University of Iowa admits colored students, but the student body as a whole does not fraternize with them, and the faculty members do not make protegées [sic] of them; for better or worse what personal recognition that a colored student here receives he has to earn by excellent work and superior traits of personality.[2]

The written exchange between Clapp and Dent followed from the premise that a southern black man could prove his ability to navigate race relations in the South at a *northern* university. It suggested that segregation shared more crucial similarities than differences across regions and shaped the role universities like the one Fuller attended played in granting graduate degrees to students excluded from higher education in their home states. Was the University of Iowa as unfriendly toward African American students as Clapp claimed? Rather than providing black graduates with the intellectual tools and credentials to chip away at a segregated society, did the music program at Iowa fail to challenge — or did it perhaps even support — systems of oppression? Or was Clapp simply playing the role of dutiful and wily advisor, who exaggerated the troubles faced by black graduates at Iowa in an effort to make the strongest case for his student? Was this a disingenuous attempt to get a star pupil into a promising academic position?

Such questions cannot be answered well without considering the historical circumstances that brought Fuller and other African Americans to the University of Iowa's Department of Music in pursuit of a graduate degree during the Jim Crow era. When Fuller and George Overall Caldwell, another African American from Texas, first entered the program in the summer of 1929 to pursue their master's degrees, Iowa became one of the early institutions of higher education to admit black students for advanced study in music.[3] Their experiences in the North were intimately connected with their life and aspirations in the South since Fuller and Caldwell could not pursue graduate study in their home state. Segregation prevented them from entering institutions of higher education that served whites, and no institution in Texas open to African Americans offered a graduate degree in music.

The story of Fuller, Caldwell, and other early black students earning graduate degrees from the University of Iowa is largely, but not solely, about the triumph over southern exclusion. As Clapp's rather bleak epistolary assessment of local race relations indicates, students at Iowa confronted exclusion in the North as well. Yet the record suggests that African American graduates found at least a few crucial members of the white music faculty, fine arts administration, and student body to support their creative and intellectual development. Their master's and PhD theses, letters, interviews, and reminiscences attest to this support and an intellectual freedom that allowed the pursuit of projects steeped in a Western musical tradition and engaged in what it meant to be black in the United States. As one doctoral recipient put it in a 1950 letter to Clapp, "I sure do miss the Seminar."[4] Although more socially isolated and constrained than their white peers, they found an opportunity in the integrated classroom, practice room, and concert hall to thrive intellectually. In this chapter, I argue that for a purposefully small, yet influential and interconnected group of southern African American scholar-musicians — who would not be sidetracked by northern race relations — Clapp's Department of Music at the University of Iowa stimulated their intellectual, musical, and professional development.

Fuller, Caldwell, and six other African Americans earned a PhD or MA degree in music at Iowa in the decade leading up to the 1950 desegregation of graduate and professional education in the parts of the South from where all of the graduate students to that point had come. This change in the law was made possible by the ongoing efforts of the National Association for the Advancement of Colored People (NAACP), a few brave, would-be law students in Texas and Oklahoma, and a US Supreme Court sympathetic to civil rights. All of the African Americans who engaged in advanced music study at Iowa until this point arrived as college graduates or as professors on temporary leave from historically black colleges and universities (HBCUs) in these two neighboring southern states. While no direct correlation exists between the university's practice of racial inclusion and this landmark civil rights victory, there is no question that African Americans' efforts to achieve the highest educational degrees in Texas, Oklahoma, and Iowa were intimately intertwined.

Integrating Higher Education In and Out of State

By the 1950s, the University of Iowa was well known among African Americans in higher education for its reputation as an institution of academic excellence that welcomed black students. New students discovered the university through what has been called "the Iowa network, an interwoven, interconnected 'pipeline' of African American alumni."[5] With regard to the Department of Music, this pipeline flowed from Texas and Oklahoma alone for more than two decades, reflecting the positive experience and powerful influence of one of the first two graduates, Oscar Fuller. The students who followed Fuller confirmed the findings of a multidepartmental study that identified undergraduate faculty influence as the most significant factor in why black students chose Iowa for graduate school.[6]

Personal motivations, primarily with regard to professional aspirations, prompted the pursuit of an advanced degree in music. As one Iowa alumnus put it, "The Ph.D. degree was like a union card, and it was becoming impossible to achieve full professorship without the card."[7] Judging by the notable track record of alumni who became professors at HBCUs, the MA degree also functioned like a "union card" that opened the institutional door to teaching.

The decision to pursue an advanced degree was not strictly a personal matter. Important external factors led institutions in the South to push their students and faculty toward graduate and professional schools. Most notably, administrators at HBCUs sought accreditation, which depended in part on the number of their faculty with advanced degrees.[8] Until at least 1950, segregation prohibited African Americans from attending in-state institutions of higher education that served white students, and HBCUs tended to offer few if any graduate degrees.[9] This meant that African Americans had to leave the legally segregated South for graduate and professional schools in the North, which posed a financial problem.

By the 1930s, many southern states responded to this problem by appropriating funds for use by faculty at HBCUs to defray the additional costs of attending graduate school out of state.[10] Historian Jimmie Lewis Franklin, who was a beneficiary of such state funds from Mississippi when he attended the University of Oklahoma after it desegregated its graduate school, emphasized the insufficiency of these appropriations as well as the unfair burden they placed on black churches, fraternal lodges, and other black groups that picked up the students' extra costs. "In short," wrote Franklin, "blacks subsidized the system of segregation."[11] Based on the actions of the African Americans who pushed for this educational aid and the students who received it, however, the alternative (i.e., no state financial assistance) seemed worse.

Of the two states from which black graduates in the music department at the University of Iowa came during the first few decades of this practice, Oklahoma first offered money for graduate and professional study out of state (although Fuller and the first students who used such funds came from the other state, Texas). Approved prior to fall 1935 university classes, Oklahoma Senate Bill 203 provided for payment of tuition, fees, and travel expenses of graduate study in educational institutions outside of Oklahoma to residents who could not attend the state university. Although the legislation made no mention of race, its reference to article XIII, section 3, in the state's constitution that forbade integrated education clarified the racially specific intentions of the bill. Eligible applicants for the award had to submit proof of their "good moral character and of ability to pursue the courses of study." The new law stated that the amount of money available to each student should mirror the amount that out-of-state students paid for in-state tuition in Oklahoma and was not to exceed a total distribution of $5,000 for either of the first two years of implementation.[12] Over the fifteen years that funds were awarded, the funds reached more than 1,900 students, who individually each year received "somewhere between $111 and $170."[13] According to historian Zella J. Black Patterson, in 1946 the state made payments to 22 music students and a total of 149 black students. By the mid-1940s the state was allocating a total of $25,000 a year but had doubled this amount by the late 1940s to ensure that all eligible students were funded.[14]

Advocates for out-of-state graduate and professional school funds in Texas experienced slower legislative success. Two years after Oklahoma passed its education bill, the Texas State Inter-Racial Commission and the State Association of Colored Teachers sponsored a similar bill in the Texas Legislature, where the Committee on Education considered it.[15] Dr. Richard T. Hamilton, chair of the Committee on Civics and Public Welfare of the Dallas Negro Chamber of Commerce, spearheaded efforts on the bill's behalf. He and his committee members attempted to get "an influential member" of the state house and senate to introduce the bill, but no one complied. The group instead paid a lobbyist, who succeeded in bringing the bill before the legislature. In a letter to NAACP special counsel Charles Houston, Hamilton asserted, "We have aroused considerable white public sentiment in favor of this legislation." Emphasizing reasons for optimism, Hamilton continued:

> Every newspaper in Dallas has editorially endorsed it, also a number of outstanding educators in white colleges throughout the State, notably among these is the President of the University of Texas who holds advanced views toward Negro education. He went so far as to say to our committee that were it not for provisions in the State Constitution, forbidding, he would favor the admission of Negro students to the University of Texas for graduate and professional work.[16]

In spite of the favorable media attention and support, along with the endorsement of Texas Governor James V. Allred and the efforts of noted white antilynching activist Jessie Daniel Ames, who met with legislators and spoke on the bill, the bill failed.[17] This initial failure represented only a temporary setback: by 1939, the state was allocating $25,000 for out-of-state schooling.[18] It was during this time that African American students from Texas arrived at Iowa to study music. Oscar Fuller, Lois Towles McNeely, and Edison Holmes Anderson completed their graduate degrees by the early 1940s, and the new scholarship aid presumably factored into their decision to enroll. "Southern states are becoming more and more conscious of their duty toward raising the educational level of its people," wrote McNeely in her MA thesis. "In a measure Negro state institutions are feeling the effects of this change in attitudes, and more and more state funds are being appropriated for Negro education."[19] Herbert Mells, a professor at Langston University, arrived around the time the Texans left and would become the first African American from Oklahoma to earn a graduate degree in music at Iowa and the second with a PhD.

While black leaders and even some white allies in Texas and Oklahoma pushed for educational bills to redress an inequality created by segregation, many whites only supported such legislation as a means for maintaining segregation. This change in perspective occurred when civil rights leaders made headway toward an even bigger goal: the desegregation of graduate and professional education.[20] For years, civil rights advocates and some segregationists recognized the legal vulnerability of "separate but equal" education given the inequality between majority institutions and those serving black students. The NAACP's strategy toward dismantling segregated education rested on how such inequality violated the equal protection clause of the Fourteenth Amendment. Charles Houston's friend and fellow Harvard Law School graduate, Nathan Margold, recommended that the NAACP use the court system to force southern border states to either create equal institutions and provide equal services or to end segregation. Houston's legal advisory committee proceeded under "Margold's theory that the white establishment was not willing to pay for truly equal separation."[21]

The 1938 US Supreme Court ruling in favor of Lloyd Gaines, an African American man who had been denied admittance to the University of Missouri Law School because of his race, emerged as a prominent early test of this strategy. Thurgood Marshall, who was trained at Howard University Law School and hired at the NAACP by Houston, represented Gaines. Marshall had previously argued successfully in front of Maryland's supreme court, which struck down segregation at the University of Maryland Law School in *Pearson v. Murray*.[22] In *Gaines v. Canada*, the US Supreme Court ruled that Missouri had to either admit Gaines into the previously segregated law school or create a comparable law school for black students. Missouri chose the latter option, creating a law school at Lincoln University. Gaines mysteriously disappeared in the months following this ruling, thereby derailing Houston's plans to attack the legitimacy of the new law school in the courts. "With *Gaines*," asserts historian Gary Lavergne, "the idea of using out-of-state scholarships to meet the test of separate but equal legally ended forever and everywhere in the United States."[23]

This outcome did not prevent southern states, including Oklahoma and Texas, from continuing to fund these scholarships. For segregationists, offering such funds to black graduate students potentially reduced the likelihood of new cases challenging the state's Jim Crow laws. African Americans understood that their efforts toward desegregation would be arduous, if not perilous; having access to state money that lightened the burden of out-of-state study made it that much easier to avoid the more difficult and dangerous path. But the strongest support for out-of-state funds came from predominantly black proponents of desegregation and those open to such change, such as University of Texas president H. Y. Benedict and University of Oklahoma president George Lynn Cross. The spirit in which well-positioned whites such as Benedict and Cross supported such appropriations likely signaled to black strategists that the time was ripe to challenge "separate but equal" education in the courts.

Ada Lois Sipuel Fisher, a recent Langston University graduate, posed the first noteworthy challenge since *Gaines* when she entered President Cross's office on January 14, 1946, to apply to the University of Oklahoma Law School. Cross denied her application, but upon the request of civil rights leader and newspaper editor Roscoe Dunjee, the president wrote a letter clarifying that race was the sole reason for her denial. By making clear that Fisher was qualified for admission in every other way, this document helped the NAACP legal team representing Fisher directly challenge Oklahoma's segregation laws in the courts.[24] In *Sipuel v. Board of Regents of the University of Oklahoma*, the US Supreme Court ruled that the state had to provide Fisher with the same opportunity for legal education that other Oklahoma residents enjoyed. The state responded by hastily creating a law school for black students at Langston University. Fisher refused to attend this clearly inferior school of law, and her attorneys filed a motion arguing that she should be admitted to the University of Oklahoma. While the Cleveland County District Court ruled that the two schools were equal and the Oklahoma Supreme Court upheld the lower court's decision, Fisher won her appeal to the US Supreme Court by default when Oklahoma attorney general Mac Q. Williamson refrained from traveling to Washington, DC, to argue the state's position. On June 18, 1949, Fisher entered the University of Oklahoma Law School.[25]

Motivated by the ruling in *Sipuel v. Board of Regents*, Langston University professor George W. McLaurin and five other would-be graduate students in various fields applied for admission to the University of Oklahoma in fall 1948. Thurgood Marshall, who also represented Fisher, chose McLaurin as the key plaintiff in a suit filed in federal district court. The three-judge panel ruled that the state had to either admit McLaurin into the education program or discontinue this program for white students, and the state chose the former option. McLaurin preceded Fisher by more than eight months to become the first African American to attend the university.

McLaurin, Fisher, and the other black graduate students admitted during this period desegregated admissions to the university, but their initial experiences within the various programs were anything but integrated. For instance, all four of McLaurin's education seminars were held in the one classroom that enabled administrators to separate him from the other students within an anteroom; he could see the professor up front, but neither he nor the white students could see each other. He and the other black graduate students ate their lunch in the corner of the cafeteria, which was surrounded by an iron chain and accessed by a side door, while an armed guard stood watch. Fisher vividly recalled attending her constitutional law course taught by a professor who had argued in the courts against her admission to the law school. She remembered "a single large wooden chair behind a wooden rail" that was in the last row of the room. "Attached to a pole on the back of the chair was a large printed sign that said COLORED." Reflecting on "what racist action or situation over the years [she] felt most acutely," Fisher concluded, "I think perhaps walking past my classmates in the law school classroom and climbing the levels up to the 'colored' chair was the most humiliating."[26]

The humiliation black students experienced within a segregated campus appeared destined to end on June 5, 1950, when the US Supreme Court reversed two lower court rulings, thus undermining the "separate but equal" principle established fifty-four years earlier in *Plessy v. Ferguson*. In *McLaurin v. Oklahoma State Regents* the Supreme Court ruled that the university's treatment of the former Langston professor differently from the white students violated the equal protection clause of the Fourteenth Amendment.[27] As a result, McLaurin, Fisher, and other black law students returned to an integrated campus in the fall. Heman Marion Sweatt, who had attempted to enter the University of Texas Law School one month after Fisher's initial attempt in Oklahoma, spent more than four difficult years fighting to gain admission. As in Fisher's case, Sweatt's race was the only factor that disqualified him and he refused to attend the segregated law school the state created in haste. In *Sweatt v. Painter*, the Supreme Court concluded that this law school and the state's efforts to provide equal segregated education failed. "It was clear from the opinion that a good-faith effort to supply equality of treatment without integration was insufficient; rather, it must be equality in fact," asserted Werdner Page Keeton, who had been dean of the Texas law school at the time of the ruling and dean of the University of Oklahoma Law School when Fisher and McLaurin struggled for admission.[28] The desegregation of higher education through *Sipuel v. Board of Regents of Oklahoma*, *McLaurin v. Oklahoma State Regents*, and *Sweatt v. Painter* provided the civil rights movement a huge momentum boost and paved the way for the *Brown v. Board of Education* ruling a few years later.

The NAACP's strategy of making the case in the courts that separate education was inherently unequal and in violation of the Constitution's Fourteenth Amendment proved successful. Southern states could not possibly create graduate and professional programs that offered black students the

same quality of education that white students enjoyed in their public institutions. This inherent inequality could be measured through objective data,
such as the number of faculty members and books in the library at hastily
created "sham" black law schools in Texas and Oklahoma, but it also registered in less quantifiable — but in the eyes of the US Supreme Court, more
harmful — ways. "The separation that Chief Justice Vinson declared uncon-
stitutional in *Sweatt* and *McLaurin*," wrote Gary Lavergne in his insightful
summation of the two path-clearing rulings, "was the separation not from
white students, but from ideas and points of view."[29] According to Vinson,
black students in segregated facilities or separated within the state institutions,
as were Fisher and McLaurin, did not benefit from the most important part
of higher education: the stimulating exchange of knowledge, the free flow of
critical discourse in and beyond the classroom between faculty and students.

In spite of its limitations, the state practice of funding out-of-state education did not appear to undermine efforts toward desegregation or slow this
process down, as some segregationists had expected. On the contrary, it may
have buttressed this process by helping educate the faculty and professionals
who encouraged the pursuit of similar educational achievement among their
family, peers, and students. Fisher, McLaurin, and Sweatt only benefited from
the examples, guidance, and support of African Americans with the type of
degrees they sought, regardless from where these degrees were earned. Even
the NAACP, which refrained from officially endorsing efforts to pass Texas
legislation for out-of-state funds, recognized the value in such legislation. In a
letter on the NAACP's desegregation strategy to A. Maceo Smith of the Texas
Negro Chamber of Commerce, Charles Houston asserted that "a practical
view of the situation in Texas would indicate that our next step is a scholarship
bill and we should like to be of assistance in helping you build up statewide
sentiment for the same."[30]

The scholarship aid from Oklahoma and Texas benefited at least some of
the southern graduate students who enrolled in the Department of Music
at the University of Iowa. Their acceptance of this money signaled a determination to earn an advanced degree despite the travel inconvenience and
unfamiliarity with northern racism. As the courts slowly dismantled Jim Crow
education, black Texans and Oklahomans at Iowa had reason to see themselves as part of the march toward integrated higher education. Registration
records offer a glimpse at this cross-country process.[31] Midway through his
second academic year of graduate study, Mitchell Southall had copies of his

transcripts sent to the Oklahoma Board of Education, which administered the provisions of the act that granted state money for out-of-state study.[32] Herbert Harris, who had copies of his transcripts sent to Texas State University in Houston a few months after the Supreme Court struck down the segregation practices that necessitated the stipend, may have been the last such aid recipient at Iowa.[33] Edison Anderson and Oscar Fuller forwarded transcripts to Prairie View, which may have been directed to the committee of deans that oversaw the administration of Texas scholarship aid.[34]

The most noteworthy recipient of scholarship aid for the study of music at Iowa is the one who, in a small way and perhaps unwittingly, gained an advantage over white students *because of* segregation. Lois Towles McNeely received consistent financial assistance from her home state of Texas in her pursuit of a PhD in music at Iowa. Over the course of two years of doctoral study, during which time she passed her qualifying exam, McNeely on three occasions forwarded copies of her transcripts to the Committee for State Aid for Negroes in Austin, Texas.[35] Only McNeely and other black Texans qualified for assistance since they could not attend the graduate schools whites attended. White Texans could attend the state's graduate programs, but they could not earn a PhD since this degree was not offered at that time.[36] These students could, of course, pursue the highest degree in a different state, but unlike McNeely, they received no state assistance. Although she never completed her doctorate, McNeely landed a faculty position at Fisk University in Nashville. The partially state-funded training that led to this professional success represented a fleeting reversal in the usual flow of privilege within the system of "separate but equal."[37]

The landmark 1950 Supreme Court rulings eliminated the need for Texas and Oklahoma to provide funds for African Americans seeking out-of-state graduate and professional training.[38] All students, regardless of race, presumably could now enjoy an advanced education in their home state without having to travel north. In the years leading up to this civil rights victory, southern black graduate students chose northern schools, in part, because they had no other choice. But did getting into these schools necessarily guarantee fair and equal treatment? As the examples of Ada Lois Sipuel Fisher and George McLaurin illustrated, segregation could exist within what might appear from the outside a racially integrated environment. In making the decision to head north to states such as Iowa, then, did black students get access to the "ideas and points of view" that were the hallmark of higher education?

Philip Greeley Clapp, Oscar Anderson Fuller, and Early Black Music Graduates

In late 1949, a few months after Ada Lois Sipuel Fisher entered the University of Oklahoma Law School, a thirty-three-year-old music professor at Langston University, Edison Holmes Anderson, decided to travel to Iowa to complete his PhD. A native of Terrell, Texas, near Dallas, Anderson earned his BA at Prairie View Normal and Industrial College near Houston, where he was a star tenor under the direction of the head of the music department and choral director Oscar Anderson Fuller. For the two years following graduation he served as principal at a junior high school back at home. Fuller, who earned his MA from the University of Iowa in 1934, encouraged Anderson to apply to his alma mater.[39] Entering in 1940, perhaps with Fuller, who returned for his PhD, Anderson completed his MA in music from the University of Iowa in 1941.[40] Like his mentor and college professor, he attended summer sessions at Iowa, which sped up the completion of his degree. Upon graduation, he became music director of Arkansas State College in Pine Bluff before serving overseas during World War II and directing volunteer military choral groups. After the war Anderson assumed duties as head of the Department of Music at Langston University the semester after Fisher graduated. Attesting to how highly the university thought of its new faculty member, Langston University granted him a yearlong sabbatical at New York's Columbia University in only his second year. By the time he told his spouse of his plans to return to graduate school in the North, he had already formed and toured widely with his A Cappella Concert Choir, the choral group upon which his reputation as a talented director rested.[41]

Gloria Edwards Anderson recalled her reservations over her husband's plans to return to Iowa. Earlier in the year he had "suffered a nervous breakdown" on a choir tour. Gloria had visited him in a Texas hospital for two months before they could return to their home in Oklahoma. The doctors concluded that "Edison must slow down," but she recognized that "there were other disturbing factors contributing to his serious illness. Segregated conditions were still rampant for blacks, and his having to travel under such conditions was disappointing, hurtful . . . sometimes causing anger." One incident at a restaurant involved being told in front of his two children to go around to a segregated entrance for service. "That was the only time the children heard their father curse," recalled Gloria, "and he wasn't about to go to the kitchen."

The proud choral director also experienced similar humiliating Jim Crow incidents while touring with the A Cappella Concert Choir, which included being denied sleeping accommodations. Compounding his trouble, soon after returning to Oklahoma, his mother died.[42]

In spite of his recent breakdown and the loss of his mother, Edison assured Gloria that he would be fine in graduate school. "I'll be studying with teachers who know me," he reportedly said. Shortly after arriving, however, his voice teacher, Herald Stark, called with bad news: Anderson was confused and Stark doubted he could handle the rigors of graduate school. "What must I do?" the concerned professor asked his would-be student's spouse. The next day Gloria flew to Iowa, where Stark and his wife met her at the airport. Describing gestures of interracial friendship that went well beyond what one would have expected in the South during the period, she continued, "They were friendly and helpful. It seemed I had known them all along. I can never forget their kindness in welcoming me to their home and assisting throughout my stay." Anderson "fully recovered" after a few weeks of "excellent treatment" at a facility in Mount Pleasant, Iowa. During his recovery, the music department head, Philip Greeley Clapp, Stark, and others remained "in close touch," remembered Gloria. "They encouraged Edison to be patient; to give himself ample time and rest before attempting school again."[43]

Like Fisher, McLaurin (who happened to be Anderson's former colleague at Langston), and Sweatt, Anderson initially found his attempt to enter graduate school thwarted. Whether or not segregation proved to be the direct cause, it clearly represented a contributing factor in his debilitating breakdown. "There are certain things in our society we can't change," wrote J. W. Sulek, his therapist, in a letter from Mount Pleasant. "All we can do is accept them, for by accepting and understanding, we save ourselves a lot of bitterness."[44] We cannot know what Anderson made of Sulek's admonition to accept and understand the reality of segregation; what is clear is that this reality weighed heavily on his mind.

Why, on the immediate heels of a breakdown and loss of a parent and when challenges to segregation in higher education gained traction, would Anderson leave Oklahoma for graduate school in Iowa? In spite of these factors seemingly working against it, his decision may be understood for its pragmatism. He wanted to earn the highest degree in his field; Oklahoma did not offer a PhD, but the University of Iowa did, and he already had a successful experience with the latter institution.[45] His decision may also signify the attractiveness of a department that bore the unmistakable impress of its creator and longtime head, Philip Greeley Clapp. More than any other professor or administrator, Clapp attracted black students to the program and attempted to make them feel welcome and supported. Indeed, his reputation drew Fuller to the university to pursue his MA and later his PhD, which he earned eight years before it was even legal for African Americans to pursue graduate or professional education with whites in the South.

Clapp set a towering example as both an educator and a practitioner of music. Born on April 4, 1888, he grew up in Boston before attending school at Harvard University, where he participated in a broad array of musical activities. After earning his PhD, only the third awarded in music by an American university, he studied in Europe and in Boston under Dr. Karl Muck, who along with Clapp's mother were the most formative musical influences in his life. In 1919 Clapp assumed duties as director of the State University of Iowa School of Music, where over the next thirty-four years he directed the completion of eighty-nine doctoral degrees. Within his first few years he developed the music school into a department with undergraduate and graduate courses that counted toward credit. Until late in his life, Clapp consistently performed, directed, and composed music.[46]

Clapp's biographer emphasized how he exerted nearly absolute control over the department. He "ruled the department with an iron hand . . . like a dictator — a benevolent one if things went the way he wished or a relentless tyrant if things went contrary." This dominance over "virtually every aspect of its faculty and students" lasted from 1919 until at least 1946.[47] It also meant he controlled who got into his department; if he had wanted to exclude certain students for reasons beyond academics, he probably would have succeeded. As a strong department leader, Clapp set the tone for how faculty interacted with students. If he had harbored deeply racist or misogynist views, the University of Iowa would not have graduated the number of African Americans and women that it did.

Still, it is difficult to form a definitive picture of Clapp's views on race because he rarely touched on the topic explicitly. He clearly did not subscribe to the scientific racism that flourished during his early professional years. In an article he penned on a Spanish ethnic group and in a subsection entitled "Of Science and Skulls," he gently lampooned eugenicists and their faith in the infallibility of science. "The result of this adoption of infallibility by science," wrote Clapp, "is that a mere layman, with no laboratory to support his mere reason, almost feels it his duty to believe all that the scientists tell him, even when they contradict themselves and one another, as they usually do."[48] His perspective, informed by his study of culture, generally aligned with those of the cultural anthropologist Franz Boas, whose seminal studies would undermine the racial sciences in future decades. This did not mean that Clapp avoided thinking in racial terms or making generalities about human populations. He occasionally spoke about Negroes, American Indians, and Jews as progenitors of their own racially unique music, but he did not promote thinking in terms of racial hierarchies, a central tenant of eugenics. "Talent, as everybody may observe for himself," he wrote in a piece about American music, "is distributed by the Creator with an almost shocking disregard for theories as to where it ought to alight. Probably every form of talent is at all times latent in widely varied types of people."[49]

Clapp's belief in the catholic distribution of talent included racial differences: the black students admitted into the music program and supported by him and certain other faculty members made this belief evident. In the summer of 1929, Oscar Fuller and George Overall Caldwell probably became the first African Americans to enter the University of Iowa School of Music.[50] Fuller and Caldwell had good reason to know each other since the latter man taught music at Bishop College in Marshall, Texas, where the former's father, Oscar Fuller Sr., served as a dean.[51] It is easy to imagine the two men, counseled by the elder Fuller, deciding to test the promising new summer school up north together; strength in numbers, they might have concluded. The surviving record indicates that Fuller Jr. and Clapp formed a relationship built on mutual respect, if not admiration. "Throughout [Fuller's] years of teaching and study," wrote Fuller's biographer about his graduate school years, "Dr. Clapp was a guiding and sympathetic advisor."[52] In the dedication of his doctoral thesis, Fuller expressed a broad appreciation for Clapp, "whose great musicianship and genuine, human insights shall remain among the most cherished recollections of my musical experience."[53] Clapp expressed similar sentiments when he described Fuller as "outstanding both as a musician and as a man."[54]

Born on September 20, 1904, in Roanoke, Virginia, Oscar Fuller Jr. grew up in an exceptionally well-educated family. His father, Oscar Fuller Sr., and his five paternal uncles all earned PhDs, while his paternal aunt earned an MA at Columbia University. Fuller Sr. took classes at Harvard College and graduated from Bates College. He completed his MA from the University of Chicago and a doctor of divinity at Union University in Virginia before becoming dean of Bishop College, a historically black institution in Marshall, Texas. While earning his undergraduate degree at Marshall, Fuller Jr. studied music under John Albert Talcott, a young, white, Canadian instructor who had recently returned from World War I and built himself a fifteen-rank pipe organ in his home. Fuller considered Talcott "a romanticist and so he and I were very good friends as well as being my teacher." After college, Fuller studied theory and composition at the New England Conservatory of Music in Boston under the tutelage of Dr. Benjamin Cutter. During his studies he learned of Dr. Clapp's reputation as a piano prodigy, elite scholar, and successful head of the music program at the University of Iowa. Dr. Frederick Shepherd Converse and the Conservatory's president George W. Chadwick encouraged Fuller to pursue an MA at the University of Iowa with Clapp.[55] Both Converse and Chadwick had experience working with exceptional African American composers: Converse taught Florence Price and Chadwick taught William Grant Still. Both from Little Rock, Arkansas, Price and Still were arguably the most significant black classical composers in the first half of the twentieth century, and among the first to have their works performed by major American orchestras.[56]

When Fuller decided to pursue graduate study, then, he did so out East and in the context of a music school removed from the direct concerns and impact of legal segregation. His father and extended family, with their elite eastern educational pedigree, offered Fuller examples of professional achievement not delimited by laws regarding their race. Yet race certainly entered the minds of Converse and Chadwick in deciding where to send their promising black student for advanced study. Perhaps one of them told Fuller that Clapp was the nephew of the famous abolitionist and Radical Republican, Horace Greeley; Fuller apparently believed in this nonexistent family connection long after Clapp's death.[57] Whether openly addressed or not, all parties understood that Fuller's options for graduate study were limited to institutions open to blacks. Clapp may have been one of the best music instructors in the country, but the University of Iowa never would have figured into Fuller's future plans without an awareness of his relatively progressive racial views.

Fuller entered Iowa's Department of Music in the summer of 1929, several years before he completed his MA. His not attending school during the normal academic year apparently reflected his own professional needs rather than an institutional discriminatory policy. For the five years leading up to his departure, Fuller was the chair of the music department at Negro Agricultural and Technical College of North Carolina (now North Carolina Agriculture and Technical State University). In the fall of 1929, he began the first of his thirteen years at Prairie View College, where he headed the music department. Like many of the African American graduate students who followed in his footsteps at Iowa, Fuller's work as a professor during the regular school year precluded his pursuing studies anytime other than during the summers except when granted a leave of absence.[58]

The Fine Arts Summer Session had two terms that spanned from June 10 to August 23, 1929. During this period Fuller and other students had the opportunity to take courses across the Department of Fine Arts, which reflected the departmental emphasis on integrating music, graphic, plastic, and dramatic arts, thus providing students with a broad program of enrichment geared toward training teachers of fine arts in high schools. Toward that end, the university brought in artists of "national prominence." According to a promotional bulletin, the program exposed students to daily demonstrations of orchestra, band, chorus, glee club, piano, history, voice, violin, and piano. The Department of Music accepted all courses toward the BA, MA, and PhD, and the university gave each fine arts credit as much weight as any other credit (a practice which at that time apparently set Iowa apart from many other institutions). The program even gave faculty and students the opportunity to "appear frequently on radio programs broadcast from university station W.S.U.I."[59] It is unknown whether Fuller went on air during his first years at Iowa, but by his final two semesters he wrote radio programs for the station. His hour-long noon luncheon programs focused on works by black composers and featured both solo and group performances.[60]

Prairie View granted Fuller a release for the 1933–1934 school year so that he could complete his MA degree.[61] He took piano lessons from Drs. Clapp and Harry Thatcher, along with courses in music history, theory, and performance. He also participated in university chorus and symphonic choir and earned his student scholarship by serving as a piano accompanist. On May 15, 1934, in the university's north music hall and after hosting his radio show earlier in the day, Fuller performed works by classical composers in a joint public recital, along with a young, white female vocalist and her female accompanist.[62] A month later he submitted his master's thesis, "The Teaching of Music in the Leading

Negro Colleges." In the acknowledgments, he thanked the administrators and teachers at the fourteen institutions he surveyed and Dr. Clapp "for his criticisms, suggestions and supervision of this thesis."[63]

When the University of Iowa granted Fuller his first graduate degree, he joined a relatively small number of African American musicians to reach the same educational heights. Out of the fifty-six music teachers identified in his thesis at the fourteen "leading" institutions, eleven had earned their MA, although it is unclear how many of these professors were black.[64] The total number of African Americans who earned graduate degrees in all fields increased dramatically during the 1930s.[65] The growing faculty at Prairie View mirrored this national trend. A document created late in the decade listed the institutions from which the 165 employees at the college attained their highest degree. Iowa distinguished itself as the state that produced the second largest number of MA and PhD degrees among the faculty, with nine members earning their highest degree from either Iowa State (five) or the University of Iowa (four). In the 1934–1935 school year, Iowa led all other states by supplying twelve of the "Instructional Staff."[66] Fuller may have been alone with his advanced degree in the music department, but he was surrounded at Prairie View by other similarly successful academics in other fields, including many with Iowa ties. College newsletters document the many faculty members traveling back and forth during the summer and regular school year to Iowa and other higher education institutions. By 1940, at least twelve faculty or soon-to-be faculty members at Prairie View attended graduate school or earned an advanced degree from the University of Iowa.[67]

Undoubtedly a number of factors influenced Fuller's decision to return to Iowa to pursue his PhD in music, including Clapp's encouragement. During this time, a tremendous amount of travel occurred between the small, historically black college in Texas and the large, public university in Iowa. In the summer of 1939, professors Rufus P. Perry and T. P. Dooley returned to and new faculty member Frank Greene Davis arrived at Prairie View with their respective doctorates from Iowa in chemistry, biology, and economics.[68] Many more faculty members began or finished their master's around this same time. Rather than coincidental, the burst of graduate activity illustrated the galvanizing effect — in the wake of the *Gaines* ruling — of Texas funding out-of-state schooling; for the first time in the history of the college, large numbers of faculty received state help to pursue their graduate degrees. The increased numbers pursuing graduate study at Iowa also reflected the success of the academic pipeline initially forged between Fuller and Clapp, which saw its first success in the completion of Anderson's MA degree.

Three years after his breakdown, Anderson returned to the University of Iowa to begin work on his PhD, which he completed in 1957. Since completing his MA, the academic pipeline expanded to include Langston University in Oklahoma, where Herbert Franklin Mells and then Anderson served as department heads. Intriguingly, four years before Mells became department head and a decade before he began graduate study in Iowa, Ralph Ellison — with great musical ambition — attempted to enroll at Langston University. After the Langston president denied him admission, Ellison attended Tuskegee Institute, where he studied and performed music with aspirations of becoming a composer. Ellison's brush with Langston and a music career represents a compelling "almost was" addition to the story of the Oklahoma–Iowa academic pipeline.[69] Anderson, however, had a good position at Langston, signaling that something more than professional development drove his decision to return to Iowa. Anderson's spouse, Gloria, recalled their family's time in Iowa City while he completed his final degree. "Unlike New Yorkers, the Iowans were relaxed and friendly," she wrote. Their family "shared remarkable and gratifying experiences throughout the busy year."[70] In her telling of it, the positives of the Andersons' time in Iowa outweighed the negatives, including the experiences of racism she relayed. In the absence of Anderson's own words, the PhD he earned may serve as evidence that the scales similarly tipped in his favor.

"A Delicate Situation": The Limits of Pluralism in the Music Department

In her doctoral thesis on African American graduate students at the University of Iowa from the 1930s through the 1950s, Madgetta Thornton Dungy focused on the experiences of twenty students. Drawing from oral interviews and survey responses, she identified how racism impacted their lives both on and off campus. Securing housing represented one of the biggest obstacles for African American graduates and one of the clearest expressions of segregation. Not until after World War II did the university start accepting black students into the dormitories. Until that time, the only options available to them were six boardinghouses and two fraternities off campus. Along with housing, students also faced segregation in city restaurants, stores, and barbershops, which inconsistently denied them service according to the individual whims of proprietors; no city policies or ordinances dictated these frustrating practices. Similarly, no written university policy forbade the presence of African Americans at social functions, such as dances, which nonetheless often functioned as racially exclusionary affairs. Furthermore, the university and businesses in town routinely denied African Americans employment.[71]

In spite of the presence of segregation, the majority of the students she contacted "were very satisfied with their graduate school experiences."[72] This sentiment seemed to reflect several factors, which included positive relationships with peers and faculty, the lack of overt racism within their respective departments, and their experience with more pervasive segregation in the South. As hardworking graduate students, their focus on doing well academically and completing their degree overshadowed many other concerns, such as the discomfort caused by occasional encounters with racism. In short, the university alumni Dungy interviewed and surveyed recalled that their lives revolved primarily around their academic department, where their academic performance mattered more than their race. The quality of their relationships with peers and faculty in their departments left a positive impression that outweighed the negative memories of exclusion they deemed peripheral to their task at hand.[73]

Unfortunately, intradepartmental concerns over race in the early 1940s threatened to undermine the focus on academics that African American alumni favorably recalled. A warning sounded from within the music department. "Without offense to either white or colored students," wrote Philip Clapp in the previously cited letter to Dillard University President Dent, "I may say that the State University of Iowa serves an area in which there is just beginning to be a color problem, and that the presence of any considerable number of colored students in any one department might create a delicate situation there." Clapp then drove home the point as it related to Dent in his capacity to recommend students for out-of-state graduate study. "I do not encourage the enrollment of a colored student in this department unless his musical ability and personality traits are such as clearly to promise that he will not as an individual arouse or reawaken any color problem in official or personal relationships with the faculty and students."[74]

To what burgeoning "color problem" Clapp referred is unclear, but he indicated it had something to do with simple math. The previous few years had seen a dramatic and unprecedented surge in the numbers of African

Americans who earned either an MA or PhD. Perhaps Clapp, the head of the music department, felt growing pressure from administrators to limit the number of black students accepted into the program.[75] The number of African Americans earning graduate degrees in the years after Clapp's letter to Dent dropped more than 50 percent from preceding years.[76] This drop in light of Clapp's advice raises the possibility that inflated scrutiny of black candidates curtailed their enrollment more than a flagging interest in the program or lack of financial means. Then again, this drop may have solely reflected the dramatic drop nationwide of males enrolled in higher education during World War II. Either way, apparently the racially charged "delicate situation" of which Clapp warned was averted.

Oscar Fuller served as the model of the type of student Clapp wished Dent and other administrators at southern HBCUs would restrict themselves to sending his way. Fuller had "won the complete respect and personal esteem of all faculty members and students whom he met, both in this and other departments." Clapp explained why:

> He is neither bumptious or servile, but quietly self-respecting; naturally he was in our department building a good deal of the time, devoting himself to this work without making any fuss about it of any kind; he has never forced himself upon anybody conversationally or otherwise but is cultivated, well informed, and fully able without embarrassment to himself or others to take part in recitations, seminars, and the numerous conversations in which our faculty and students have unhesitatingly included him.

In contrast with these examples of smooth relations, Clapp then explained a situation in which he assumed the southern president would be especially interested:

> When Mr. Fuller came to us for his second period of residence, the courses which he had to take brought him into a number of small classes and seminars with some Southern white students; I could see at first that the latter felt not too favorably about close contact with any colored student in the classroom, although they made no immediate complaint and made no trouble in the classrooms or the building; within two or three weeks everyone of these Southern, — two men and two

women, — commented to me about the excellence of Mr. Fuller's work
and expressed admiration for his manners and behavior, and very soon
were treating him exactly as if he were a white student of talent and
character.[77]

This assessment of Fuller's skill at negotiating a seemingly isolating racial
climate points to the types of challenges other African American students
faced during this period. It also indicates that the black students bore the
burden of adapting to the cultural expectations of white students, faculty,
and administrators; neither Clapp nor other whites at the university appeared
ready to embrace cultural differences. The aging department head, who did
more than any other Iowan administrator to attract Fuller and other African
Americans to the music department, exhibited a critical shortcoming identified by Dr. Philip G. Hubbard in his book on diversity at the University of
Iowa. As noted in the introduction to this volume, Hubbard asserts that in
the period preceding his arrival in the 1950s as only the second black faculty
member hired by the institution, "The presence of African Americans in the
[university] community was accepted only to the extent defined by the least
tolerant member of the majority."[78] Clapp made the truth of this claim explicit
in his letter to Dent by focusing on the responses of southern whites to Fuller,
whose success of character was measured by his ability to defuse their racism
and win their respect. Apparently no one in authority intervened directly on
Fuller's behalf. One wonders how Clapp would have responded had the white
students not accepted Fuller.

The high stakes riding on Fuller's ability to allay racial tensions through
his talent, charisma, and social acumen is suggested by a similarly charged
situation relayed in the memoir of celebrated jazz sideman William Oscar
Smith. Smith completed his PhD at the University of Iowa fifteen years after
Fuller completed his, and the campus had become more welcoming toward
African American students over this period. Smith described the university as
"a musicians' paradise," with supportive faculty and a strong sense of community. "When word got around that someone was in trouble," Smith wrote, "the
faculty and members of the business community came up with help." One of
these members of the business community, a white bar owner who employed
Smith's jazz trio, expressed his dislike over black men dating white women.[79]
This experience presaged an event that threatened to derail his plans to complete the PhD. After passing his comprehensive exams, Smith was invited to

a faculty party. His spouse was unable to attend, so he went with a young, white female classmate named Alice. He was the lone person of color at the party, and he "was afraid that people would not realize the true nature of this situation since . . . most of them did not know me or Alice." Confirming his worries, a red-faced professor directed him to take Alice home and return to the party. Upon his return, he was met by the British musicologist for whom the party was thrown:

> Dr. Westrup was interested in my background but also in Alice's back-ground. I begged off as I knew very little about her. The party eventu-ally broke up, and I went home disturbed. If they were thinking what I thought they were thinking, I could see all of my hopes for a Ph.D. flying out the window. First thing in the next morning I went to [the musicol-ogy professor] Mr. Luper's office and explained to him that Miss Cisco was a classmate without a car who had asked me for a ride. I also added that she was the girlfriend of the guitar player in my trio . . . , that I was simply doing her a favor, and that my wife couldn't come because of an emergency. His reply was, "I'm glad you told me."[80]

Forced to operate within this tricky social arrangement, where the student had to prove him- or herself both as an exceptional musician and a master in the arts of race relations, it is surprising how many African Americans com-pleted their graduate degrees. The fact that all of the early graduates until the 1950s came from the South may indicate that initially the program was not a good fit for African Americans from areas such as Chicago who rejected the perceived need to tolerate any degree of white hostility and desire for black deference. It also suggests that Clapp may have understood his role as training black cultural leaders who would thrive in HBCUs as much for their ability to effectively interact with whites according to the conventions of segregation as for their music talent. This was a practical objective in light of the dependence by such schools as Prairie View College and Langston University on white politicians and policy makers for state allocations, which directly affected these institutions' chances of accreditation.

If Clapp failed to create a climate that celebrated cultural difference and shunned intolerance, he at least helped provide an opportunity for black aca-demic success and a degree of meaningful interracial contact; many of his African American students succeeded in making the program work for them, and they left with fond feelings toward the school and certain members of the faculty. These feelings attested to the attitudes and actions of the department's domineering head, who through his classroom interactions with black students set an example for his white colleagues and students. The southern white students who initially resented Fuller's presence in class probably would not have come to accept him, no matter how skillful his comportment and exceptional his music talent, if Clapp had not demonstrated through his words and deeds that Fuller belonged. No existing evidence suggests that any black music students at the University of Iowa experienced the type of humiliating in-class segregation that George McLaurin and Ada Lois Sipuel Fisher faced.

The master's and doctoral theses produced by the eight African Americans to complete their graduate degrees at the University of Iowa by 1950 attest to the guiding and supportive presence of Clapp. In the acknowledgments of her 1942 MA thesis, the first African American woman at the school to complete a graduate degree in music, Lois Towles McNeely, expressed her "deep appreciation to Dr. Phillip [sic] G. Clapp for his many helpful suggestions and under whose direction this thesis was prepared."[81] McNeely, who completed her MFA the following year, wrote her MA thesis on the history of music education at Wiley College in Marshall, Texas, where she attended as an undergraduate. As a grade school teacher and resident of Texas, she may have heard of the University of Iowa music program via Fuller's reputation, which Dr. Oscar Fuller Sr., a dean at Bishop College (also in Marshall), would have been in a position to spread locally. McNeely's gift as a pianist would have especially appealed to Clapp, a piano phenomenon in his own right. After leaving Iowa and teaching at Fisk University, McNeely toured overseas as a concert pianist. Her talent drew the attention of legendary pianist Arthur Rubenstein, who offered her coaching. By the time she debuted in New York, some critics likened her piano playing to the inimitable voices of Marian Anderson and Paul Robeson.[82] Her exceptional beauty, which led her to pursue modeling amid her music career, may have been a mixed blessing for her reputation as a pianist; she never garnered the critical accolades of either Anderson or Robeson.

Herbert Franklin Mells, who in 1944 became the second African American at Iowa to earn a PhD in music, jointly dedicated the symphony he wrote for his dissertation to Clapp and his wife, Mildred Ethel, "for her advice on many matters of detailed importance." He praised Clapp, his "teacher and advisor for that type of instruction which emanates from a bounteous reservoir of successful experience, creative artistic skill and musicianship." In addition to noting his musical prowess, Mells thanked Clapp for "generosities that immeasurably contributed to [his] efforts for achievement here at University of Iowa and to [his] professional status in general."[83] These unnamed "generosities" apparently extended beyond what one might identify as strictly professional duties. To a letter Mells sent upon returning to Langston University after earning his PhD, Clapp responded with a long, witty, and heartfelt letter that evoked a closeness reserved for friends. "We greatly miss you here," wrote the animated elder before describing the comical lengths to which he went to supply four-part harmony for the choral conducting students. He expressed his desire for the orchestra to perform Mells's symphony and noted, upon his former student's request, his conveying of greetings to his "many friends." "We shall have to write some more letters which naturally we wish to do anyway," hopefully averred Clapp, "so let me hear from you again, and soon."[84]

Clapp's letters to his current and former African American students offer insight on a man whose warmth and intelligence could transcend racial barriers. They expressed genuine care for their recipients, even if such sentiments were predicated primarily on the deep respect he had for their musical talent. The same could be said of the letters sent by these students, who couched their care and respect for Clapp in formal prose aimed to appeal to their mentor's sensibilities. Judging by their frequency and tenor, the letter exchanges satisfied on both ends; they also suggested a desire for meaningful contact across racial lines. Through the written word, Clapp and his students fostered collegial relations if not legitimate friendship that might not have always been possible through face-to-face contact.

Postlude as Prelude

Addressing the good reputation that Iowa's graduate programs enjoyed among African Americans, Philip Hubbard identified music professor Himie Voxman among four department heads who were especially supportive of black students. Hubbard did not mention Voxman's immediate predecessor, Philip Clapp, who created the graduate department and probably had more impact on African Americans earning MA and PhD degrees in music than any other individual in any institution during his lifetime. Years after Voxman's retirement, Clapp's biographer asserted that the elder head's arrival in 1919 "was arguably [Iowa City's] greatest cultural boost to date."[85] This "cultural boost" may be understood to include his success in fostering an educational environment that allowed for, if not embraced, racial diversity and which Voxman continued to nurture. "His legacy should be talked about as much as possible," asserted the critically acclaimed black composer Thomas Jefferson "T. J." Anderson, because "Clapp was responsible for so many [high-caliber] African American composers going to Iowa."[86]

Clapp died on April 9, 1954, one month before the monumental *Brown v. Board of Education* decision that signaled the death knell for legal segregation in the United States. Had he reflected on the struggles waged by graduate and professional school–bound civil rights leaders of the period — including Ada Lois Sipuel Fisher, George McLaurin, and Heman Sweatt — he might have come to appreciate the unique position of his department, educating the next generation of music professors at HBCUs in a South headed toward desegregation. Perhaps he noted a similar trajectory in his own community and school, which in the wake of World War II began to eliminate its own barriers, including the informal policy of excluding black students from the residence halls.[87]

If Clapp failed to appreciate the increasing momentum of the civil rights movement, his worsening health and, more important, loosening grip on his department may have been to blame. After an illness in 1946 that diminished his energy level, the "benevolent dictator" of the music department increasingly became a target for those who wanted new leadership. By June 1951, the dean of the School of Fine Arts, Dr. Earl Enyeart Harper, took steps to force Clapp out of his position. At Harper's request, Voxman began to prepare budgets and assume other departmental administrative duties. Harper appointed a three-person executive committee composed of Herald Stark, Thomas Turner, and Voxman, which had to sign off on all of Clapp's official business. This same year his second wife, Mildred, left him. In spite of his failing health, his diminished executive power, and the administrative efforts to oust him, Clapp held control for as long as he could. He was relieved of his administrative duty on July 1, 1953, and then in March 1954, three weeks before Clapp's death, the Iowa Board of Regents named Voxman department head.[88]

The passing of departmental authority from Clapp to Voxman accompanied another noteworthy transition. In June 1950 — the same month the US Supreme Court struck down legal segregation in graduate and professional education — James Timothy Ashford entered the University of Iowa's music department. A few months later, Mai Olive Prather joined him at the start of the academic year. When Prather completed her MA and Ashford his PhD, they became the first African American graduates without any direct educational ties with either Texas or Oklahoma. Up until their arrival, everyone had either taught or attended (and in the case of Oscar Fuller, Herbert Franklin Mells, Mitchell Southall, and Edison Holmes Anderson, both taught *and* attended) college in one or both of these states. Six of the eight Iowa alumni had direct ties with either Prairie View College or Langston University. No longer were African American graduates channeled exclusively through this academic pipeline, from the music departments of Fuller and Mells, most notably, to the department of Clapp.

This shift signaled departures and changing leadership in the music departments at Prairie View and Langston as well. Upon earning his PhD at Iowa, Fuller assumed duties as music department head at Lincoln University in Missouri.[89] The new music head at Prairie View had no direct link to Clapp, and music students from this college stopped arriving at the University of Iowa. Langston had successive heads with Iowa degrees. Mells served in the position from 1935 until the mid-1940s, when he left to head the music department at Tennessee State University.[90] After serving overseas during World War II, Anderson replaced Mells at Langston, where he stayed for more than thirty years.[91] Anderson sent one of his standout students, Mitchell Southall, to Iowa, where he earned an MFA and a PhD by 1949 before returning to Langston to teach. This homecoming turned out disastrously for Southall, who allegedly fell victim to the stress and insecurities of his new boss, Anderson, and unscrupulous acts by the administration. As Southall told it in letters to Clapp, Anderson "violently assaulted" him over a dispute involving practice facilities, and the administration worked to cover up the event. "I cannot give you all of the details of this four year loss of time here," wrote Southall, "but in the near future, I shall take the time out to drive up there and discuss it in detail with you." In his measured and empathetic response, Clapp avoided taking sides and recommended that Southall find a position somewhere other than at Langston.[92] The soon-to-be phased-out mentor writing to his former student encouraging him to leave the institution at which so many of Iowa's African American graduate students attended or taught provides a melancholic image of an era drawing to a close.

Regardless of the mid-twentieth-century personnel changes at Prairie View, Langston, and Iowa, the academic pipeline formed by the heads of the music departments at these institutions made a profound impact on the music education at HBCUs around the country. Rather than signaling its disintegration, the fact that new graduate students at Iowa started to come from states other than Texas and Oklahoma represented its success. New channels formed over the 1940s and 1950s as graduates from Langston and Prairie View obtained their MA and PhD degrees and accepted positions at institutions with which they had no previous close connection. For instance, after leaving Langston, Southall taught at Lane College, Southern University, and Miles College.[93] Other HBCUs at which early Iowa graduates taught included Rust College (George Overall Caldwell), Fisk University (Lois Towles McNeely), Grambling State University (Earl Preston Harris), Savannah State College (Herbert C. Harris), and Friendship Junior College in Rock Hill, SC (Tallie Mozee).[94]

Distinguished alumnus William Oscar Smith described how the pipeline worked. Hired as director of graduate studies by Mells at Tennessee Southern University, Smith recalled that his boss "planted the first notion in my head about going for a doctorate specifically in music at his *alma mater*, the University of Iowa." He took the advice and completed his PhD in music at Iowa in 1957. Back at Tennessee Southern, Smith "became very close" with faculty member Eddie Goins. "I was able to influence him to go to my school."[95] Goins finished his PhD in 1962.

Regardless of the paths taken to the University of Iowa, the Department of Music benefited immeasurably from the presence and output of the African American students who initially came from the South and eventually arrived from all parts of the country. Fortunately, Clapp, Voxman, and other faculty and administrators recognized this reality and worked to make a hospitable and dynamic place for all students. Their efforts played a part in creating the department that Smith called "a musicians' paradise."[96]

I NEVER THOUGHT OF MYSELF AS AN OUTSIDER

⁙

entered the University of Iowa as a freshman art major in the fall of 1958, having graduated from Muscatine High School during the previous spring. Prior to my senior year in Muscatine, Iowa, I had spent middle school and the first three years of high school at Chester High School in Chester, Illinois, located about sixty-three miles southeast of Saint Louis, Missouri. Both institutions were racially integrated, having a school population that was roughly 97 to 99 percent white. Prior to my family's relocation to Chester, I had attended racially segregated public schools in Alton, Illinois, where all classmates, teachers, and school administrators were African American.

My father, the late Rev. Fred L. Penny, was ordained an AME [African Methodist Episcopal] pastor, and his first pastoral assignment was to Mount Pisgah AME Church in Chester, his boyhood church. Although Chester was and remains a mostly white small community, my paternal roots there date back to 1850 and a number of older citizens remembered my grandparents and my dad as a young boy.

My siblings and I immediately adapted to the relocation from an all-black environment to one that was considerably more rural and nearly all white. We had a strong sense of who we were as individuals and were not discomfited by the overnight demographic change in our environment. It made no sense to me that I should see myself as being more "different" from my new classmates than they were from each other. The most important differences that I noticed among them were social class–related, and these became more sharply defined as they advanced to the higher grade levels. Except for the occasional use of the infamous N-word by a few whom I found easy to dismiss, the nastiest social discrimination that I witnessed was white-on-white class discrimination. For me personally the class pendulum swung wide as the friendliest youngsters tended to come from opposite extremes of the class spectrum, the middle class not so much. To this day I tend to attract people who are polar opposites.

The only other African American pupils with whom I attended school at Chester were cousins. The black school population at Muscatine High School was likewise very small. While opportunities for a social life for high school–aged blacks in a predominantly white setting were very limited in the 1950s, I still managed to make it work for me. I did not shy away from attending dances and other recreational activities, but I mostly concentrated on my studies, attaining placement on Chester High School's academic honor roll for two years in a row. In middle school, I had been one of two pupils to represent my school in a county-wide spelling bee during both seventh and eighth grades. Despite being the only African American pupil in most of my classes, I was somewhat high-spirited, proud, and a little rebellious, refusing to feel stigmatized or stymied by being black and poor. I wasn't about to let any self-esteem issues get in my way. I recognized early that like my more privileged white counterparts, I had been issued a brain at birth and had a responsibility to use it. Chester had excellent public schools, giving me access to a solid educational foundation. As far as I was concerned, neither blackness nor poverty constituted a valid excuse for failure to optimize such opportunity to the fullest extent possible. My father, gregarious and outgoing, was an eternal optimist who constantly held up a positive view of the future to his children, keeping them motivated to move forward.

The described background is what I brought with me when I was accepted by and entered the University of Iowa, an event simultaneous with my father's assignment to Bethel AME Church of Iowa City. Demographically, Iowa City felt like business as usual since again, my family had relocated to a community that was mostly white. In 1958 the African American population of Iowa City was so small that, except for one's own family, an entire week could pass without seeing another black face off campus. Most of the African Americans that I got to know in Iowa City were University of Iowa students. Although I did not pledge, I attended a number of Alpha Kappa Alpha (AKA) social functions. Later, a younger sister did pledge and become an AKA member. Also, in time, more black students began to attend Bethel, where they were able to worship [and] receive counseling, advice, and comfort from my father. Each Sunday, after morning service, a fellowship meal was served, providing an opportunity for black students to interact with each other, discussing the various issues of the day, great and small. Despite Bethel being a historically black church, people of all races were welcome. My father maintained an open-door policy for all. These interactions were very valuable in terms of human relations and understanding, which were helpful to black students who had come to Iowa City from more segregated communities that had larger black populations.

Once black students were able to get past feeling "different" in an "alien" environment, they tended to benefit academically as well. I was aware that tutoring was available to those entering the university from high schools or other educational institutions that were lacking in certain resources and requirements in those pre–affirmative action days. I always felt that those who were earnest about enhancing their life's chances could find what they needed. I admired the University of Iowa's faith in its ability to educate all who made it through the door and wanted to learn.

Weekend recreation tended to consist primarily of Saturday night house parties, most of which were attended by students of all races. Women who lived in the dormitories had a 1:00 a.m. curfew so most would begin leaving the parties around 12:30. My sisters and I usually left at this time also. We often heard later by word of mouth that the parties got wilder after 1:00 a.m., but most of them were relatively sedate prior to 1:00 a.m. with lots of dancing, conversation, and fellowship with peers. I was not too familiar with the bar scene, downtown or elsewhere, and was not attracted by it. With the possible exception of my dad's rogue cousin, I'd always found drunks boorish as well as boring. My sisters and I always left whenever we found ourselves at any gathering where few were left who could still form complete sentences. It was rather bizarre to see any of one's friends roaring drunk. It was as though "space aliens" had abducted him or her and sent in a crazy look-alike as a replacement. We were not opposed to drinking when done in moderation and the drinkers knew when to stop.

My undergraduate experience at the University of Iowa resulted in greatly expanded exposure to the world of visual fine art and fine arts in general. I eagerly embraced this exposure. Although I had innate artistic talent, my visual understanding of the world was limited and a bit corrupted by popular but unsophisticated imagery favored by an uninitiated teenager. I could draw very well but had no clue about what constituted "art." I'd had a sheltered upbringing in small towns and didn't get out much. Needless to say, I was quite naive about the visual arts, a fact that I soon recognized without having to be told and set about to explore the new approaches and learning experiences offered by the School of Art. Under the tutelage of such internationally esteemed luminaries of the world of fine art as Professors James Lechay (life drawing), Eugene Ludins (painting), and Mauricio Lasansky (printmaking), I learned how to "see" a new way, much improving my visual and spatial understanding of the world. This was ultimately liberating, enabling greater creative possibilities and enhanced artistic expression, whether representational or more abstract. I also enjoyed interacting with a fellow African American classmate in studio art — a very talented graduate student named Leon Hicks who went on to distinguish himself in a collegiate art faculty position in Florida.

In addition to the studio art classes, there were art history and theory classes where I learned to identify a number of artists' styles and approaches from throughout the globe and from different periods in history. Along these lines, I was very happy to see the acquisition of the famed Elliott collection of African art for the university's Museum of Art, which contains some unique and amazing art pieces. I still strongly urge everyone to see this exhibit.

In addition to the visual arts, I had been a classical music lover since the age of three. I could sight-read music and loved to sing so I auditioned successfully for the University Chorus, then under the baton of Professor Herald Stark of the University's School of Music. Although not a music major, I would later study piano privately with several teaching assistants. I had studied piano as a youngster but felt there was room for improvement. Private vocal study would come much later when I was no longer enrolled as a student. After joining the University Chorus, I met two gifted African American graduate students, Eddie Goins and Wendell Whalum. Both of these men were doctoral candidates who also sang in the chorus and would soon make their mark in choral music. Mr. Whalum also served as organist at the First United Methodist Church of Iowa City. Recently, upon reading the small print at the bottom of the page of hymn #358 in the current edition of the AME Hymnal, I saw that this traditional spiritual had been arranged by Dr. Wendell Whalum. Further investigation revealed that he had arranged eight other hymns in the book. I was amazed to discover this University of Iowa connection in my church's hymn book, a copy of which I purchased for donation to the Rita Benton Library of the School of Music.

Since my family didn't have much, we attended a great number of world-class on-campus performances and other events that were free. Once every month or two I rounded up all five siblings, and we attended a University of Iowa Symphony concert. Sometimes I took my parents if they weren't busy. Prior to coming to the University of Iowa, I had virtually no access to live performances of any genre of music or theater. All I could do was gaze longingly at the arts and entertainment pages of the *New York Times* or the *St. Louis Post-Dispatch*. There was only a single radio in the house and no television until I was well into my senior year of high school. Later, one of my younger brothers would earn his undergraduate degree from the School of Music, and he is now a jazz musician and composer in Minneapolis. He thanks me for "dragging" him to all those concerts when he was a child. Exposure to these performances helped him discover his own musical gifts as a jazz prodigy when he was ten or eleven years old.

The availability of a number of distinguished lectures was much appreciated. The most memorable among these was the visit of Dr. Martin Luther King [Jr.] in the fall of 1959. Dr. King spoke to a standing-room-only crowd in the Main Lounge of the Iowa Memorial Union. I shall never forget meeting him following his talk and the ensuing question-and-answer period.

I was underweight and not particularly physical, but I had to take some time away from all the arts and great lectures to fulfill an undergraduate physical education requirement, so I studied modern dance, archery, and body mechanics. Swimming, however, did not go so well and I still cannot swim. In those pre-Afro days, most African American women did not go out without first straightening their hair, which, unless permed, would revert back to its natural texture when wet. This was a great hindrance to learning how to swim, and bathing caps did not help much. I enjoyed all the other activities, but body mechanics proved to be the most life changing in terms of greatly improving my posture and overall body alignment, as revealed by before-and-after photos taken by the instructor. This physical training has served me very well ever since.

I was two weeks away from college graduation when I discovered, or rediscovered, that I could also write. A book report had been assigned in the art history class on Italian Renaissance art. To my immense surprise, I received a grade of A on my book report with brief but very positive remarks from Professor Wallace Tomasini written in the margins of the pages. Prior to that assignment, my collegiate writing efforts had been somewhat indifferent and uninspired — something to get through and get over with. What was so different about this particular assignment remains a total mystery to me. In my freshman rhetoric classes, I had proven better at speaking than writing. I had written as a child but had allowed this talent to gather dust despite owning language skills. After this resurrection of a long-neglected ability, my interest in writing and written material was renewed, and thereafter I began to help my siblings and other students, from across a broad ethnic and socioeconomic spectrum, with their writing assignments. My help consisted primarily of correcting grammar and sentence structure and encouraging greater clarity of content. By sheer providence, absolutely everyone that I helped earned an A on his or her paper. It seemed that "A" papers had become contagious. Ironically, many of the papers that I helped with involved analysis of the work of various writers, ranging from William Shakespeare to James Baldwin. I subsequently have also helped a few foreign-born individuals — for whom English was not native — to write letters and other papers so that they could be better understood by their mentors, sponsors, instructors, etc. One young woman was a recent arrival from Germany whom I helped with a paper so that her instructor would know that she understood the subject.

Looking back on all of the above, I find both the physical and demographic changes of today's Iowa City a far cry from the town I moved into in 1958. But I liked it here and stayed.

THE FINE ART OF REPRESENTING BLACK HERITAGE

Elizabeth Catlett and Iowa, 1938—1940

Like the narrator of Ralph Ellison's *Invisible Man*, Elizabeth Catlett found that her education was framed by the realities of segregation. Catlett's trailblazing experience as an African American student of fine arts at Iowa reveals the tension surrounding integration in the Midwest. This chapter examines Catlett's formative educational years and concentrates on her master's work. Her artistic study and emergence as an internationally respected sculptor highlights how her time at Iowa prepared her to confront difficult issues of racial identity and agency. In the late summer of 1938, Catlett was just twenty-three years old when she rode the train from Washington, DC, to Iowa City to attend graduate school at the State University of Iowa. In another testament to the strength of the pipeline between Iowa and historically black colleges and universities (HBCUs) — an issue other essays in this collection address — Catlett chose Iowa on advice from acquaintances at the historically black university North Carolina College for Negroes in Durham (now North Carolina Central University) who had attended the university in Iowa City. When Catlett saw the school catalog, she realized she might be able to afford the tuition that was a reasonable seventy-five dollars per semester, with no out-of-state fee. The fact that she could also study with Grant Wood (1891–1942), a "real artist who was teaching," convinced Catlett to apply.[1] In June 1940, Catlett became the first student to graduate with a master of fine arts degree in a studio art. In addition to her degree in sculpture, two other MFA degrees were awarded in June 1940. This marked the first time this unique degree was conferred in the United States.[2]

Undergraduate Molding:
Training in the Nation's Capital

In 1935, during the middle of segregation and the Depression years, Catlett graduated cum laude with a bachelor of science degree in art from Howard University in Washington, DC. Howard was not her first choice. Catlett was awarded a scholarship to Pittsburgh's Carnegie Institute of Technology but was refused admittance when the college determined she was African American. So Catlett entered Howard, which boasted the first art department at a historically black university. She entered with the support of one semester of tuition saved by her mother and scholarships that covered the balance of her enrollment.[3]

As an art student at Howard, Catlett had several primary influences. Chief among them was her professor James A. Porter, author of *Modern Negro Art* (1943), who taught drawing and painting, Mexican art, Latin American art, and African art. Porter believed that art created by African American artists should be part of the mainstream art history canon.[4] She also studied with James Lesesne Wells, who taught printmaking and crafts; James V. Herring, who founded the department of art in 1921 and the art gallery in 1928 and taught European and American modernism; and Loïs Mailou Jones, a professor of design whose painting fame distinguished her as one of the few black visual artists of the 1930s whose fame reached Europe. As discussed by Brenson and others, Catlett said that she didn't study with Professor Alain Locke because while Porter and Herring believed in the integration of a diversity of Western and non-Western styles created for the public at large, Locke was convinced that African American artists should be primarily influenced and connected to African ancestral traditions and should create art for the African American public. Catlett largely supported Porter and Herring's views.[5]

Initially, Catlett studied seriously with Jones, a black woman who was fast becoming an important force in Harlem Renaissance circles, but she grew tired of value studies and poster design. Nevertheless, they remained lifelong colleagues and friends. Jones, an up-and-coming black female artist, graduated from the school of the Museum of Fine Arts, Boston, and studied African art at Columbia University before Herring persuaded her to teach at Howard.[6] She proved to be an important resource for Catlett, who was still defining her interests. In her junior year, Catlett changed her major to painting with Porter, who encouraged her to become a full-time artist.

Catlett was extremely familiar with both Western and non-Western art. The Howard University Gallery of Art presented regular loan exhibitions under the direction of curator Alonzo J. Aden. Catlett recalled seeing her first exhibition of African art in the gallery. A selection of high-quality reproductions from the Barnes Foundation collection of both European and African art made a strong impression on her. She also remembered traveling to New York City to see exhibitions of works by Georges Rouault and Vincent Van Gogh.[7] Whereas the public museums in the North were open to all individuals at the time, in the South they were closed to African Americans. This fact became significant in the academic year following Catlett's graduation from Iowa when, as head of the art department at New Orleans's Dillard University, she successfully fought to gain admittance for her African American students to a Picasso museum exhibition that had been closed to them because of their race.

Sculpture was not taught at Howard, but Catlett had access to the wide range of public art situated around Washington. By the 1890s, the District of Columbia was home to an abundance of sculpture on a scale found nowhere else in the country. Observers of the monuments and statues could identify the principal modes by which the artists visually asserted power and constructed United States identity. Subjects were often historical figures such as US presidents and military figures, men portrayed as "national heroes" via the literal positioning of the grandiose statues on towering pedestals.[8] The impact of receiving firsthand training from observing these monuments to U.S. character undoubtedly sowed the early seeds of Catlett's notions of the relationship between art and civic identity.

These public monuments and the art created by the US government New Deal art programs were beneficial to Catlett as both an undergraduate at Howard and, later, as a graduate student at the University of Iowa. When Catlett attended Howard, Public Works of Art Projects (PWAP) commissions were made available to students. Catlett recalled an opportunity to design and complete a mural for Minor Teachers College located near the Howard campus. Professor James Porter provided Catlett with a book on the murals of Diego Rivera, and with further research, she discovered the Mexican muralists. Although Catlett was unable to complete the project due to her studies and other activities, she identified with the political, societal, and cultural goals of the muralists. From this experience, Catlett witnessed and began to appreciate that discipline and perseverance were essential if one was to become a professional artist.[9]

In discovering this idea, Catlett joined a number of other black artists affiliated with historically black universities and colleges who enjoyed an established network providing global connections and opportunities. Artists such as Aaron Douglas and Hale Woodruff formed enduring relationships with universities that put them in contact with other artists. Professional artists working on New Deal art projects also formed state-to-state interpersonal networks. The experience of working on projects often provided a heightened sense of community without race, gender, class, or religious distinction. The expression of this collective sensibility could be projected through the subject matter and goals of individual artists. In Stacy Morgan's enlightening book, *Rethinking Social Realism: African American Art and Literature, 1930–1953*, she asserts that complementary modes of operation were established for some African Americans employed by New Deal programs. Morgan suggests that employment in the art programs could make possible both professional integration and the development of a self-determined aesthetic.[10]

When Catlett prepared to begin her graduate work at Iowa, the network of New Deal artists between Washington and Iowa was already established. The PWAP and affiliates included Howard University and Grant Wood, director of the Iowa PWAP in 1933 and 1934. Catlett's sculpture professor, Harry E. Stinson (1898–1975), who taught sculpture courses at Iowa from 1929 to 1940 (Stinson had received a BA in geology and art from Iowa in 1921), was head of the Iowa PWAP sculpture division under Wood. Some of Stinson's sculpture was partially created in university buildings, as were Wood's murals. Stinson and student assistants made several civic sculptures in the school studios, including a cast stone wall relief depicting soldiers located in the northeast entry of the Iowa Memorial Union.[11] Wood and Stinson's PWAP and civic project work formed a connection for Catlett with her PWAP mural experience and reflections on the Washington public sculpture tradition.

Taken together, Catlett's undergraduate training and experiences in Washington, DC, prepared her for the new relationships she would form in Iowa. As she embarked on a new phase of her artistic training, the ideas and core aesthetic sensibility at the heart of her artistic approach took root. She was aware of Danish sculptor Christian Petersen, who also worked for Wood and possibly influenced Catlett's later work. This link is significant because after completing murals at Iowa State College (now Iowa State University) in Ames, Petersen continued to work for the college, where he completed several public sculptures, including the 1941 limestone *Fountain of the Four Seasons*.[12] One of the four female American Indian figures of which the fountain is comprised represents a woman holding an infant. The subject and style of the Petersen figure bears a resemblance to Catlett's thesis sculpture, *Negro Mother and Child.* Catlett likely met Petersen and saw his work when she traveled to Ames in spring 1940 to kiln fire her terracotta figures. The path from DC to Iowa was filled with great promise.

A Student with a Mission:
Sculpting Black Humanity at Iowa

In the late 1930s and early 1940s the Department of Graphic and Plastic Arts was undergoing significant change. Art historian Joni Kinsey notes, "Iowa was a hotbed of aesthetic controversy and innovation, a place where the American Scene clashed with the avant-garde in ways that were central to the ongoing national debate over the future of American art."[13] The conflict that came to a head between Lester Longman, the chair of the program who promoted international modernism, and Grant Wood, the renowned artist and professor who was perceived as regionalism's principal cheerleader, climaxed during the years Catlett studied at Iowa. As the two men struggled to define the relationship between modern art and regionalism, they altered the course of American art. According to Kinsey, the "avant-garde's encounter with the American Scene at Iowa had far-reaching consequences" that "helped establish perceptions of American Scene painting, regionalism, and modernism down to the present day."[14] This is the departmental storm Catlett entered as she began her master's work in Iowa and continued to refine the artistic interests that would define her career.

When Catlett enrolled in the program at Iowa, the MA degree could be obtained after one year or thirty credits, and the MFA could be secured after two years or sixty credits. The second year was to be spent "with exclusively studio subjects."[15] At Iowa, Catlett initially focused on painting, but after the first year her efforts and passions switched to sculpture. Catlett recalled, "I did my first carving in high school that I remember distinctly. We had to do a carving out of a cake of Ivory soap, and I did an elephant. I just cut it out. And then I thought about it all afternoon and night, which I now realize was very strange, to see how to make it look more like an elephant."[16] This focus and intensity that marked her turn to sculpture represented the essence of her approach to her academic program.

Catlett was an excellent student (see table 1). Catlett's diverse course sched-ule attests to her artistic curiosity. But at Iowa, Catlett also wanted to learn everything she could about sculpture. Because metalwork was not offered in the art department, Catlett enrolled in the engineering department's Manu-facturing Processes undergraduate course for instruction in techniques for the manipulation of metals, including soldering, forming, and lost wax casting. In this class Catlett made a sand cast and a wax cast for bronze sculpture. Two of these were included in her thesis exhibition.[17] She had already realized that she would need to develop her own voice to make the most of her studies at Iowa.

Among several influences on Catlett as a graduate student at Iowa were the courses taught by Horst W. Janson, who studied and taught at Iowa from 1938 to 1941. Janson had recently emigrated from Munich, Germany, to the United States, and he had not yet authored the seminal yet widely criticized textbook *The History of Art* (1962). Catlett was enrolled in Janson's Medieval Art and Architecture and Northern Renaissance Art and Architecture. Catlett recalled that "he was a young man who had just come to the United States and he was a really tough art history teacher."[18] She did not mind the challenge and valued the opportunity to work with serious instructors who demanded the best from students enrolled in their courses.

Students at Iowa also had an opportunity to work with Jean Charlot (1898–1979), a French American painter and illustrator known for his murals and close relationships with the Mexican muralists. As a visiting artist at the university during the summers of 1939 and 1940, Charlot created two fresco murals in the art building, no longer extant. *St. Christopher* (1939, fresco, 10 × 2 ft.) was located in an art school classroom and *Woman with Cradle* (1940) was located in a basement corridor of the building. Both murals were composed of one section executed by Charlot and several additional sections by students.[19] Charlot also completed two lithographs at the university in 1939, two versions of the title *First Steps* printed by instructor Francis McCray, and two etchings printed by Charles Okerbloom in 1940.[20]

The presence of Charlot's murals and lithographs in the school, as well as his November 1939 exhibition in the Iowa Memorial Union of twenty-two paintings with primarily Mexican themes, almost certainly nurtured a grow-ing interest in Mexico and printmaking for Catlett. A short newspaper article describing Charlot's November 1939 exhibition notes, "Charlot developed a consuming interest in the life of the common people of Mexico and in the ancient American art of the Maya and Aztec. With River(a), [José] Orozco

TABLE 1. Elizabeth Catlett's Courses and Grades

1938–39 SCHOOL YEAR			
Course	Instructor	Fall Grade	Spring Grade
Oil Painting	Catherine Macartney and Grant Wood	A	A
Sculpture	Harry Stinson	A	A
Watercolor Painting	Catherine Macartney	B	B
Medieval Art and Architecture	Horst W. Janson	B	A
Northern Renaissance Art and Architecture	Horst W. Janson	B	A
Figure Construction	Grant Wood	A	-
Life Drawing	Francis McCray	-	B
1938–39 SCHOOL YEAR			
Course	Instructor	Fall Grade	Spring Grade
Seminar in Art Criticism	Lester D. Longman	A	B
Oil Painting	Grant Wood	B	B
Anatomy	[first name missing] Dawson	A	A
Sculpture	Harry Stinson	A	A
Manufacturing Processes	[no name given]	B	-
Fresco Painting	Harry Jones	-	B
Thesis	Harry Stinson, Grant Wood, Lester D. Longman	B	A

SOURCE: Adapted from Alice Elizabeth Catlett Mora, 1938–1940 transcripts, Office of the Registrar, State University of Iowa.

and others, he did monumental frescoes on the walls of new government buildings. Through all of these ran the theme of the continual struggle of the peasant farmers against domination."[21] Although Catlett would not travel to Mexico until 1946 when she received a Julius Rosenwald Fellowship to study in Mexico City, her exposure to Mexican art and ideas is rooted firmly in her Iowa graduate training.[22]

With Grant Wood as her primary influence at Iowa, Elizabeth Catlett developed a figural style characterized by simple, broad planes. Wood — sounding a similar note as his contemporary in theater, Edward C. Mabie, who is discussed in chapter 3 — suggested to his students that they work from what they knew intimately. He supported Catlett's desire to build on the idea that the personal and the political could be the same thing. From Grant Wood, Catlett received support for her preference to realistically represent what she knew at a time when abstraction was beginning to take hold. She combined regionalist approaches and a growing knowledge of the Mexican mural movement with the visual languages of modernism, Mesoamerican art, West African art, and German expressionism. In a sense, Catlett's artistic exploration reflects the dueling notions at the heart of Wood and Longman's philosophies. Pondering her Iowa experience with Wood, Catlett explained:

> I found out for the first time from the way he worked that creating a work of art has a process. . . . He made us begin with a line drawing. First he said, "What are you going to do? It should be something you know most about." I decided to do a little black girl ironing; I knew a lot about ironing. Then we did a diagram, from which we reworked our line drawing. Then we did a drawing on brown wrapping paper using charcoal and chalk to get the values straight, and only then could we go into a painting, where we were limited to three or four colors. And as we learned what we could do with those colors, then we could add other colors.[23]

Catlett described the limited palette Wood assigned as "ivory, black, white, yellow ochre and Indian red."[24] After a while Wood allowed the students to "add a little Alizarin Crimson and mix a little white with black to make a blue."[25]

The reworked drawing was based on the principle of dynamic symmetry, adding slight distortions, which strengthened the drawing. Through her career Catlett continued to distort and exaggerate for expressive emphasis. Catlett noted:

> Something about the way Wood worked fitted right in with the way I liked to work. I like to work exactly. My aunt taught me how to knit and it took me a long time to learn because I never wanted to have a dropped stitch and I never wanted it to be dirty. I wanted it to be exact which is why I imagine I sand wood and stone instead of leaving the tool marks.

I like smooth surfaces and things finished. And he worked with his hands a lot. I remember Lois Jones being very dainty with what she was doing and I remember Grant Wood rolling his hands up and getting them down in the paint. He used to take a piece of Masonite and paint, white lead paint on it, and then sand it.[26]

Like other African American students pursuing degrees in University of Iowa art programs, Catlett's tutelage under Wood had a profound impact on her creative development. She arrived at the university with a strong sense of her individual artistic technique rooted in her cultural upbringing and cultivated at Howard, where she distinguished her singular method from Jones's less physical work. When Catlett began working on her master's degree, Wood's approach complemented and inspired her.

Although Catlett did not study printmaking at Iowa, she recalled, "I remember I made some Christmas cards once in lithography . . . they had a little thing on the board of how to do a lithograph and they were real little lithographs. And I put about five of them on one stone so I printed all of them . . . it was like 10 printings."[27] There is no doubt Catlett would have observed Grant Wood drawing on the lithography stones provided to him by Associated American Artists (AAA) for some of the sixteen lithographs he created between 1938 and 1940. Catlett would have noted that his precise draftsmanship, compositional approach, and sensitivity to tonal nuances and contrasts were ideally suited to the medium, and that he was a thoughtful and conscientious artisan who treated printmaking as seriously as he did painting. Later in her career Catlett would become recognized for both her sculpture and her prints.

Catlett was not only impacted by Wood's aesthetic techniques, but she was also likely inspired by his philosophy regarding introducing art to the public. Wood liked the idea of making art available to the public at very low prices. In a 1938 letter he wrote, "I am so thoroughly convinced of the value of the five dollar original lithographs as the most effective means of producing an art-minded public for the future, that I would be delighted to sign a long-time exclusive contract with AAA tomorrow. A contract based on the five dollar print — depression or no depression."[28] At Iowa, Catlett learned that public sculpture, murals, and printmaking were capable of reaching mass audiences.

In addition to learning from her courses and professors, Catlett consistently pursued her interest in the history of art by visiting art exhibitions and the art library. She believed "the more art you look at the more you understand and

the more you learn about art."[29] As a student at Iowa, Catlett had the opportunity to view many art exhibitions in the Iowa Memorial Union. Exhibitions
held from fall 1938 through spring 1940 included *War Etchings by Goya and
Dix; Drawings by American and European Artists; Archipenko, Sculpture and
Painting; Beckmann; Fifty Prints from Associated American Artists; Thomas Hart
Benton, Paintings, Lithographs and Drawings;* and *Jean Charlot, Paintings, Lithographs and Drawings.*[30] This consistent and broad exposure to art, together
with her rigorous training and supportive instruction, positioned Catlett to
commence her master's work with confidence.

A Thesis for African American Community

The realities of Catlett's life at Iowa undoubtedly fueled her desire to craft
sculpture that spoke to the importance of African American relationships in
a country that failed to see them as equals. She completed her master's work
on a campus where African American students were banned from living in
campus dormitories until 1946. When Catlett arrived in Iowa City, several
African American students met her train and helped her find a room in the
one-story shotgun boardinghouse of a Mrs. Scott. Catlett recalled this communal welcoming and mused, "They were just there."[31] Like many other black
students, she paid ten dollars a month rent for the room. In her second year,
Catlett lived in a different boardinghouse for African American women and
paid twenty dollars per month for the room. For a few months in that house
Catlett shared a room with author Margaret Walker.[32] Catlett remembered
that in her first year, eighty African American men and eight African American
women students were enrolled at Iowa.[33]

Several dissertations describe the situation for African American students,
who were forced to look beyond the university for everything from housing and eateries to clothing stores and hair care. For example, at the time,
Towner's department store did not allow African American men or women
to try on clothes.[34] Of course, for many students like Catlett, shopping for
new clothes was a luxury they rarely could afford. After her tuition and room,
Catlett had thirty-five dollars per month from her mother to live on. She sold
her beautiful handmade winter coat for extra money and then purchased a ski
jacket and pants, which were much more practical for the weather in Iowa.
When she ran out of money for food that she usually purchased in the student
union, Catlett would go to Vivian's restaurant: "I would say, 'Vivian, do you

want any help? And she would say, 'Oh, yes. So I would make hamburgers and serve people and would eat there, but I would miss a little time from school."[35] Describing her social life, Catlett commented, "I spent all day at the art department until late at night and on weekends.... I played bridge with Vivian and two other ladies on Wednesday afternoon because they had good food."[36] An active swimmer and working summer pool lifeguard in Washington, DC, Catlett revealed in Dr. Clifton H. Johnson's 1984 interview that she broke the racial discrimination barrier in the University of Iowa gymnasium swimming pool.[37]

Even as she faced the hurdles erected on a segregated campus, Elizabeth Catlett explored many possible paths of inspiration to determine her final thesis subject. As she strove to create a monolithic sculpture that reflected both tradition and modernity, she decided to represent the bond between mother and child. Catlett's relationship with her own mother was of seminal significance. Catlett's father died before she was born, leaving her mother on her own to raise Catlett and her two siblings. Catlett's mother also shared family stories regarding enslaved ancestors, a legacy not far removed from her life since three of Catlett's grandparents were slaves. These familial realities conveyed occasions of forced, broken bonds. In interviews and documents throughout her career, Catlett shared the story of the horrific incident of the kidnapping of her pregnant grandmother's grandmother who gave birth to a stillborn baby on the slave ship, and of her great-grandmother, whose daughter was taken from her and sold.[38]

Catlett wanted to infuse her master's project with the spirit of this inheritance. Completing at least one piece of sculpture in a medium other than plaster for the advanced degree was also of uppermost importance to her.[39] Catlett's written thesis includes five black-and-white photographs: a sheet of preliminary sketches, a sheet of sketches of the final idea, the clay model, the plaster cast and limestone sculpture in progress, and the completed sculpture. The methodology of the sketches evolved from Professor Porter's drawing instructions at Howard, which he prepared from George B. Bridgman's approach to drawing.[40] Bridgman was an artist and lecturer who taught figure and anatomy drawing for more than forty-five years at New York City's Art Students League and published six books on anatomy for artists. The box forms of Catlett's thesis sketches represent the major masses of the figure (head, thorax, pelvis, appendages), which she linked with lines to create "wedges," or simplified, interconnecting forms of the body.

In her thesis, Catlett describes the construction of four small clay figures, one of which was a larger standing figure, which she ultimately discarded because it was deemed more suited for bronze, not stone. Catlett wrote that she selected the seated position for the figure based on her observations of mothers and children in the community because the "two always seemed closer, always more compact; and compactness is one of the characteristics of stone."[41] She proceeds to describe the primary aim of the sculpture: "To create a composition of two figures, one smaller than the other, so interlaced as to be expressive of maternity, and so compact as to be suitable to stone, seemed quite a desirable problem. The implications of motherhood, especially Negro motherhood, are quite important to me, as I am Negro as well as a woman."[42]

In a conversation with Mary Gibbons, Catlett revealed that she took the pose of her model to feel it in her own body.[43] From the model, Catlett formed a clay figure, which was fired and then cast in plaster. Using a piece of Indiana limestone one and a half times larger than the plaster cast — an expensive purchase requiring a disciplined effort — Catlett began to "rough out" the main masses with a claw hammer and refine it with a hammer and point, tooth and flat chisels. She employed pumice stone and water and stone rasps to smooth the surface. With increasing familiarity, Catlett made decisions about the surface textures based on her own technical discoveries. Describing the process, Catlett wrote:

> [The] texture on the mother's hair originated through an accidental discovery that the large tooth chisel driven straight in gave an interesting rough surface. A smaller tooth chisel gave texture to the baby's hair; and a claw hammer used on the base was responsible for its rough effect. The undraped sections on the mother and child were than [sic] sanded to obtain an even finish. It seemed more effective, however, to leave a little variation in the drapery, and so it was worked over with a tooth chisel and flat chisel.[44]

Negro Mother and Child, sadly now lost, was exhibited at the 1940 Tanner Hall Art Galleries of the American Negro Exposition in Chicago, held July 4 through September 2, where it won "First Honor" for sculpture. The exhibition of more than three hundred pieces selected from more than five hundred entries by a jury headed by Donald Cayton Rich of the Art Institute of Chicago was curated by Howard University Gallery of Art curator

Alonzo J. Aden.[45] African American artist Hale Woodruff designed the cast bronze awards. Historian Adam Green describes the exposition as an often forgotten example of African Americans proactively shaping their lives and communities.[46] In *Modern Negro Art* (1943), Catlett's former professor James Porter described *Negro Mother and Child* accordingly: "The simple round massiveness of the work exemplifies good taste and soberly thoughtful execution. It avoids those pitfalls of sentimentality . . . [of] . . . so many academic bores who pumice the marble until it resembles a pin cushion [*sic*] more than a work of art. The negroid [*sic*] quality in Mother and Child is undeniable, and the work has poise and a profound structure."[47]

Catlett's sculpture has affinities with several of her contemporaries. William Zorach's 1931 *Mother and Child* was a significant influence, as were female African American sculptors from the first half of the twentieth century Selma Burke, Meta Warrick Fuller, Edmonia Lewis, Nancy Elizabeth Prophet, and Augusta Savage. In 1934, Savage became the first African American artist to be elected to the National Association of Women Painters and Sculptors, and she was also the first director of Harlem's Community Arts Center, where Catlett was later employed. Following in Savage's footsteps, Catlett allowed her art to speak to the importance of black community through representations of powerful black women and black mothers and children, themes she repeatedly explored over the course of her entire career. By a quirk of fate, a few years before Catlett began her rise, Ralph Ellison had initially traveled to New York with a letter of introduction from his Tuskegee art professor to secure him a place in Augusta Savage's West 143rd Street basement studio.[48] The young Ellison likely never imagined that an artist of Catlett's caliber would one day create a memorial in honor of him.

Ironically, the undergraduate mechanical engineering course Catlett took outside the art department became the focus of a disagreement within Catlett's committee. The members included Janson, Longman, Stinson, and Wood. Initially Dr. Longman did not want to accept the course toward the degree, even though Catlett also had four graduate credit hours transferred from Howard University. Catlett described her conversation with Dr. Longman in his office:

"Miss Catlett, you have to put in an application for your degree." And I said, yes. And he said "well I would advise you to put it in for a Master of Arts degree because you can't get an MFA degree because you haven't had any printmaking." And I said "I have had some printmaking and I have done some lithography since I have been here." . . . And I said "why didn't you tell me this last year, because I could have applied and received the MA in one year." So I applied for the MA, but I was very angry.[49]

Considering the larger feud unfolding between Longman and Wood concerning modern and regionalist art, Catlett may well have found her work and progress toward the new degree caught up in her professors' dueling views. According to Catlett, it was Grant Wood who fought for Catlett's entitlement to the MFA. Catlett described Wood as "a very wonderful person . . . he had a delightful sense of humor. When I told him I wanted to change my major to sculpture from painting he said 'that's alright I don't mind you changing.'"[50] After she completed her oral exams for the MA, Grant Wood telephoned her and said, "I have something to tell you. We are going to try and get you the MFA degree. Come prepared for a battle."[51] Catlett added that everyone on her committee except Dr. Longman thought that she should receive an MFA if the sculpture professor (Stinson) was going to receive the same. "They asked me to sit outside for at least an hour and a half. I could hear loud voices with the arguing going on inside." When they invited her in, Wood stood, offered his hand to her, and said, "Let me be the first to congratulate you. You are going to receive the Master of Fine Arts."[52]

After graduating from Iowa, Catlett was appointed chair of the art department at Dillard University in New Orleans, Louisiana. Like many African American UI graduates who accepted positions at HBCUs after they left Iowa, she quickly assumed responsibility, playing a leadership role in the development of the art curriculum. Although Catlett once professed, "I didn't want to be a teacher, I wanted to be an artist,"[53] she later averred, "I have always wanted my art to service black people — to reflect us, to relate to us, to stimulate us, to make us aware of our potential. Learning how to do this and passing that learning on to other people have been my goals."[54] The themes and approaches set forth in Elizabeth Catlett's Iowa thesis *Negro Mother and Child* (1940) would largely endure for the remainder of her long career as her work continued to acknowledge the weight of the past and the force of the present, pointing toward the future.

Indeed, the steadfastness of her aesthetic philosophy make it of little surprise that she was chosen to complete the *Invisible Man* monument in 2003, just nine years before her death. The fifteen-foot-high, ten-foot-wide bronze monument features a large figure in motion who asserts his presence through Catlett's playful cutout motif: when viewers look at the sculpture, they see through it, re-creating Ellison's invisible theme. Catlett followed her vision in designing and realizing the piece even when the organizers had other ideas. She recalled, "When I went to Washington, D.C., to chat about the work, I walked into the meeting room and there were 15 people sitting there telling me where the sculpture was going to go, what it should look like, what materials I should use. I let it go on for a while, and then I said, 'I'm not listening to you.' They were very surprised."[55] For Catlett, like many other black Hawkeyes, Ellison's premise resonated personally. Discussing her memorial to Ellison in a 2003 National Public Radio interview, she admitted, "I, as an artist, a black woman artist, have been invisible in the art world for years."[56] This no longer need be the case.

A DIFFERENT KIND OF BEAUTY CONTEST

attended Jack Yates High, one of the three black high schools in Houston. During my senior year, my guidance counselor discovered my interest in theater. She knew a teacher at another black school who had pursued doctoral studies in performing arts at the University of Iowa, and she urged me to talk with him. I did, and based on our conversations, I applied and earned admission to UI. My decision to attend a school over a thousand miles away did not faze my family. To understand why, I have to describe my upbringing.

I'm an only child of a single mother, but despite my father's absence, you might say that I really had three parents. My mother loved me, and my grandmother basically raised me. My aunt who had no children of her own treated me like a daughter. Though each of these women invested heavily in my future, my grandmother led the pack. She wanted at least one person in her family to attend college, and even if the school were on the moon, she would have tried to make it happen. When I received the chance to go to the University of Iowa, she, along with the rest of my family, got busy figuring out how they could send me to school. They created a plan, and in summer 1955, I departed for UI.

I traveled to Iowa City by train. The trip took two days, but it was really fun because that year four black kids from Houston entered the University of Iowa. We partied all the way to the university, but when we reached the campus, the celebration ended. None of us knew anything about the town. As we settled into our new surroundings, we realized that many miles separated us from our loved ones. My initial experiences captured the difficulty of such separation.

Freshmen had to go through an orientation, so we arrived a little earlier than the upperclassmen. At one welcoming function, I met a young, white male. We struck up a friendship, and after getting my address he invited me on a date. A few days later, he canceled our plans. I never saw him again. Through episodes like this one, I learned that even when you move across regions, certain mind-sets still flourish in America. This lesson stung a little; however, it did not surprise me. Growing up in Houston, I lived in a Jim Crow society. The year before I graduated, the Supreme Court ruled segregated schools illegal, yet in 1955, nothing had changed yet. Because of my background, I did not come to UI believing that the school would cater to me. I expected that white boys wouldn't date black girls and that black students wouldn't have the same privileges as whites. Such situations did not dampen my enthusiasm for being there; rather, they taught me to lean on my friends.

My peers and I were accustomed to making our own community. In Iowa City, we pursued that activity with a vengeance. When the upperclassmen returned to campus, I quickly learned that the black students maintained a lively social network. Greek organizations played a key role. During my first semester, the Kappas sponsored a mixer to make sure that all incoming students mingled with the people who were already there. Black students didn't have access to campus facilities, but the Unitarian church allowed us to use their basement. Even as we faced discrimination, our camaraderie grew because we found solutions together. We looked out for one another. That caring explains why I have very few, if any, bitter memories of UI. I shared my family's excitement about the adventure of higher education, and being in college made me so happy that only something cataclysmic could have soured it for me. If my black friends buffered me from such disasters, then my white peers propelled me to an unexpected accomplishment.

I stayed in Currier Hall, the biggest female dorm on campus, and of the one hundred black students enrolled at the University of Iowa, only a handful of us lived in that residence hall. Most of the white women in Currier attempted to show me that they weren't prejudiced and that they were just good folks. During fall 1955, the Miss State University of Iowa contest gave them a forum in which to display their convictions. The Miss SUI competition involved housing units from all across the university. Each of these residences would put forward candidates who would vie to be crowned the campus queen. Since I had only been in school almost three months, I didn't know about the contest, and even if I had known, as a freshman, I had neither the audacity nor the planning to run for the title. Despite my reluctance, when the elections for Currier were held, my dorm mates chose me as one of the finalists. I appreciated their support and depended on their help even more in the next phase of the selection process.

After the dorm competition, the remaining candidates stumped for votes campus-wide. This part of the campaigning began with a kickoff event in the student union. During the event, each finalist introduced herself to the crowd. As we did, most of us used a skit or a clever little gimmick to make ourselves memorable. J. P. Cochran, a terrific guy and a graduate student in theater, served as my creative director. When he found out that I was a finalist, he brainstormed a great idea for my skit. He knew that I came from Houston, and since Mitch Miller's "The Yellow Rose of Texas" got played a lot then, J. P. thought that my skit and my campaign slogan should be linked to the song. He wrote a script, and my friends from the dorm performed it. For a couple of weeks after the kickoff event, we made the rounds. Only men could vote, so once we contestants got decked out in our finest dresses, somebody would pull up in a really pretty car and off we would go to the dorms and fraternity houses trying to convince male students that we should be their campus queen. The campaigning took place during a designated period and in scheduled places, so everybody had a chance to interact with all the voters. In order to have successful public appearances, my peers did lots of private work.

The black women in my dorm sat up night after night making little paper yellow roses, and I would hand out these tokens every place we went. Because they had the largest room, Lowetta Hightower, Julie Fisher, Audrey Dixson, and the Moore sisters regularly handled flower duty. At some point, almost all of my black sisters helped. They also got together all of their finest gowns so that I never had to go out in the same dress twice, and one of them, Julie Fisher, had a beautiful fur coat. I'm all decked out in somebody else's clothes every night. That was just an example of how, as a community, our folks came together to support this effort. I mean it was really a community effort, and I couldn't have done this by myself.

The voting took place via secret ballot and happened on one day. Usually officials tallied the votes, and during the big winter ball the night after the election, they announced the winner. That year, the results leaked out before the dance, and by the time the school shared the results, many people already knew that I had won the crown. Stories about my victory appeared in all the newspapers before it was even formally announced on campus. I got a call from a reporter about eleven o'clock in the morning the day before the dance. Stories about my victory not only appeared locally, but within a few days, the story traveled around the globe. I heard from people as far away as Europe and Africa. In addition, individuals from all over the US sent me newspaper clippings from their local papers. There was a full-page color photo in *Look* magazine as well as in *Jet*. During all of this attention, I even received a telegram from Mitch Miller!

The news of my triumph broke just a few days after Thanksgiving and only a few weeks before school was recessed for the Christmas holidays. As word of the honor spread, my friends again gave me their support. I had a dress — my own dress this time — that I was going to wear to the crowning ceremony. Although this dress was white, it was short. By the time I arrived at the dorm, my girlfriends had already decided that I should wear a long flowing gown, one that would be more fitting for a queen. Tricka Harris had this gorgeous white dress that was yards and yards and yards of toile, and they all agreed that I would wear this gown. They pressed it, making sure it didn't have a wrinkle anywhere, and I wore that dress to the ball. When I got back to Currier that night, my dorm mates had decorated my floor like a queen's palace, and my room was the throne. They had wrapped everything in aluminum foil and decorated every square inch of space. My peers, starting with my very special roommate Gerri Spencer, gave me a great reception. When I arrived home for the holidays, the reaction was even more impressive. I got off the train in Houston, and the whole town, including the band from my alma mater, turned out for a big parade. My supporters mobbed the train station, and the hometown hosted a huge celebration. This moment created a high for everybody including my high school teachers, family friends, and church members. Everyone basked in this accomplishment, and more than anybody else, I soaked in the excitement. This feeling did not last.

Although I had been recognized at an official crowning ceremony before I left Iowa City for Houston, as far as the university was concerned, that moment at the Fire and Ice Ball marked the beginning and the end of my reign. The school leadership never officially acknowledged me as the campus queen. Traditionally, Miss SUI had reigned or been acknowledged at certain events. Instead of allowing me to fulfill those duties, the university canceled those appearances. Initially, I thought that shifts in local schedules dictated these changes; however, when a Big Ten engagement did not happen, I realized that I would be unlike any other Miss SUI. Our football team went to the Rose Bowl, and in prior years, the campus queen had been on the parade float. During the year that I was Miss SUI, they bypassed me and reached back to invite the last year's Homecoming queen. They excused this slight by explaining that she was a graduating senior so this would be her last chance to be honored while I — as a freshman — would have many other opportunities. No such opportunities materialized because not only did the university leaders cancel everything during my reign but also they promptly took steps to ensure that a "mistake" like a black queen could never happen again. The administration drafted new rules governing the Miss SUI contest, and these rules gave the administration unprecedented powers in the selection process. In the future, they would be able to produce whatever result they wanted.

In other publications, I have stated that I felt no bitterness about these experiences, and with the benefit of further reflection, I still believe that's a very honest answer. I chose not to dwell on the university's prejudice because doing so, in essence, granted the institution the power to invalidate what we did. For me, our effort should never be shortchanged. Winning Miss SUI signaled a watershed because of the time at which it occurred and the social dynamic that prevailed. In the 1950s, white universities weren't electing black campus queens every day; therefore, UI's inability to accept that it had created an environment where that could happen made me think "shame on them." Equally important, the students who cooperated in the face of intolerance deserved to have their really important accomplishment celebrated. If the university wasn't big enough to embrace their courage, then the school would have to cope with that loss in dignity. My main concern then and now is recognizing the phenomenal individuals who helped me do something that I never could have done alone.

At the time that I became Miss SUI, I was very young. I turned eighteen while I was at home on Christmas vacation. Because of my youth, I didn't fully appreciate what my experiences meant. Reflecting on these events today, I see that this moment deeply influenced my early adulthood. My confidence increased, and even more important, my appreciation for my peers soared. The people I met at UI were amazing. In the face of incredible odds, they pursued and achieved an unprecedented result. I tried to thank them then, and now I use every chance I get to let my friends know how much I appreciated their support. Young people who are reading these remarks today may not know what the social climate was like in 1955 when all of this took place. Suffice to say that even at UI with its long tradition of tolerance, there were many individuals who did not see black people as equals. My friends knew that these opinions existed on campus, and despite that difficulty, they still put time and energy into my candidacy. Their faith impressed me, and through the election process, I met some remarkable people that are still a part of my life today.

In 1998, during one of our reunions, the Iowa Black Alumni Association (IBAA) presented me with a plaque that commemorated my election as Miss SUI 1955. This occasion allowed me to revisit the events that defined my time at UI, and the process proved instructive. During the program, a university representative made some remarks, but frankly, I don't remember a word he said. I do, however, remember what he didn't say. He did not apologize for the university's failure to validate our accomplishment in 1955, nor did he make any offer to correct that wrong. In the face of such neglect, the sentiments of my fellow IBAA members provided a stark contrast. Barbara Miller, presenting on behalf of IBAA, spoke in tones that brought me to tears. Following Barbara's presentation, the other folk in the room that night showed me their continued affection. Their goodwill continues to be what matters the most to me.

When I was on campus in spring 2013, I sensed that the interconnectedness that had sustained me was missing for many of the young black students there today. This situation saddened me. All of these years later, and they still seem to feel marginalized and disconnected. On top of that, they are not unified. Back in the '50s, we all supported each other; one black student would never walk past another without exchanging a good word. We felt that our survival depended on having each other's back. I know that much has changed since then and that we live in a very different world, but maybe we would be better off if some things had not changed. Iowa still launches the careers of its black students, and while they are on campus, they collect important memories that shape their lives. For me, Iowa was a place of warm lifelong connections. Not only did I form vital friendships but also I met and married my husband, an alumnus of UI. We have been together for fifty-seven years, and from that campus connection, I pursued an eventful path.

After we were married, I left Iowa to become an army wife, yet mindful of my grandmother's wishes, I remained committed to my education. I later completed my undergraduate degree at Roosevelt University in Chicago. After undergrad, I began work on a graduate degree in social work at Loyola. My husband and I eventually settled in New Jersey, where we have remained for forty-six years. I completed my MSW at Rutgers and had a very rewarding career as the first full-time social worker for a predominantly white, upper-middle-income school district just outside of Princeton. In addition to my work with special populations within the student body, I was encouraged to bring programs on diversity into the district. Additionally, I participated in the district's efforts to recruit more minorities onto the professional staff. After twenty-nine years, I left the school district to become a licensed clinical social worker in a small, private mental health agency in the same community. Two years ago I retired and am now a volunteer on the board of a local halfway house for women in recovery. I am the proud mother of three and equally proud grandmother of three more. Whether it is appropriately acknowledged or not, UI lurks in the backdrop of these developments. Good and bad together, I would not trade my time there.

STAGING AUTHENTIC AFRICAN AMERICAN CHARACTER

Regionalism, Race, and UI Theater

On July 18, 1936, Fanny McConnell (who would later become Fanny Elli-son) wrote to President Bluford at North Carolina Agriculture and Technical College, a historically black college in Greensboro. She opened her letter by highlighting her credentials:

> On June 1, 1936 I graduated from the State University of Iowa with a Bachelor of Art's degree and a major in Dramatic Art. I am prepared to direct a little theatre movement in a college and, also, to teach the various theatre practices that students are obliged to know in order to produce effective results in acting and the staging of plays. The subjects included in Dramatic Art which I might teach are: Acting, Stage-make-up, Voice and Diction, Phonetics, and some Stagecraft. I also am able to teach Dramatic Literature, English, Shorthand . . . and typewriting, and Public Speaking.

Fanny closed her missive by offering to provide a reference from "Miss Helene Blattner, University of Iowa, Iowa City, Iowa."[1] Her determination to draw attention to her work at Iowa reflects both her awareness of the cutting edge nature of the UI theater program as well as the unique position she held as a black graduate from the institution in 1936. Additionally, she seemed confident that her professor would attest to her capacity for producing good work in the realm of drama.

Fanny also publicized her graduation in the *Nashville World*. In June 1936, the newspaper announced, "Chicago is proud to greet Miss Fanny McConnell who has returned from Iowa City where she was just graduated from the State University of Iowa. Miss McConnell majored in dramatic art" and "is now one of the few trained Negroes in that field." The article proceeds to proudly proclaim, "She was the only Negro student to graduate from that department and did some very fine things while there. She directed several plays; was given the leading role in radio productions, and did interpretive reading at which she earned a commendable reputation." By attending to the details of Fanny's training, the newspaper underscored her distinctive status. Fanny's letter to President Bluford — along with a letter she sent to Yale in August 1936 inquiring as to whether she might "register in the Department of Drama at Yale"[2] — makes good on the promise at the end of the propitious Nashville article: "Miss McConnell hopes to find a position as a teacher, preferably in dramatic art, by fall. She hopes further to continue her work at Yale University."[3]

Fanny viewed her undergraduate work at Iowa as valuable training that she was determined to develop and transfer to the black community. She believed the art of drama could meaningfully impact the position of African Americans in the United States, and her conviction found crucial philosophical support at the State University of Iowa. Her 1934 arrival in Iowa City proved an auspicious moment for students studying drama. Though the inception of the University Theatre traces its roots back to the 1920–1921 academic year when it was formally designated the Department of Speech, no more than five years had passed since the department was renamed the Department of Speech and Dramatic Art to reflect its special focus on drama. Thus, 1929 witnessed the founding of the School of Fine Arts just as a new focus on drama emerged.[4]

The person responsible for shaping the theater program played a central role in making it an attractive program for African American students. A Wisconsin native who held bachelor's and master's degrees in political science, Edward Charles Mabie had been serving as head of the department since 1923. By October 1934, he was charging ahead with plans for a new building to house the drama department.[5] Although he was initially hired to teach debate, Mabie quickly became a transformative force in the world of theater. Professor Glenn Merry mused, "[Mabie] was what I needed in debating, but my theatrical department was pitiful. Ed had a great originality and ignored what it was to overwork. . . . Ed was a dramatic personality with an unmitigated temper. So I turned him loose; you know the results. He was a creative genius."[6] Eccentric, earnest, and extremely passionate about authentically portraying the Midwest to the rest of the country, Mabie strove to revise pedagogical approaches to theater on university campuses. While by no means an ardent supporter of black equality, Mabie nevertheless saw a definite symmetry between the staging of genuine regional character and the development of African American character in US drama. As a result, he supported black students who came to Iowa in pursuit of both undergraduate and graduate degrees in all facets of dramatic art.

Mabie's devotion to carving out a new identity for theater arts at Iowa ensured that Fanny was not alone in seeking Iowa as a training ground for developing African American drama. After she completed her undergraduate studies in 1936, a number of African American students entered the Department of Speech and Dramatic Art to pursue graduate work. This cohort that matriculated through the program from the late 1930s through the 1950s went on to become major forces in African American theater and on the campuses of historically black colleges and universities (HBCUs) in particular. Just as Fanny sought employment at North Carolina A&T, the black graduates who followed her viewed their degrees as crucial credentials necessary for changing the face of training future African American students of drama. These theater practitioners entered advanced degree programs at Iowa on the heels of the Harlem Renaissance and major stage success stories such as Langston Hughes's *Mulatto* (1935), the longest-running Broadway play by an African American until Lorraine Hansberry's *A Raisin in the Sun* debuted in 1959. Under Mabie's direction, however, Iowa encouraged theater students to view their *training independently* from Broadway's artistic philosophy. Mabie counseled students to infuse staged productions featuring their region and culture with a dose of reality necessary for American theater to become a vehicle for introducing US diversity in forceful, authentic terms.

The black students who enrolled in UI's theater department took Mabie's artistic philosophy to heart. As the struggle for racial equality shifted into high gear during the 1940s, UI theater majors looked beyond the racial difficulties suffusing their daily educational experience and anticipated their future contributions to the teaching, creation, and production of black drama. They viewed their time in Iowa City through a lens of future possibility. Iowa was not free of racial prejudice, and even progressive educators such as Mabie did not always treat black students equally. Unlike his peer, Philip Greeley Clapp, whose career in the music department closely paralleled Mabie's tenure in the Department of Speech and Dramatic Art, Mabie was not as supportive of black students during their studies or after their graduation from his program.

African American students concentrating on dramatic art, like their black peers in other departments, faced the disorienting reality of enjoying access to world-class training in the classroom while simultaneously suffering the discomfort of racially biased policies throughout Iowa City. Jim Crow was not officially sanctioned on campus, but as other chapters in this volume note, practices barring black students from local businesses were widespread. Notwithstanding this difficult reality, over a twenty-year period beginning with Fanny's undergraduate studies, the Department of Speech and Dramatic Arts awarded degrees to black students who profoundly influenced the world of African American drama. This chapter touches upon these students' experiences at Iowa from the 1930s through the 1950s — and provides glimpses of their professional work — to examine how Iowa theater training influenced the artistry of black UI graduates and proved the centrality of the large white public university in the work of creating a pluralistic US society.

Creating Art Out of Ethnic Conflict: The Roots of UI's Experimental Theater

The story of African American students who pursued degrees in theater during the dawning days of Iowa's drama program cannot be told without a serious contemplation of E. C. Mabie's leadership and vision for the department. Mabie aimed to establish Iowa as a theater powerhouse. In 1935, he hosted the National Theatre Conference at the State University of Iowa, and he was proud to have the announcement of the new director of the Federal Theatre Project (FTP) delivered in Iowa City. President Franklin Delano Roosevelt's Works Progress Administration was determined to put artists back to work during the Great Depression while continuing the cultivation of authentic American art. The appointment of Hallie Flanagan, an Iowa native and graduate of Grinnell University, to lead the Federal Theatre Project promised to emphasize the trailblazing work unfolding in the states of the Midwest far away from New York City. Like Mabie, Flanagan shared a deep belief in the potential of the regional stage to portray the diversity of American character that Broadway productions invariably missed, ignored, or egregiously caricatured. As one of her first appointments, she designated Mabie to oversee the midwestern region. In her tentative plan for dividing the country, she selected Mabie to preside over North Dakota, South Dakota, Minnesota, Nebraska, Iowa, Kansas, and Missouri. In a letter to Mabie, Flanagan designated these states "Yours, of course," and explained, "I confess to some disappointment as to some of these divisions; on the other hand, I realize that the midwestern area was too gigantic a setup for any one person, even a person with superhuman energy!"[7] She was well aware of the ambitious work Mabie was carrying out in Iowa, and she worked hard to keep him involved in the Federal Theatre Project.

Flanagan also viewed African Americans as a crucial part of the success of American theater. When production plans and organizational efforts encountered difficulties in many regions she supervised as the director of the FTP, she remained careful to celebrate the accomplishment of the black units. In a September 1935 telegram, she praised the progress Elmer Rice was making with the Harlem Negro Unit of the FTP, also known as the Negro Theatre.[8] As director of the New York region, Rice proudly announced that the Negro Unit's initial show would debut between January 15 and February 1, 1936. He noted several works that he hoped to bring to the stage, including *St. Louis Woman* by Countee Cullen and Arna Bontemps, an untitled play by Zora Neale Hurston, Frank Wilson's *Walk Together Children*, and a special production of William Shakespeare's Scottish play later dubbed the "Voodoo *Macbeth*."[9] Mabie, however, remained somewhat skeptical of the federally driven program, its potential for success in the Midwest, and the role African Americans would play in its productions.[10] In stark contradistinction to Rice, Mabie sometimes seemed reluctant to advocate on behalf of black actors. As director of the midwestern region of the Federal Theatre Project, he offered little support to Harry Allen, an FTP administrator committed to including African American theater professionals. Allen alerted Mabie to his plans in a 1935 letter: "We are sending for your approval and signature two theatre projects; the first, to provide work for colored professional musicians, actors, and amateurs from the relief rolls, to be organized into a minstrel unit. This project is very much desired by Mr. Hill and by leaders among the colored people here in Des Moines."[11]

Mabie responded to one inquiry regarding the availability of African American actors in Iowa by curtly noting, "With regard to the other project for colored vaudeville troupe, I have no evidence of any kind that there are any professional negro theatre workers on relief in Iowa."[12] Allen, state director of Professional and Service Projects, an FTP government director, challenged Mabie's assertion in a January 1936 letter to Hallie Flanagan. Allen promised:

A complete report will follow very soon and will show, I feel sure, that there are sufficient qualified professional theatre workers among the colored people here in Des Moines and Polk County to justify the operation of such a project. . . . The negro theatre workers with possible qualifications have in most instances been assigned by our Labor Division to the pick and shovel type of employment; and when they registered, having no idea of the possibility of work along theatre lines, they were put down as common laborers or in some other classification.[13]

Allen followed up his letter to Flanagan with a note to Mabie: "Enclosed find letter I have just written to Mrs. Hallie Flanagan, which indicates our activity in making a vocational survey of the professional negro theatre workers in Polk County." He goes on to reiterate, "As I indicated to Mrs. Flanagan, there are no doubt a sufficient number of professional colored theatre people to justify a project, but I know you must have facts and proof and we will get you this information as quickly as possible."[14]

Mabie remained unconvinced of both the existence of African American theater professionals in sufficient numbers to legitimize FTP work and the true goals of the government program in the Midwest. His obstinance with regard to Allen's proposals seems to stem from a deeper distrust of the politics surrounding the project rather than opposition to the inclusion of black theater professionals in Iowa. This fundamental suspicion of the FTP together with his passion for the departmental work consuming his energies at UI led to Mabie's resignation as a regional director. He wrote to Flanagan to explain his decision: "I wouldn't tell you all this except that I do want you to know that I am sincere in the statement that I believe I can better serve the theatre in this region by giving my attention to my own department at this critical time." Moreover, he questioned the quality of the work the FTP pursued:

In the seven States in my region one unit involving 20 persons has been organized about the Omaha Community Playhouse. If theatre persons are given control of appointees and policies in Minnesota there is a possibility of organizing a good theatre company. All other units in this region are mediocre variety units which have little possibility. Work in this region is principally a social service. In Iowa and Minnesota administrative officials do not want State or regional theatre directors to control policies or appointments. Nebraska officials, too, according to Mrs. Paul Gallagher's report, have delayed and interfered with the

Omaha Community Playhouse project. The prospect for the completion of distinctive theatre work is not bright.[15]

Mabie refused to participate in a theatrical project that relegated artistic excellence to a secondary position behind politics. The prospect of ceding operational control to government appointees who lacked an understanding of the Midwest also struck him as untenable. Considered from this point of view, his opposition to production projects for professional African American actors in Iowa may say as much about his reservations concerning the FTP as it does about his commitment to supporting black drama. In any case, his resignation allowed Mabie to return his focus to the Department of Speech and Dramatic Art at UI.

His renewed and now singular concentration on developing the UI theater program proved propitious for black students invested in employing the stage to work out issues related to racial conflict. Although the Depression was ravaging the country, a large gift from the Rockefeller Foundation allowed Mabie to dream big for his new theater building and the program it would make possible. The 1936 completion of the state-of-the art building — whose construction Mabie minutely monitored — signaled the leading status of Iowa's drama program and heightened its attraction for African American students. In addition to the modern building, the philosophy at the heart of Iowa's drama department made it a natural destination for African Americans devoted to developing black theater.

A pioneer in his advocacy for regional theater, Mabie carefully articulated what he described as the "experimental theater," which would "produce new plays interpretive of the life of Iowa, Nebraska, Oklahoma and Dakota country. The history, character, land and customs of this region as it is written into plays will constitute the materials of the program of the experimental theater." Moreover, Mabie declared, "The men who work in Iowa will not need to keep one eye turned to Broadway hereafter. They can grow to full stature, work, live, and die west of the Mississippi, if they choose. Ten years from now, what the New York theatre wants of Iowa, it must go to Iowa to buy, and that is as it should be."[16] Mabie clearly hoped to extend what he described as Paul Green's success. In describing the North Carolinian's achievement, Mabie noted:

> Paul Green, in these plays and in his interpretation of negro life, has proved himself "first playwright" of the regional theatre. For him and others like him, it is to be hoped that regional theatres established in the

important population centers across the country will be espoused by the people of the region round about and will become as permanent and vital to the cultural life of the community as is the library or the school. With the municipal art gallery, the symphony orchestra, espoused by the city or the state, and the theatre as much a part of the life of cities of the West as it is of New York, plays like those of Paul Green's will become treasures of a living American theatre.[17]

The connection Mabie draws between Green's portrayal of African American life in the South and the larger relevance of regional drama clarifies his interest in black themes in his experimental theater, an investment that found success early in his tenure as department chair. Indeed, in 1931 Mabie celebrated the success of *The Tree*, a play Richard Maibaum wrote for his master's thesis at Iowa that went on to become the first antilynching play to be performed on Broadway. Maibaum, a Jewish student of German descent, maintained a close relationship with Mabie as his career took off in both New York and Hollywood, and he frequently credited his success to his Iowa training.[18] He recalled, "It was an amazing place, Iowa. Full of inspiration and enthusiasm and experimentation" and a "do-it-yourself" mentality. Mabie, Maibaum declares, was at the center of Iowa's burgeoning theatrical philosophy as well as his own forming aesthetic: "I met the man there who was to prove a great influence on me. . . . Mabie was . . . responsible for Iowa's thrust in fine arts. He was a powerhouse — a broad, chunky, big-voiced eccentric who didn't suffer fools, shirkers, or phonies gladly. A very, very difficult man, but unique. He believed profoundly in regional theatre." Reflecting back on the inception of *The Tree*, Maibaum recalled, "I gave it to the 'boss,' as we called mabie [*sic*], to read, and he was enthusiast [*sic*] about it. When I was an upper soph we put the play on in a tiny experimental theatre in Iowa City; and I played the lead and directed it. Paul Green, the Pulitzer Prize-winning playwright . . . from North Carolina, came to see it and encouraged me."[19]

Mabie's enthusiasm for plays framed around racial conflicts he felt uncovered the complexity of midwestern life did not, however, lead him to rubberstamp plays simply because of their subject. For instance, when Maibaum first shared his plans for "A Soul Goes Marching," Mabie responded positively until he discovered weaknesses in the work. Hoping to secure his mentor's approval, Maibaum explained his idea for the play in terms of both race and regionalism: "The idea is simple. . . . John Brown's body lifts itself from the grave and goes walking the middle west. He organizes the vacillating farmers and saves their acres, cut down now, as he was in 1858, by the law....Of course, it isn't John Brown after all, but only looney old Jeff Keever, who is under the delusion that he is the great abolitionist." Maibaum proceeded to muse, "A SOUL GOES MARCHING strikes me as an ideal play to inaugurate our new theatre when it opens. It is a play that springs directly from my love of the middle west, a part of the country that will always mean the word 'freedom' to me." What is more, he warns, "The end of the third act makes the lynching in THE TREE seem tame so far as exciting drama goes."[20]

Mabie's response was unequivocal in its enthusiasm: "What a thrilling letter! I am all stirred up about *A Soul Goes Marching*. Your central idea appeals to me as a grand one. I am waiting for the 'script eagerly."[21] Nevertheless, after reading the script in its entirety, Mabie counseled, "I think you need to spend a few weeks near to the soil and to the situations in which these events took place....A more intimate study of the actual situations would enable you to write with authority and would convince me that you have something important to say. Just now I am convinced that you do not know your farmers."[22] Even as Mabie pushed Maibaum toward developing a more realistic presentation of Iowa farmers, he clearly saw the utility of interweaving issues of race and regionalism to make for meaningful drama. He sought to distinguish the kind of drama produced in Iowa from the Broadway stage that was too often satisfied with sensationalism over authenticity, and this meant pushing his students and protégés to discover the truth of midwestern character. Maibaum took this lesson to heart as he neared the Broadway opening of *A Soul Goes Marching*. In an interview with the *Des Moines Register* he explains why New York audiences would be interested in an Iowa play that explores racial tensions: "Because ... Iowa is American. It's as American as Calvin Coolidge taking his oath as president by the light of a kerosene lamp. And the farm rebellion is typical of Iowa and its American tradition."[23]

Mabie's relationship with Maibaum offers an important window into his philosophy for the experimental theater and why it proved attractive to African American students. The "boss" established unwavering standards for good drama regardless of the subject. He was also intuitively alive to the ways both the history of US race relations and its contemporary difficulties shaped particular regions of the country. Mabie advocated for drama that dared to scratch beneath the surface of stereotype, and he pushed his students to draw on their individual wells of experience. Just as he warned

Maibaum that his farmers failed to capture the midwestern farmer truthfully, he encouraged his African American students to write plays that would add to the vitality, depth, and honesty of the US stage. Advocating for the production of new dramatic works became an essential element of his philosophy and his legacy.

Mabie was intensely aware of the dearth of material featuring the black experience in American drama. In an April 1933 letter, he noted his own difficulty in finding plays for black students to produce:

> A group of colored students here in the university are very anxious to undertake something interesting in the theatre. They have persisted in their interest all year so I know a group of about twenty of them are thoroughly sincere. Would you think about the matter a bit and tell me of any plays for negroes which you think would be appropriate. I have considered Paul Green's play, *Potter's Field*, which I understand has just been tied up again with another option. Of course, these youngsters grin all over when I ask them if they would like to do *Green Pastures*. Do you know whether that is available? Are there any other interesting 'scripts for negro players?
>
> I am going to use two negro youngsters in a new play of Conkle's during the summer. I want to keep their interest and enthusiasm alive because I think it is likely to prove a very good asset in connection with certain experimental work in the future.[24]

The "boss" saw training African Americans interested in drama as valuable to his plan for expanding his idea for experimental theater. Of course, his latent racial stereotyping in noting that the students "grin all over," as well as his appreciation for Green's often socially backward work, reveals the extent to which he was a man of his time. Nevertheless, his willingness to include black students in the work of E. P. Conkle, his former student and colleague, underscores his investment in expanding opportunities for African Americans in theater.

While he may not have consistently championed the civil rights movement, Mabie never wavered in his support for excellent theatrical art that probed the struggle for equality. He even wrote to Langston Hughes as he endeavored to find new material for his African American students. His 1935 letter to Hughes is direct:

A group of negro students here at the University would like to make an experimental production of a new play. While I was in New York recently I was told that you have a new play which might be appropriate. If you have such a play and it is available for production by amateur group [*sic*] of negro students I would be glad to hear from you and if possible to have the privilege of reading the manuscript.[25]

Hughes, who was then living in Mexico, answered promptly to grant permission for his play to be used by black students at Iowa. Hughes explains, the play "is called *Mulatto*, and it is a dramatization of the story *Father And Son* in my recent book THE WAYS OF WHITE FOLKS." After assuring Mabie that his agents can send a copy to Iowa and "are quite willing to release the play for amateur production," Hughes closes the letter by acknowledging that a "couple of little theatres" were considering staging his work, and he suggests that the department chair think about a one-act from his story "Mother and Child": "I'd appreciate it if you would turn it over to the Negro group."[26] Like Mabie, Hughes clearly understood the importance of getting his work out of New York to amateur and small theaters open to experimenting with new material.

Mabie's exchange with Hughes underscores the extent to which he developed his ideas of regional theater in conjunction with his exploration of race on stage. His philosophy made certain that the story of the University of Iowa's theater department was intertwined with the story of integration. A *Daily Iowan* article published in 1934 underscores the confluence of this history by highlighting the emergent status of Iowa's art programs at the very moment that students such as Fanny prepared to enter the Department of Speech and Dramatic Art. The article notes, "Iowa gained fame first as a center of science" and "it is only in the last few years that the University of Iowa has assumed a new role — center of a growing feeling for art in the middle west. And in this new role University theater has played an important part."[27] The arrival of several African American students majoring in drama signaled one more way that UI theatre contributed to the special work Iowa pursued in its contribution to reimagining American identity.

Fanny and the Quest to Recast Black Character

Fanny's difficult path to achieving her bachelor's degree brought her to Iowa City determined to succeed. She entered the State University of Iowa in 1934 as a junior transfer student from Fisk University in Nashville, an institution she did not wish to leave. Fanny had worked hard to finance her studies at Fisk, where she cobbled together scholarships and work-study program opportunities to realize her dream of a college education. In an appeal to one potential benefactor, Judge Hueston, Fanny laid out her case for why he should support her pursuit of her undergraduate degree:

> To you, I realize my personal emotions are incidental, but the plans which I purpose to work toward, I feel, will not be incidental, for they are for every living Negro, as well as myself.
>
> I should like to major in English or Literature as a means of preparation to later do extensive research work in Negro literature. Out of the ten million Negroes in America, the percentage that is familiar with Negro history and literature are not worth mentioning. I am an average Negro girl, and in all of my school experience, my teachers were so taken up with teaching the bravery of Washington and the remarkability of Dickens that I never knew of a Toussaint Louverture, or an Alexandre Dumas. . . .
>
> I want to help glorify that which is fundamentally valuable to the Negro. It is a big job, even to help, and one must have due preparation. I am asking you to assist me in my start. The results of my work would be neither rapid no[r] brilliant, but reasonably productive and conscientiously acquired, I assure you.[28]

Fanny consistently viewed her educational progress as training to prepare her to impact the broader position of black Americans. As she made clear to Judge Hueston, she never imagined herself as intellectually gifted or exceptionally talented. Her grades from both Fisk and Iowa show her to be a B-average student who made Cs as often as she made As. Fanny was distinguished, however, by her sincerity, drive, and commitment to racial uplift.

In addition to the letter she sent to Hueston, Fanny sought support from the Alpha Phi Alpha African American fraternity and several sources at Fisk. She ended up working for James Weldon Johnson, the eminent poet and major force within the Harlem Renaissance. On her résumé, she described working as Johnson's private secretary and noted, "Because of Dr. Johnson's interest in me as a writer he placed at my disposal his very valuable library and at every hour that I was with him sought to teach me as much as I could absorb."[29]

Although it seems that Johnson was unable to continue employing Fanny beyond her sophomore year at Fisk, he supported her advancement and even wrote a recommendation letter on her behalf two months before his untimely death. She clearly made a strong impression on him as his assistant. When Fanny's funds ran out at Fisk, she was distraught. She explained to one potential supporter, "I have found Fisk to be ideal. It has worked marvels with me, both in health and temperament. To get back next year means more to me than I can ever explain."[30] She later confided to her second husband, Ligon Buford, that when she visited Howard University with a friend in the early 1940s, she greatly enjoyed it because it "was so much like Fisk."[31]

Notwithstanding her love for Fisk, when financial difficulties made it impossible for her to complete her undergraduate work there, Fanny optimistically transferred to the University of Iowa. Her move from Nashville to Iowa City was almost certainly a difficult one. Numerous pictures from her Fisk days feature Fanny stylishly dressed with other young women and men, posing all over campus as well as around town. She was clearly a popular young woman, and she had confidently confided to her mother, "I think I am the best looking girl in the freshman class. I am going to make it my business to be one of the smartest too."[32] She even took pictures with Johnson, cementing her position within the who's who of black academia. By stark contrast, her photos at the University of Iowa are almost exclusively solitary portraits of her posing in front of the Old Capitol or sitting in the grass on the lawn before the capitol. Fanny came to Iowa with a serious sense of purpose that appears starkly divorced from her days filled with socializing at Fisk.

Fanny's registration cards document her full course load during her two years in Iowa.[33] Her first year of classes covered mainly general requirements, including a wide range of areas from French and Spanish to algebra and stenography. By the fall semester of 1935, however, she dove into her major in dramatic arts. Fanny took interpretive reading, British drama, costume, classical music, radio, playwriting, and individual speech. The syllabus from Contemporary British Drama shows the wide span of plays she read, and her copious notes from all her classes attest to her diligent study habits and purposefulness. She was also conscientiously developing her sense of dramatic criticism. In a formal response to the first performance of *Bird in the Hand*, Fanny began by declaring, "BIRD IN HAND was not a very provocative play. One saw it and immediately forgot it. This was not due to the fault of the actors, but to the fault of the play itself."[34] Her professor's brief comments on her paper suggest that he agreed with her assessment. Fanny was determined to succeed but she was equally committed to developing an independent, critical voice.

By the time she began her second year of coursework at Iowa, Fanny was busy participating in a number of departmental productions, some of which undoubtedly nurtured her interest in African American drama. Maibaum's *The Tree* had been performed on Broadway in 1932, and by 1934, Maibaum was back in Iowa working as an assistant in the Department of Speech and Dramatic Art. He understood the impact racial explorations had on the university stage. Recalling the impact of *The Tree* when it was first performed in Iowa City, Maibaum explained, "I saw that play lift them right out of their seats. I knew it was a success. A woman fainted, and the next day, one of the professors called up Director E. C. Mabie and said, 'Dammit, Mabie! You oughtn't to put on things like that. I walked the floor all night.'. . . I knew I had something."[35] When Maibaum produced *Birthright*, his anti-Nazi play about a cultured Jewish family who lives in Germany through Hitler's reign, Fanny was part of the costume crew. She was almost certainly aware of Maibaum's cutting-edge work interrogating racial violence in the United States, and participating in the staging of his politically powerful *Birthright* likely proved a stimulating welcome to Iowa.

Fanny also worked as part of the costume crew for the 1934 performance of Sidney Howard's *Yellow Jack*, and she served on the property crew in the December 1934 staging of Virgil Geddes's *Mud on the Hoofs*. During the 1935 season, she worked on the lighting crew for Marcus Bach's *The Happy Merger*, the building crew for Susan Glaspell's *Alison's House*, and the stage crew for Dan Totheroh's *Distant Drums*. Although Fanny did not play an official role in the April 1936 production of Andre Obey's *Noah* — she was probably busy preparing for graduation by this moment — she could not have missed either the fanfare surrounding its performance or the critical focus on race. A Cedar Rapids newspaper offered a succinct summary:

> The play deals with the tribulations of Noah who turns to his animals for understanding when his family fails to have confidence in the 40-day ark trip. In the end even the animals leave Noah, and his three sons desert him for the corners of the earth where they were to establish the yellow, the black, and the white races, respectively. Left alone, Noah's slightly questioning faith in God is re-affirmed by the appearance of the rainbow.

That one of the last Ethiopian strongholds to fall was that of the son
Ham's descendants is a pertinent contemporary fact.[36]

The strange appendage of the final sentence proclaiming the "contemporary"
pertinence of Ham's descendants verifies that for Iowans, a play about Noah's
ark continued to foreground contemplations of African Americans' existence
in the United States.

Fanny graduated from Iowa feeling fully prepared to contribute to the world
of theater. She returned to Chicago and by February 1937, she was working
for Susan Glaspell under the auspices of the Federal Theatre Project. Fanny
served as a "playreader," which she explains meant that she read "play manuscripts and prepared criticisms of them, with the view of selecting productions
for the Federal theatres of Chicago." She specifies that a "knowledge of all
phases of the theatre was necessary, in addition to a special knowledge . . . of
dramatic literature dealing with Negro problems."[37] Glaspell sought Mabie's
advice when she initially considered hiring Fanny. Writing to him in November 1936, Glaspell related, "This morning a Miss Fanny McConnell, a negro,
came in to talk to me about play-reading. She tells me that she is from the
University of Iowa and has worked in the Dramatic Department. I found her
intelligent and think she can be helpful to us, especially as we need her viewpoint in the selection of plays for our Negro Theatre."[38] Thus, while Mabie
worked to extricate himself from the responsibilities of the FTP, Fanny was
determinedly clearing a path to participate in the national program to burnish
her credentials in theater.

Although Fanny worked for the FTP for only five months, she remained
committed to developing her expertise in drama. During the summer of 1937,
she served as a counselor and teacher of drama and speech for the Wabash
Young Men's Christian Association (YMCA) camp, and the following year,
she joined the Board of Education of Museum Extension Aid, where she
prepared lectures on topics as diverse as the history of costume to Shakespeare and John Milton. With this experience under her belt, Fanny was
soon prepared to assume a leading role in the production of drama. She was
determined to apply her training in theater from the University of Iowa to
strengthening black drama, and she believed that founding a black theater
company would be the most direct way to impact African American play production. In March 1938, Fanny founded the Negro People's Theatre (NPT)
and served as its primary director.

Her approach to organizing the NPT bore her trademark seriousness and organizational skills. Its constitution clearly outlines the goals of the theater group and Fanny's sense of the importance drama might play in seeking equal rights for African Americans. Article 1 of the constitution explains:

> The object of this organization is to serve as a cultural nucleus for the expression of creative talents devoted to the theatre and allied arts, the latter of which include the dance, writing, music and graphic and plastic arts, essential [sic] the presentation of plays and artistic expressions dealing with the varied aspects of Negro life in association with other peoples and which is intended to lift the intellectual and cultural horizons of the community.[39]

Fanny's investment in connecting theater to other art forms harks back to her Iowa training. Reflecting on the artistic vitality of the university in the early 1930s, Maibaum recalled the exhilarating atmosphere and philosophy permeating theater in Iowa: "The University was two-hundred miles from Chicago, so culturally it was a matter of do-it-yourself. There was so much going on — poetry, music, drama, art."[40] Mabie played an instrumental role in creating the doctorate of fine arts on the University of Iowa campus, and he earnestly argued that the disciplines comprising the fine arts were worthy of such academic recognition. To drive this point home, he advocated a closer working relationship between scholars in related fields: "*What is needed is some cooperation and help from professors of fine arts, music, art, drama, painting, etc.*" (emphasis in original).[41] Fanny could not have missed Mabie's fundamental belief in such an interdisciplinary approach to art and theatre, and she adapted this core idea to the creation of the NPT.

The maiden production she directed for the NPT was Langston Hughes's *Don't You Want to Be Free?* Fanny forthrightly drew from both Hughes's idea for his Harlem Suitcase Theatre, which he founded in 1937, as well as his material. She was also inspired by the generous encouragement Hughes provided when he visited with members of the NPT during his trip to Chicago in 1938. Writing to Hughes in April of that year, Fanny thanked Hughes for the "confidence and encouragement" his visit provided to the founding members of their enterprise. Additionally, she suggested possibilities for further collaboration that might impact not only the individual fortunes of the Chicago-based NPT but other black theater groups as well:

We are grateful for your invitation to establish friendly alliance with your theatre group there in New York. Perhaps in time the alliance could be an official one, with not only an interchange of ideas, plays and favors, but the planning of a mutual program to which your group, ours, and possibly the one at Richmond could work toward and be responsible for. By such organization it seems that stability and perpetuation of Negro progressive theatre would be more or less assured.[42]

Fanny's bold suggestion to Hughes also reflects her familiarity with the FTP and its interest in black drama. Her work with Susan Glaspell surely heightened her sensibility to the federal program's investment in new works for black performers, and FTP director Hallie Flanagan made no secret of her excitement about the dramatic work being staged by the units of African American theater workers. As Negro Units continued to enjoy success in multiple regions across the country, Flanagan had appealed to Mabie for additional advice regarding material for black actors. A 1937 telegram inquired, "Can you suggest brilliant professional producer for our Negro company in either Anthony and Cleopatra or Lazarus Laughed."[43] Fanny self-consciously worked to ensure that future such requests would not go unfulfilled.

The successful NPT production of Hughes's *Don't You Want to Be Free?* confirmed Fanny's sharp theatrical eye. Melissa Barton describes this inaugural production as "the toast of the South Side" and evidence of Fanny's shrewd maneuvering between the more conservative and progressive spheres of black Chicago.[44] Fanny struggled to convince her young theater company to take on Hughes's radically hued drama, but she argued that the stage was the perfect space to work through the knotty issues related to race and class vexing the Chicago black community. As Barton quotes, Fanny explained that the realism at the heart of Hughes's play would aid their mission to "point out what [is] wrong with the world" and "release pent-up resentment."[45] Fanny believed the NPT could genuinely influence race discussions in Chicago, and although she was not politically radical, she understood the power the stage wielded as a space for prompting difficult conversations. In a letter announcing an upcoming meeting, she reminded NPT members, "We are not just a group of people organized to give plays, but we are a group attempting to supply a community need."[46] She urged her youthful peers to embrace the audacious nature of their project: they sought nothing less than to provide the diverse

segments of black Chicago with the "articulation and decent educational recreation" that spoke keenly to their individual needs.[47]

In a more expansive letter to the group, Fanny expanded upon the stakes
of their endeavor:

> A permanent theatre for the Negro people represents an immense ideal,
> an ideal which has long, long been neglected. Certainly the Negro has
> as much to say as any other peoples on the face of the earth. . . . What is
> wanted, and what you must surely agree is needed, is a theatre in which
> plays that are vital and significant unto us as human beings, not martyrs
> or mountebanks, but just mere human beings who hunger and love and
> fight as normal people of any race or creed.[48]

In a draft of the letter, Fanny expounded, "Even if we had not the wealth of
telling material from our current lives from which to draw as a source for
theatre, we have a heritage . . . of great Negroes who stood alone in their day
and cried out against the outrages toward their people. . . . We will give them
due tribute. We'll reincarnate them in the theatre. There is no more effective
or enduring monument. May be [we] can do in the theatre what our history
books don't do in school."[49] Harking back to her letter to Judge Hueston when
she sought support for her college education, Fanny continued striving to
correct the educational challenges facing black children.

She generously shared pointers with fledgling theater companies across the
country even as she worked to keep the NPT afloat. By late 1939, the financial
hurdles for the troupe and challenges within her marriage to Ligon Buford,
the business manager of NPT, necessitated Fanny's resignation as director
of the NPT. Yet even as she stepped down, she could point to some impressive accomplishments. A December 1938 letter inquired whether she might
bring *Don't You Want to Be Free?* to England and assured Fanny, "This would
be a novelty in Europe and I should say would be very successful as we have
never had this type of entertainment over here before."[50] Although Fanny
could not take advantage of this opportunity, she never wavered from her
fundamental belief that her individual projects only made sense in light of
the broader impact her work in black theater might have on the development
of a multifaceted African American arts tradition. This sensibility remained
a mainstay of her aesthetic beliefs and fueled her unwavering support of her
husband's artistry as a novelist. What is more, her philosophy was replicated

by black graduates from the UI Department of Speech and Dramatic Art from the late 1930s to the 1950s. Mabie's legacy was rich indeed.

The Path from UI Advanced Degrees to Invisible Man

When Fanny left Iowa City in 1936, the door to pursuing master's and doctoral degrees in theater swung open more widely to prospective African American students. Mabie's commitment to advanced degree programs in the arts bore fruit in the form of increased opportunities for black students eager to secure the credentials necessary for establishing and expanding theater degrees at HBCUs. Examining the work these students completed at UI together with their experiences in Iowa City illustrates their artistic talent, their personal tenacity, and the magnitude of their strides in the world of theater. From the 1930s through the 1950s — the formative period of Mabie's departmental leadership — African American graduates from Speech and Dramatic Arts translated their Iowa degrees into the development of university theater programs, the creation of institutes for black teachers in secondary schools, and the publication and production of acclaimed professional work across a range of performance arts. In broad terms, their work on advanced degrees positioned their creative, pedagogical, and organizational accomplishments to prepare the nation for the world-premiere staging of Fanny's future husband's award-winning novel *Invisible Man*.

*   *   *

Thomas Pawley's experiences at Iowa underscore both the challenges and the rewards that students who followed in Fanny's footsteps encountered during the 1930s and 1940s. Unlike Fanny, who grew up in a home without a father, struggled through night school to earn her high school diploma, and fought to secure funding to finance her undergraduate education, Pawley arrived at the University of Iowa with his bachelor's degree in English in hand and a certain confidence born of his academic background. His father had been a professor at Virginia State College in Petersburg, Virginia, so Pawley grew up on a college campus. Although he had no previous formal training in theater, he arrived in Iowa City in 1937 eager to begin working on his master's degree in the Department of Speech and Dramatic Art. Pawley recalls that he had "read numerous dramas especially those of Shakespeare and been a very active

participant in the Virginia State College Theatre Guild."[51] A private meeting
with Mabie resulted in his initial course schedule that included Advanced Acting as well as the Experimental Theatre Seminar, a class Pawley took with Tom
Williams, who was only a few years away from discovering fame as Tennessee
Williams. Pawley admits that he arrived to Iowa with dreams of pursuing a
career in acting, but his instructors asked him, "What are you going to act
in? We need playwrights." Pawley explains, "That's why I went into playwriting."[52] Indeed, many people described Mabie's main accomplishment at Iowa
in terms of his dedication to producing original material. Norman Felton
unequivocally declared, "The great contribution of Mabie to the cause of
playwriting was to *make* writers *write*."[53]

Pawley describes his theater work at Iowa as immensely practical and often
exciting. He recalls being "surprised (and delighted)" when E. P. Conkle selected his first sketch, "Ku Klux," for production. Noting that Mabie encouraged students to "explore [their] regional origins, in [his] case the American
Negro," Pawley focused his sketch on "the appointment of Alabama Senator
Hugo Black, an ex-klansman, to the Supreme Court."[54] He chose Williams,
who boasted a southern accent, to play the role of the black minister. Although
Pawley considered a variety of themes in the sketches and plays he produced
for his coursework,[55] when he settled down to work on his MA, he focused
exclusively on black themes. His master's thesis, submitted June 5, 1939, includes three one-acts: *Jedgement Day*, *Smokey*, and *Freedom in My Soul*. In his
acknowledgment, Pawley singles out Mabie and Conkle for special thanks
before expressing his "appreciation for both the encouragement and the criticism given [him] in the preparation" of the three plays.[56] His dissertation
similarly offers Mabie special thanks, but Pawley admits that he never saw
the chair of the department as a mentor. Mabie's theatrical philosophy and
work ethic rather than personal support distinguished his relationship with
African American students.

For instance, in thinking about his master's thesis, Pawley recalled Mabie's
objection to one of his plays. All three of his one-acts attest to the varied
ways Iowa's program encouraged students to study diverse elements of their
regional subjects, but Pawley remembers that his plays were not uniformly
well received by the "boss." The first one-act, *Jedgement Day*, is a comedy
centered around a black man who refuses to go to church with his wife only
to dream that he awakes on Judgment Day. In the vein of Charles Dickens's

A Christmas Carol, Zeke commits to changing his life, but before he can demonstrate his newfound salvation, drowsiness overwhelms him and he lazily returns to sleep. Interestingly, photographs Pawley included in his thesis from the performance show all the actors in blackface. In his description of the experimental production of the play in the introduction to his dissertation, Pawley simply notes, "The comedy was performed by white students in Negro make up and represented an interesting contrast."[57] Conversely, the photos from *Smokey* feature black and white actors sharing the stage. This piece set in a Georgia jail contemplates the explosive issue of lynching. The black man Smokey has killed a white man whom he discovered in bed with the black woman he loves. Although the white deputy and sheriff attempt to carry out their charge to protect Smokey from the growing mob outside the jail, all the men realize that not only is Smokey sure to be lynched, but the other black man in the jail, Blue, will also likely be murdered by the mob. The play ends with Blue following Smokey into the crowd to fight a losing battle with their manhood intact. In discussions of this play, Pawley recalls Mabie declaring, "This is just propaganda!"[58] This response is curious given Mabie's unreserved support for *The Tree*, but Maibaum's lynching play principally probed white male psychology. Whatever the logic of Mabie's assessment of Pawley's lynching drama, Pawley found both a supporter and a defender in the department in the person of Marian Gallaway, whom he describes as his truest advocate and mentor in Iowa.

The final one-act in Pawley's thesis approaches black men's determination to defend their masculine identity from exploitative labor conditions. *Freedom in My Soul* focuses on African American employees at a Long Island summer resort. Their deplorable wages and horrid living quarters inspire the men to rebel against their white employer by planning a strike. The play ends with Ace, the lone black man to resist joining the strike, experiencing an epiphany: his face lights up and he wonders whether his fellow workers are right. Together the three plays demonstrate Pawley's enduring interest in studying black male character in radically different American settings, a theme he continued to pursue in his dissertation with greater success and sophistication. Although the late 1930s ushered in the emergence of well-known black playwrights including Langston Hughes and Theodore Ward — men who found success with politically forceful plays such as *Don't You Want to Be Free?* (1938) and *Big White Fog* (1938) — Pawley's penetrating exploration of black male psychology proved unique. Moreover, Mabie undoubtedly recognized the powerful originality of his student's work because he invited Pawley to return to Iowa to earn his doctoral degree.

After earning his master's, Pawley temporarily taught at Prairie View A&M before joining the faculty of Lincoln University in 1940. As a resident of the segregated state of Missouri, he was eligible for state funding that promised to support his doctoral studies at any institution outside of Missouri. Like Fanny, Pawley also initially sought to attend Yale, but when he requested letters of recommendation from Iowa, he met with resistance. Instead of receiving letters to complete his application to Yale, Pawley received a long-distance phone call from Mabie. Pawley was surprised to hear Mabie declare that he wanted his former student to return Iowa to earn his doctoral degree. What is more, his recollections of the difficulties Iowa City posed for him as a single black man made Pawley reluctant to return now that he was a married man and a father. To convince him, Mabie promised Pawley an apartment for his family and a special fellowship. Pawley accepted Mabie's offer, and when he arrived in Iowa City, he discovered that his professor had pulled strings to have his family placed in special housing for veterans. Pawley laughingly recalls his appreciation of Mabie's hard-bargaining tactics: "He was the boss!"[59]

Back in Iowa City as a doctoral student, Pawley again turned his attention to African American masculine identity. *Crispus Attucks* and *Messiah*, the full-length plays composing his dissertation, demonstrate Pawley's artistic growth as a doctoral student. In *Crispus Attucks*, he offers a radically expanded view of the black man who was the first American casualty of the Revolutionary War, while *Messiah* portrays the life of Nat Turner. Pawley infuses both full-length plays with theatrical heft by turning to historical figures. In the case of Crispus Attucks, Pawley portrays his main character as a man pulled into the dispute between the colonists and Great Britain when his son is killed by a careless British soldier. Attucks must transition from thinking solely in terms of his individual hopes for a bright future for his son to working toward attaining freedom for a country that promises a future where all black men are free. Pawley transforms the scant historical record that tells a conflicting story of the death of Crispus Attucks into a vehicle for developing an emotionally complicated black man whose participation in the fight for American liberty gives rise to African American interlocking considerations of fatherhood, freedom, and individual agency. Similarly, *Messiah* offers an innovative picture of Nat Turner. In Pawley's hands, Nat leads the bloodiest slave insurrection in American history fueled by his sincere belief that he follows God's will. In his final moments, he realizes his mistake and dies from the physical trauma of his undertaking rather than at the hands of the white legal system. Pawley's title and multifaceted presentation of Nat Turner depart from the historical record to evaluate black masculinity from a more nuanced vantage.

Pawley's probing explorations of African American men's responses to the reality of their existence in the United States unfold against the lived reality of his experiences in Iowa City as both a master's and a doctoral student. Like that of many black students, his initial interest in Iowa resulted from word-of-mouth reports. Pawley recalls a friend telling him about a university in the West that had a new attitude about creative work and was one of the most liberal institutions of the Big Ten even though it was "out there in the cornfields."[60] Pawley arrived at the University of Iowa determined to succeed and willing to look beyond the racism that was standard beyond the campus and occasionally invaded academic spaces, too. The openness of his white classmates, however, often surprised him. Pawley recalls sitting in a seminar with another student who repeatedly referred to Negroes as "darkies." But by the end of the term, he claimed this student as one of his closest friends. His classmate declared, "I'm going to take you to get a beer," but this turned out to be a difficult task given the segregationist policies that blanketed businesses in Iowa City.[61] They searched for hours before finding an establishment beyond the city that agreed to serve them.

In fact, white students' progressive approach to forming relationships across racial lines sometimes proved detrimental to black students' educational success. Arthur Clifton Lamb, an Iowa native who earned his bachelor's degree in dramatics, English, and Spanish from Grinnell College and his master's degree in playwriting from UI in 1940, discovered that his creative talents alone could not ensure his scholastic success when he returned to UI to pursue his doctorate. Lamb's master's thesis, a full-length play titled *Beebee: The Drama of a Negro Lady Doctor*, follows the experiences of a homely black woman who is determined to be a doctor and serve the poor African Americans of her small town. His deft handling of the structure, dialogue, and inclusion of explosive contemporary issues exhibits his playwriting talent. Moreover, Mabie received a letter from Barrett Clark in 1952 inquiring about Lamb's *Roughshod Up the Mountain*, a play Clark thought might be appropriate for Broadway. Clark proposed that Mabie send Lamb's play to Audrey Wood, Miriam Howell, or Annie Laurie Williams, all "women of intelligence and culture."[62] These women were also powerhouse agents. Wood, for instance, represented Tennessee Williams throughout the height of his career. Notwithstanding Lamb's promising start, when a night watchman discovered him and a white female student in a compromising situation in the basement of the drama building, his doctoral studies came to an unceremonious end. Pawley recalls learning about Lamb's dismissal from the program when he accompanied the Lincoln debate team to the University of Iowa in 1954. Mabie pulled Pawley aside to discuss Lamb's expulsion. The "boss" lamented, "I just had to let him go."[63] As soon as the news of Lamb's interracial romantic liaison spread, Mabie was forced to take action to protect the integrity of the department. Thus, Lamb was not allowed to complete his doctorate at Iowa.

Like Lamb, Whitney LeBlanc found the university's strict policies regulating interactions between black men and white women difficult to tolerate. After earning his master's from Iowa in 1940, LeBlanc returned to UI to pursue his doctorate in the mid-1950s. He continued to hone his directing work while he also participated in productions as an actor. One performance placed LeBlanc rehearsing opposite professor Arnold Gillette's daughter, JoEllen. After weeks of developing the play with his white costar, a professor refused to allow LeBlanc to complete the performance when he realized it required the black male student to kiss JoEllen Gillette. LeBlanc chafed at the racism that too often superseded a professional approach to theater, and his refusal to submit himself to such injustices led to him leaving the program without his doctoral degree.[64]

Despite such incidents endured by fellow students, Pawley describes his time at Iowa as an exhilarating, pioneering experience. He was one of the first African American students to be inducted into the Purple Mask Society, an honorary drama group originally organized in 1922 under Mabie's leadership. Its creed specifies that members be selected on the basis of scholarship, which was determined by maintaining at least a 3.0 grade point average on a 4-point scale in dramatic arts, meritorious service to the theater, and a cooperative attitude. This distinguished the Purple Mask Society from the Scarlet Mask Society that required a 2.5 grade point average. To be elected into either society, nominations were given to faculty members, and a majority of positive votes were required for election. The societies published the names of successful honorees in their hometown newspapers. According to its creed, the Purple Mask Society was also devoted to uniting theater leaders on campus with outstanding alumni, encouraging scholarship to extend the benefits of theater, considering the means to raise production standards, and uniting those entering professional careers in theater.[65] Pawley vividly recalled sitting near the rear of the theater one May day in 1939 when Marian Gallaway "smacked a purple mask" over his head.[66] He had not expected to be inducted into the society.

Pawley's successful matriculation through the Department of Speech and Dramatic Arts paved the way for a number of African American students who completed their advanced degree work in the 1940s and 1950s. In addition to the aforementioned Whitney LeBlanc (MA 1940, pursued doctoral studies, 1954), these graduate students included James Butcher (MA 1941), Winona Lee Fletcher (MA, 1951), and Ted Shine (MA 1958). Iowa became a recognized pipeline for African American students seeking an advanced degree in theater arts, and the growing number of black UI graduates led directly to the development of drama programs at HBCUs throughout the country. Butcher, LeBlanc, and Shine all spent time instructing students at Howard University; Pawley, Lamb, and Shine taught at Prairie View A&M State University; Pawley, Shine, and LeBlanc also worked at Lincoln University; Fletcher proved an integral force at Kentucky State University; Shine began his career at Dillard University; and Lamb also instructed students in drama at Shaw University and Johnson C. Smith University before joining the faculty at Morgan State College, where he remained for more than twenty-five years. This list — which is by no means comprehensive — demonstrates the impressive legacy the University of Iowa's theater program claims with respect to the development of drama at black colleges and universities. Many of these graduates placed their devotion to teaching black students ahead of their personal creative careers, a testament to their training at Iowa as well as their devotion to expanding black drama.[67]

Iowa graduates and faculty also played a pivotal role in addressing the dearth of black instructors of theater and drama in secondary schools. In *The Black Teacher and the Dramatic Arts: A Dialogue, Bibliography, and Anthology* (1970), Pawley and William Reardon examine the necessity of improving theater programs at HBCUs to increase the numbers of African American drama teachers in black communities. Reardon, a white professor who taught as an instructor, assistant professor, and associate professor in the UI theater program from 1953 to 1961, went on to become a consistent advocate for minority participation in theater arts. When he secured a 1967 grant to support training secondary school teachers in theater and drama, Reardon was

shocked to receive only three applications from HBCU graduates amid a pool
of more than one hundred applications. Determined to discover the roots
of the problem, he reached out to Pawley and Owen Dodson, the longtime
chair of the drama department at Howard University. Both men agreed to
help Reardon, and with their assistance, Reardon developed a new proposal to
the United States Office of Education, Disadvantaged Youth Branch, seeking
support for an Institute of Black Repertory Theatre planned for the summer
of 1968 on the University of California–Santa Barbara campus. The organizers expanded application qualifications in hopes of increasing their interest
pool, and in the end, they selected forty-one participants from two hundred
queries about the institute.[68]

Reardon and Pawley established their newly formed repertory in Santa
Barbara for two months during the summer of 1968, in which time they presented eighteen performances of various kinds. Participants also dedicated
significant time and energy to addressing the challenges of teaching drama
in black colleges, secondary schools, and underprivileged communities. At
the conclusion of the institute, Reardon and Pawley published a report that
includes a "Dialogue" section that pulls no punches in criticizing the state
of drama instruction across the nation at HBCUs. Forthrightly tackling the
many obstacles undermining the growth of theater programs in black institutions, they lament the wide failure of these schools to look to the stage as
one means of answering black students' demands to be involved in educational discussions of identity amid the turmoil of the civil rights movement.
They note the paradox in their contemporary reality that found a nation of
citizens more open to minority participation in professional theater, movies, and television while HBCUs neglected to commit funds and support to
drama departments to develop this talent. Returning to many of the points
Fanny identified in explaining her passion for theater, Reardon and Pawley
insist on the necessity of moving past African American prejudices against
performance so black theater practitioners might arm students with the skills
necessary for sharing the creative history of black Americans and developing
broader aesthetic tastes in the black community. By addressing the difficult
history of drama in African American culture, Reardon and Pawley present
the late 1960s dilemma as a challenge between the modern ideas and progressive educational mentality held by many black theater professionals compared
to the provincial, outmoded mind-sets dominating too many college administrators and professors at HBCUs.

Their study highlights how professors and graduates from Iowa's theater program strove to increase the numbers of black theater practitioners across the United States. Both of the report's authors were heirs to Mabie's theatrical philosophy, and traces of his frank, no-nonsense style persisted in their method. Moreover, Reardon and Pawley's assessment of the general state of black theater — and the persistent issue of the desperate need for material — proved essential to expanding black theater as well as teaching African American audiences to appreciate dramatic performance. The emergence of acclaimed twentieth- and twenty-first-century black playwrights such as August Wilson and Suzan-Lori Parks stand on their shoulders and point to the little-recognized yet enormously significant position the UI theater program played in shaping the modern African American dramatic tradition.

Anticipating the importance of Wilson's and Parks's award-winning work, Ralph Ellison published articles that stressed the importance of producing plays focused on African American life. In fact, before he ever met Fanny, he too connected with Langston Hughes as well as with black playwright Theodore Ward, who collaborated with her in Chicago. Ellison met Hughes almost immediately after he arrived in New York in 1936, at a time when the famous poet and playwright was deeply involved with the stage. *Mulatto* was still running on Broadway, and Hughes was heading to Cleveland to work with the Gilpin Players, who were staging some of his plays. Hughes introduced Ellison to leftist politics and new literary forms that profoundly impacted his aesthetic philosophy.[69] Hughes proved instrumental to Ellison's growing confidence as a critic of art. By the time he reviewed Ward's *Big White Fog* in 1940, Ellison confidently declared that Ward's play represents "a fresh source of incalculable possibilities" that "has begun to pour its strength into the stream of the American theater." Ellison in his review proceeds to deplore the history of American theater that denied black "playwrights an opportunity to secure that working knowledge of their craft, which until recently was only to be acquired through contact with the commercial stage."[70]

Ellison's comments reveal his prescient understanding of the significance of the American stage as a space in which to examine race relations. His words also reveal the intriguing convergence of his experience with the theater and his future wife's work within the dramatic form. Both Ellisons clearly understood and esteemed the stage as a powerful site to explore cultural identity.[71] Although Ellison was ultimately hesitant to see *Invisible Man* translated to a medium other than the novel,[72] one can imagine his delight in seeing it finally emerge as part of a larger discussion of the African American experience in white universities during the middle of the twentieth century. Christopher McElroen, the director and producer of the world-premiere stage version of Ellison's novel, understood how the subject matter of *Invisible Man* recalled the experiences of students like Fanny who similarly sought to improve both their individual careers and the portrayal of African American culture more broadly. Consequently, McElroen's successful production of *Invisible Man* might be seen as a triumph that not only reflects the staying power of Ralph Ellison's mid-twentieth-century literary masterpiece but also the rich tradition of black playwrights whose training at the State University of Iowa contributed to opening the US stage to such deliberations. In that respect, the 2011 residency that focused on both Ellison and the mid-twentieth-century black experience at the University of Iowa was only fitting.

IOWA WAS ONE MORE STEP TOWARD MY FUTURE

⌐ ⌐ ⌐

The University of Iowa has always been a part of my life. My father entered the U of I for his undergraduate studies in 1919, and I grew up listening to stories about his love for the Hawkeyes. He attended medical school at Howard University in Washington, DC, and interned at its Freedmen's Hospital. After finishing his education, he married my mother and returned to Iowa to start his family and his medical practice.

My father's deep appreciation for the U of I extended beyond his stay on campus. I have fond memories of our family traveling from our home in Fort Madison to Iowa City for football games. Before and after each contest, we visited with Kenneth and Hulette Belle. While we were at their home, a variety of people assembled there. Duke Slater, Dr. Lee Furgerson, Dr. Gage Moore, attorney Lawrence Oliver, Arch A. Alexander, and their families are just some who come to mind. For a young child, it was a unique experience to see so many Black professionals in one social setting. These adults debated politics and talked about the newsworthy topics of the day. From them, we children learned lessons that would come in handy when we furthered our education.

In 1946, the oldest of my four siblings, Virginia, informed my parents that she wanted to attend the University of Iowa. The U of I barred Blacks from living in the dormitories then, and my parents told her that she could not go to a school that was not fully integrated. Rather than deny her request outright, my father contacted Virgil Hancher, the U of I president, and urged him to end housing discrimination in the dormitories. His efforts, along with the social pressures of the 1940s, forced the university to change its "unofficial policy." When Virginia stepped foot on campus, she was one of the Currier

Five, the first five black female students who integrated the dorms. She told me about some of the discrimination that she encountered. For example, she described being called down to the Dean of Women's Office because the proctor saw her socializing with white students at the 10:30 p.m. bed check. While she received punishment, the students with whom she chatted were never disciplined. After attending the U of I for three years, Virginia left and attended college in Minneapolis, where she studied medical technology.

My sister Geraldine was the next sibling who had to make a decision about where to attend college. She chose to go to one of the historically Black colleges and universities (HBCUs) — Howard University. As I began thinking about higher education, the experiences of my siblings influenced my perspective. Because I knew about the challenges that Virginia faced, the University of Iowa was not on my short list of potential schools. In addition, I did not share Geraldine's attraction to HBCUs. My first choice was McGill University in Montreal, Canada. After visiting the grounds, I fell in love with the surrounding mountains, parks, and lakes. That campus and the surrounding city seemed like the perfect place to be a student. Although I really wanted to go to McGill, as a fallback plan I also applied to the University of Wisconsin. My McGill dreams ended when I was not admitted there, so in the fall of 1950, I enrolled at the University of Wisconsin–Madison. My first year at Wisconsin was ideal; I loved everything about the experience. I returned to the university the following year, but after the first semester I began experiencing some serious health challenges. I returned home to Fort Madison following final exams in early 1952.

Upon returning home, I underwent several surgeries. During the spring semester of 1952, while recuperating, I took some correspondence courses from the University of Iowa. Since I wanted to be close to home while my health remained a concern, I decided to apply to the University of Iowa for the fall semester. I entered the College of Liberal Arts in May of 1952, and that fall I moved into S304 of Currier, a large private room in the same building my sister helped integrate.

Even though the university was not segregated, many individuals on campus had little or no experience with being in the company of Black people. I found that the most prejudiced women in the dorm seemed to be from rural Iowa. Having never seen a Black person before, except on television, they felt that characters like Kingfish on *Amos 'n' Andy* and Rochester and the Ink Spots on *The Jack Benny Program* identified all Black people. Their reactions showed a strange mix of curiosity and stereotype. Some women just wanted to know how your hair felt; others were concerned that you would get too close to them and talked openly about why they thought you were different. For the most part, I escaped the discrimination that my sister experienced years earlier.

Even with all of the students who had never met a Black person before, my two and half years at the U of I were mostly uneventful and enjoyable. In the morning, I would wake up, go downstairs, and have breakfast in the dining hall. There were days when the walk down Clinton Street to classes seemed very special, particularly in autumn when the leaves were falling. At those moments I would think this is what college is supposed to be. I also remember watching the Joe McCarthy hearings [in spring 1954] in the basement of Currier with my fellow students.

On occasion, I would go to the Union and listen to music. I also enjoyed attending football and basketball games as well as track meets with friends. I did not, however, feel totally involved in extracurricular activities. As I look back, I think I might have been more active and met more people through church, but I was Catholic and went to Mass on Sundays while most of the Black students went to services at Bethel AME [African Methodist Episcopal]. That congregation meant a lot to them, and I often heard my peers talk about different church events. In the fall of 1954, I tried to get more connected with campus life by volunteering to supervise testing for incoming students. However, three or four days before testing started, I became very ill and ended up having a major operation.

Since I was already registered and moved into Currier, I returned to the university after my surgery. I had missed several weeks of classes, so I spent endless hours at the library surrounded by textbooks and reference materials, struggling to catch up. My actions yielded no fruit. I ended up dropping some courses but finished the semester with a few hours still intact. I returned to campus after Christmas to take my finals, but when they were over, I went home. I was emotionally and physically exhausted from having undergone more than ten surgeries while trying to attend college.

To keep me interested in my undergraduate studies, my parents kept suggesting other colleges for me to consider. One of the schools they recommended was Ohio State. I eventually applied, was accepted, and started classes there in the spring quarter of 1955. Although the environment differed totally from the U of I, I enjoyed my time in Columbus, Ohio. I didn't have any other medical issues before I graduated from Ohio State in December of 1956.

Since graduation, my life has been very rewarding. I worked with a talented team to launch the Community Action Agency in Southeast Iowa. In that organization, I had a wonderful career doing things that I could support very passionately. I also counted it a great honor to be selected to serve on a number of committees, councils, boards, and commissions from the local to the national level. My husband, George, who received his BA and MA from Iowa, and I continued the tradition of taking our children to Iowa City for football games and visiting the home of Kenneth and Hulette Belle. Through this ritual, another group of youngsters had the experience of watching the next generation of Black professionals and their families debating politics and talking about current events. Our three children all chose to attend the U of I, and each of them received their BAs from the university. Two, Milton and Virginia, also earned their Juris Doctors. The third, Lois Ann, received her MBA from the University of Chicago.

Over the years, I deepened my relationship with the university. I became active in the Iowa Black Alumni Association (IBAA) and raised money for the organization by working at its concession stand during home Hawkeye football games. I represented the IBAA on the University of Iowa Alumni Association Board of Directors, and subsequently served as president of that board. I also joined U of I's Friends of the Library Board and recruited individuals to donate their papers to the Iowa Women's Archives. My sister, Virginia, and I both are contributors. Along with my husband, I continue to support programs at Hancher, the university's performing arts venue. We get tremendous enjoyment from attending performances. Through all these experiences, I can truly say that my relationship with the University of Iowa community has had a lasting impact on me.

In 2008, when George and I downsized and wanted to relocate, it seemed natural to move from Fort Madison to Iowa City. After years of never appearing or being low in the rankings, the university and its surrounding areas finally topped my short list. In many ways the shift felt like a homecoming.

OBSCURED TRADITIONS

Blacks at the Iowa Writers' Workshop,
1940–1965

Herbert Nipson, Michael Harper, and Margaret Walker attended the Iowa Writers' Workshop between 1939 and 1965. Although they did not matriculate at the same time,[1] these illustrious individuals reveal how black graduate students in creative writing embody telling yet little-noted examples of civil rights struggle. They confirm that after blacks entered white schools, their academic growth often hinged on complicated exchanges in dynamic departments. In the cases of Nipson, Harper, and Walker, their creativity blossomed as the workshop transformed from a regional entity into an internationally recognized writing mecca. Books such as Mark McGurl's *The Program Era: Postwar Fiction and the Rise of Creative Writing* (2009) chart this evolution and hail broadening attempts to understand both post–World War II literary production and late twentieth-century higher education.[2] Even though McGurl and peers such as Loren Glass and Eric Bennett provide incisive discussions of the Writers' Workshop, their analyses rarely engage black students.[3] This oversight limits our understanding of the workshop by concealing the program's role in shaping black cultural expression. In addition, this omission robs the university — which justly touts its racial tolerance — of the ability to celebrate its first wave of black graduates in creative writing. By moving Nipson, Harper, and Walker to the center of understanding the workshop, this chapter explores how these students' sojourns at the University of Iowa helped shape their professional identity as well as the development of the most prestigious writing program in the world. More broadly, these explorations demonstrate how blackness at UI tested American pluralist ideals.

Nipson, Harper, and Walker arrived at Iowa after going to white institutions as undergraduates. Their early experiences introduced them to general patterns of racial interactions in higher education, but their arrival at UI demanded a more complex grasp of the relationships among blackness, art, and democracy. As talented graduate students, they discovered a university that simultaneously offered technical tutelage and measured indifference. On the one hand, Nipson, Harper, and Walker entered a campus where the leadership of dean of letters Norman Foerster, English department chair John Gerber, journalism department chair Wilbur Schramm, and workshop director Paul Engle brought unprecedented prestige to the institution. These leaders' charisma and professional stature enhanced the university's curriculum, and because UI did not discriminate in admissions, black students benefited from studying with these luminaries. Yet even as Nipson, Harper, and Walker embraced opportunities created by forward-thinking administrators, they contended with the cultural assumptions that guided the workshop's teachings on technique, content, and taste. The New Criticism, a literary philosophy that stressed formal precision and eschewed political commentary, gained traction in the workshop during the same span when Nipson, Harper, and Walker studied there.[4] Even though they reveled in the exposure to such cutting-edge intellectual innovations, the black students found that their artistic ideas challenged both the faculty and their fellow students. The dialogue between their creative ambitions and the reactions of their teachers and classmates provides a lens for viewing civil rights–era striving. To understand the significance of such a vantage, Nipson's, Harper's, and Walker's master's work and careers must be considered.

Although their educational trajectories led them eventually to enter different parts of the US workforce, Nipson, Harper, and Walker all became important molders of black bourgeois taste. For thirty years Nipson labored at *Ebony*, a publication devoted to black trendsetting. His efforts shaped lifestyle decisions for a crucial sector of the African American public. Harper taught at Brown University until he ranked as the longest-standing professor in the English department. From that post, he sponsored festivals and edited anthologies that advanced the study of black literature. Walker spent much of her career teaching at Jackson State University, one of the historically black colleges and universities (HBCUs) in Mississippi. From that position, she influenced undergraduates as well as the graduate students who would enter the professoriate. By staffing *Ebony*, an Ivy League school, and an HBCU, Nipson, Harper, and Walker served as cultural ambassadors who exemplified the compatibility between black artistry and democratic participation. Their careers and creative philosophies were colored by their Iowa Writers' Workshop experiences. Through Nipson's, Harper's, and Walker's odysseys in a white, midwestern, public university, we witness the tense interracial negotiations that prepared them to contribute meaningfully to a racially diverse US society. Indeed, their years at the workshop represent concrete studies in the liberty labor that makes and remakes the United States. By exposing integration as a daily adjustment of the US conscience rather than a dramatic moment of opening a formerly blocked threshold, these students clarify the link between UI and the national civil rights movement. Their illumination of such historical textures makes them invaluable models.

Tutelage in Taste:
Herbert Nipson before Ebony

Herb Nipson arrived on the University of Iowa campus in the immediate aftermath of World War II. Like many returning veterans, he exulted in the educational opportunities afforded by the GI bill. But even as his enthusiasm for intellectual growth soared, his encounters with the UI housing situation tempered his mood. According to Walter Sullivan, one of his Iowa Writers' Workshop contemporaries, finding lodging in Iowa City was "ridiculously difficult" even for a white married couple.[5] Nipson described the specific prejudices against "married Black students" as a particularly bittersweet part of his introduction to UI.[6] This intolerant practice could have proved disorienting for a worldly, ex-military man, but Nipson arrived in Iowa prepared to face such realities. His upbringing in Clearfield, Pennsylvania, together with his undergraduate days at Penn State formed the sturdy foundation of an optimism and work ethic that shaped Nipson's approach to his graduate studies and colored his emotional response to the challenges UI presented.

Clearfield, in the view of Nipson's neighbor Earl Caldwell, was a spot where black parents had "a chance to build a safe space for their children."[7] While the city did not boast a large black population, its "small town, everybody knows everybody" atmosphere bred a tendency to "judge people by something other than the color of their skin."[8] This community sentiment, along with the economic hardship that defined Nipson's youth, inspired his hardworking, matter-of-fact mind-set.[9] Nipson saved money for college by working at a "clay products" plant and as a bellhop "at the leading local hotel."[10] After hitchhiking from Clearfield to Happy Valley in 1936, he enrolled at Penn State. When he arrived in State College, the university dormitories were closed to him, and restaurants and rooming houses sometimes withheld their services. Notwithstanding such racial discrimination, he "plunged into campus life with a vengeance."[11] His plunging into the chasm between scholarly development and racist restriction occurred on a campus where there were only thirteen black students out of a total of six thousand.

Armed with this social preparation as well as his war experiences, Nipson in June 1946 commenced his postgraduate study of creative writing at Iowa. He studied journalism as an undergraduate, but in the Writers' Workshop, he finished a master's and started on a doctorate that both focused on fiction writing. His movement between these two majors highlights larger changes in the fields of writing and publishing. Whereas late nineteenth- and early twentieth-century writers of both poetry and fiction often cut their teeth as journalists, the post–World War II class that Nipson joined stood poised at the fork of two professional roads.[12] They could continue the trend of practicing their craft in newspapers, magazines, and other serial publications, or they could pursue study in creative writing programs such as the workshop. The emergence of such graduate training gave them the option of making a living as a teacher and creator. Nipson's move from journalism to creative writing occurred within this context; however, his race further complicated his path. When he initially pursued journalism, Nipson's friends and family warned him that there was "absolutely no future in" the field "for any black journalist."[13] Earl Caldwell, a highly esteemed reporter whose career began about twenty years after Nipson's, echoes these sentiments. He observes that during "those early years . . . black reporters" worked for "black publications" since "mainstream . . . newsrooms were occupied . . . almost entirely by white men."[14] Although some black writers during the 1930s and 1940s regularly appeared in journals associated with the Communist Left, Nipson's forays into journalism occurred at a remove from the sites of interracial exchange associated with the urban metropolis.[15] Nipson avoided flirtations with white radicalism; instead, he pursued dreams that challenged mainstream white prejudice. When he decided to pursue a degree in creative writing, he revealed the full extent of his pre–*Brown v. Board* commitment to unsettling racist assumptions.

While Nipson studied at Penn State, he likely heard of the success that black novelists such as Zora Neale Hurston and Richard Wright enjoyed in the 1930s. News of Hurston's and Wright's triumphs probably impressed him; still, the Depression-era calculations that suffused his undergraduate life compelled him toward the difficult yet pragmatic option of journalism. At the same time that he made such utilitarian choices, Penn State instructors including Theodore Roethke exposed him to the attractions of the literary life, and as an undergraduate, he entered a short story writing contest and won an award. This experience perhaps sparked a plan of action that endured through his graduation in 1940 and his military service from 1941 through 1945. Regardless, his enrollment in the Iowa Writers' Workshop not only reflected the rosier postwar economic forecast but also a no-regrets outlook that pervaded his life. His daughter notes that from "his early days," Nipson "had an attitude that nothing is impossible."[16] The determination that led him to test the conventional wisdom about blacks and opportunities in mainstream journalism similarly shaped his belief that creative writing could be a career. His classes in the workshop both affirmed and challenged such convictions.

The heart of creative writing instruction during Nipson's time at Iowa was a seminar system where student work was publicly presented and then criticized. Describing this process in a 1947 newspaper article, Paul Engle, then the director of the Writers' Workshop, stated, "Each meeting consists of the reading of manuscripts by, customarily, two students, and the detailed criticism of them, first of all by the staff of the writing program acting as a critical panel and then by the students themselves."[17] This straightforward description accurately captures the process of a meeting, but James Hall, a student at the same time that Nipson attended, captures the spirit of these classes: "In their different ways, the workshops were brutal places. If one needed to be loved, to be praised, to be sentimentally encouraged, our manuscript sessions were not the place. Perhaps it was a sign of deep involvement, but when my own stories and poems were mimeographed and discussed, I went home limp, with a headache."[18] Hall's sentiments aptly capture the intensity of workshop seminars, but he also conveys Nipson's somewhat peripheral position in the workshop. In the same 1973 letter from which the Hall quotation is taken, Hall remembers Nipson only in terms of his military service and his editorship of *Ebony*. This sort of writing around Nipson becomes a leitmotif of his workshop experience. There are no specific accounts of students' or teachers' reactions to Nipson's work. Although classmates place him on the scene during workshop exchanges, no one, not even he himself, alludes to his compositions. A famous workshop episode illustrates this situation.

Flannery O'Connor, one of the most highly esteemed workshop graduates, was on campus at the same time as Nipson. Although the class had discussed her work before, she had never read a story herself. She did so during the spring semester of 1948. Writing about this event, Jean Wylder, O'Connor's closest friend in the workshop, observed that the class was "so strangely moved by her reading that afternoon" that Wylder deemed it "the most memorable Monday the Workshop has ever had, before or since."[19] Gene Brzenk, another student who attended the session, puzzled over his reaction to it more than twenty years later. In a 1972 letter to Wylder, he writes, "I'm really very interested to learn sometime whether the reading I've described created the same impression on others who might have been there —[Andrew] Lytle, Herb Nipson, Mary Mudge, and others of our time."[20] Brzenk's reference to Nipson suggests that he remembers him as an individual over and against the collective of fifty or so people who made up the workshop. Despite this individuation, Brzenk confirms Nipson's ostensible position as a fellow onlooker and never as the scrutinized artist.

Nipson understood the state of affairs. He agreed that "everyone in the workshop recognized [O'Connor's] talent." If this universal recognition meant that class members offered "little criticism of her writing," then it did not mean that they felt her skills alone explained the billing that she received within the workshop.[21] Hank Messick, a peer of Nipson, suggested Flannery O'Connor "was in with [Paul] Engle."[22] Expanding on this notion, Nipson averred, "The implication that Paul Engle played favorites is not unfounded. Engle was looking for stars who would bring fame to the young workshop and he favored those whom he thought would be successful. Everyone knew that Flannery was good and most of us knew that she would get favored treatment."[23] The favoritism that Nipson notes often assumed the form of regular appearances on the mimeographed sheets that indicated the works to be discussed in the workshop, but it also determined who received the fellowships that companies sponsored.[24] Whatever form favoritism took, it produced a tiered system featuring shining lights surrounded by those upon whom their beams shone. Nipson's inclusion in the latter category marked him as a part of a sizable contingent deemed less talented than O'Connor; nonetheless, her continued overshadowing of him illustrates an important facet of the workshop's legacy.

For the most part, the Iowa Writers' Workshop celebrated only graduates who went on to be stars. This self-interested selectivity governed how students were treated after they left; however, during their matriculation through the program, they mingled widely. Joseph Langland declared that between 1946 and 1949, "a number" of workshop students "used to meet one night a week to read our work to each other and comment upon it." Listing the members of "one such group," he named "Flannery O'Connor and James B. Hall, novelists, and Herbert Nipson, writing short stories then and now the managing editor of *Ebony*."[25] Nipson's inclusion among the small group suggests that he enjoyed the outside of class "friendly criticism sessions" that some individuals thought taught "as much as" the formal "workshops."[26] For many workshop participants, these sessions consolidated their sense of belonging. Nipson recalled them fondly, and some forty years later, he counted folks like Langland friends with whom he wanted to reconnect. What is more, he never expressed the anxiety that Hall recounted. Instead, he charted his own path that bridged a dual interest in journalism and creative writing.

Nipson appreciated his creative writing classes; nonetheless, his continued dedication to journalistic endeavors rather than his association with famous names such as O'Connor propelled his professional odyssey. His active membership in Sigma Delta Chi, the national journalism honor society, as well as his work for the *Daily Iowan*, UI's student newspaper, unearthed his passion for the collaborative atmosphere of the newsroom.[27] Such collaboration vividly contrasted the life of the creative writer, as described by Engle, "the old and bitter way of sitting down alone in your own room and pounding your typewriter and your head."[28] By pondering this contrast, Nipson cultivated a blended sensibility that proved the most enduring benefit of his Iowa sojourn. As a journalist in Iowa City, he built on his undergraduate experience working for the *Penn State Collegian*. There, he had received credits as both a writer and an editor. For example, in an October 11, 1938, edition of the paper, he posted the story "Harriers Upset Jaspers as Bill Smith Sets the Pace," about his cross-country teammates, and by 1939, he assumed the position of assistant sports editor. At Iowa, he again served on the student paper's editorial board. While his roles were similar, the focus of his contributions was distinct.

Nipson did not write for the *Daily Iowan*; rather, he served the publication

by providing photographs and acting as a photo editor. Since for student papers, prior experience often yields to current necessity, his transition from
composing stories to taking and arranging pictures might just reflect staff
needs. Personnel concerns no doubt played a role in Nipson's decision to
hone his photojournalistic skills while he pursued creative writing degrees;
however, other developments in his education suggest that he purposefully
pursued nonwriting opportunities at the newspaper. Nipson's academic work
at UI occurred in two phases. From 1946 to 1948, he worked on an MFA focused on short fiction. He wrote a collection of short stories to meet the requirements for that degree. After he received his MFA, Nipson began work
on his PhD in creative writing. He continued that program from June 1948
to June 1949. Surprisingly, that span coincides with Nipson's largest number
of credited photos in the *Daily Iowan*.[29] What is more, it also dovetails with
his employment as "a graduate assistant in the photo department at the journalism school."[30] He expanded his association with a department outside of
the workshop at the very moment that he was working on a terminal degree.
Through this expansion, Nipson experimented with wedding the creative
protocols of the workshop with the alternate practice of journalistic endeavors. His experiments yielded impressive recognition.

In July 1949, *Popular Photography* magazine announced that Herb Nipson
earned a first place prize in the Sports Action category at the April 1949 Iowa
Press Photographers convention. His photograph, "Fighting Jockeys," had
initially run in the *Daily Iowan*. Dramatizing how he measured the value of
the university, this prize aptly symbolized Nipson's bifurcated experiences in
journalism and creative writing at UI. Where he existed as an overshadowed,
if connected, personality in the Iowa Writers' Workshop, he was a decorated
contributor to the campus's journalistic activities. He netted statewide recognition for his photography and obtained coveted teaching assistantships
in journalism. Although his workshop classmates were receiving lucrative
fellowships and plum teaching assignments related to writing, Nipson forged
a superlative reputation in a different, if allied, UI department. His efforts
showed an attempt to fuse the "considerable self-discipline" that his peer
James B. Hall deemed a defining trait of workshoppers with the collaborative creativity exhibited in compiling newspapers and other serial publications. Through workshop sessions, Nipson noted the aesthetic awareness that
kindled "sympathies . . . for art." He saw a dedicated faculty's and an impassioned student body's commitment to lighting "small torches of enlightenment

... across America."[31] If he understood these ambitions for an individualized art, then he sought to extend them to spheres where robust group effort served a mass reading public. His short fiction clarifies how the forging of this sensibility formed another facet of the workshop's midcentury project.

Nipson's MFA thesis, "'The Handball Court' and Other Stories," consists of five short pieces of fiction. Tightly plotted and cleanly written, the works are remarkable both for their preoccupation with the alienating effects of class ascendency and for their explorations of figures in transition. Although "Look Down the Long Dark Barrel," the final story in the thesis, depicts a lynching, it — like the other pieces — dwells on white perspectives. Gene Jarrett and others have warned that the temptation to demand a manifest text of blackness is dangerous; however, the tradition of black writers portraying white characters suggests that an allegory often lurks in these narratives. Nipson's work justifies such suggestions. Capturing the stark divide between a male executive and his wife and children, "The Handball Court" contemplates materialism as a substitute for emotional connection. "The Deer Hunt" investigates similar territory when it juxtaposes a father and a son whose contrasting visions of manhood lead to violent conflict. Nipson's fiction recalls writings by D. H. Lawrence and Sinclair Lewis as it suggests that money alone will not ensure happiness. In the context of postwar civil rights activism, it also offers a commentary on redeeming the opportunities afforded by social progress. This commentary emerges through portraits of individuals reentering society after the travail of war.

"The Joy Forever" and "The Return," the third and fourth stories, respectively, in Nipson's thesis, present protagonists who are World War II veterans. As these men return from fighting, they struggle to imagine a way to "tie up" prior "years and the new ones."[32] This grappling with impoverished imagination and enhanced opportunity emerges as a hallmark of Nipson's musing on the workshop and its relevance for influencing art's place in midcentury black life. Within Nipson's work, failed imagination recurs as the true tragedy of modern existence. In keeping with his moderate politics, he does not demonize middle-class comfort or military action; instead, he laments the decline of taste. As he hints at the importance of maintaining tried-and-true virtues, he suggests that adjustments in vision present the best chance to heal a democracy beset by polarizing inequities. Nipson's writings reflect a conviction born of his experiences at UI. Recognizing that doors of opportunity were real, he also acknowledged that few of the academic possibilities open to a black man in the United States in the 1940s came with instruction manuals. When he entered the workshop, he saw it as a training ground for discovering his expertise. The program's robust debates about aesthetics and artistic style led Nipson to embrace a career in creativity. *Ebony* provided him a platform to profoundly shape the lifestyle messages to and about the American black middle class.

Herbert Nipson never finished his PhD in creative writing. In 1949, he left the Iowa Writers' Workshop and joined the editorial staff of *Ebony*, at a time when the magazine was only four years removed from its founding. John H. Johnson, the publisher, imagined that *Ebony* would be a black counterpart to *Life*, the glossy national monthly. Joining a staff supervised by the radical white editor Ben Burns, Nipson fit the lessons that he learned at UI into a broader set of skills. Nipson, first under Burns's supervision and then with increasing creative control, noted that African Americans who relocated from the South to urban spaces enjoyed aspirational accounts of racial peers who succeeded in the United States. To build the magazine's circulation, Nipson, as he defined his editorial style, presented black entertainers and athletes in triumphal profiles. If his editing celebrated black access to mainstream trappings, then in stories about discrimination and lynching, it also acknowledged the persistent facts of racial injustice. Nipson's balancing of inspiration and caution not only reflected social realities but also his own postwar training at UI. Just as the GI bill defined immense opportunity in Nipson's life, his winding path through the workshop and the journalism department marks an oxymoronic delineation of progressive education and frustrated ambition. This ambivalent reality does not sour Nipson on American democracy; rather, it reinforces the need for a black mind-set that accurately absorbs the nation's civic landscape. In collaborating on content for *Ebony* over a thirty-five-year career, Nipson couples ethical compulsions and aesthetic illumination, a blend that honors his UI days.

Through this stewardship of black bourgeois taste, Nipson joins the negotiation about when, where, and how African Americans enter some inlets of the American mainstream. His time at the Iowa Writers' Workshop provided a view of the unique, revelatory power of art and confirmed for him the complicated social and economic realities that swirled around creative processes in a multiracial environment. Because of such provisions, his approach to cultural orchestration featured a black-nationalist neoclassicism, a blend of Afrocentric pride and new humanist universalism. The University of Iowa official response to his success is telling. Nipson's name graces page 39 of the 2013–2014 University of Iowa Gymnastics Media Guide. Along with such luminaries as Tom Brokaw, he is lauded as an alumnus who "took time to consider" his "future" and thus established himself as a leader in his field. This boilerplate recognition could be dismissed as inconsequential; nevertheless, Nipson's inclusion in these sorts of university marketing materials provides an intriguing window into his relationship with the workshop.

Nipson actually exists among a stock group of exemplary UI achievers. If he has made his way into Iowa lore in this sense, his underdeveloped association with the workshop raises curious questions. The beginning of UI's claiming of Nipson's career is his 1977 induction into the Iowa School of Journalism Hall of Fame. Occurring roughly five years after Nipson had received a distinguished alumnus award from Penn State, Iowa's belated recognition nonetheless reflected timeliness. It coincided with Nipson's assumption of the executive editorship of *Ebony*. Where the School of Journalism thought that it should vaunt the legacy of a student who never even took a degree from that unit, the Writers' Workshop remained mum on Nipson. Twenty years later, on the occasion of Nipson being recognized as a UI distinguished alumnus, the reaction remained similar. Nipson has never been appropriated by the workshop. Although his affiliation with Iowa exists because of that unit, his visibility as a Hawkeye stems from the promotional agenda of individuals from a different part of the campus. This could be a reflection of his artistic inferiority, yet his highly influential position in the black publishing industry mitigates against deeming him a workshop failure. Indeed, Nipson may represent the workshop's most pervasive impact on black cultural expression, yet he remains even now a hidden Hawkeye writer. A look at the next major black voice in the workshop suggests the consequences of the university's calculated indifference toward its black pupils.

Michael Harper's Blues:
It Serves You Right to Suffer

Michael Harper sketches his time on the University of Iowa campus in stark terms: "I was the only black in the workshop in 1961, and I survived that year through relations with other blacks who happened to be at Iowa at the time."[33] His survival strategy differs from Nipson's, but many circumstances surrounding his stay are similar. Like Nipson, Harper was "the only one" during his tenure in the Iowa Writers' Workshop. Leigh Ann Randak and Lynn Koos, curators of an exhibit at the Johnson County Historical Society and the African American Museum of Iowa, describe these midwestern moments of singular black presence amid a white majority as inevitably filled with both "pride and sorrow."[34] Harper's workshop experience acutely illustrates their claim. Although he was single when he arrived in Iowa City, Harper encountered the same lodging challenges that a married Nipson faced fifteen years earlier. He viewed that difficulty as a formative exposure to "America as a schizophrenic society."[35] In many ways, the inability to turn a house into a home emerges as the leitmotif of Harper's experience in the workshop. What makes his perspective all the more noteworthy is its contrast with the outlooks of his white peers.

John Gilgun — a student who entered the workshop in 1957 — declared that "1959 was an interesting time in Iowa City." Developing his perception, he observed, "There was a sense of new beginnings, a sudden proliferation of moods and movements. Renaissance II opened, with poetry readings and jazz concerts; and the Iowa Defender began to publish its first issues. . . . In March the first picket lines appeared in front of Kresque's [Kresge's] and Woolworth's — students protesting segregation of lunch-counters in the South. . . . The 50's were over and the 60's had come in."[36] Gilgun's assessment reaffirmed accounts that cast Iowa City as a forward-thinking, midwestern "Athens." Harry Barba, whose tenure at the workshop spanned from 1959 to 1963, insisted that "with exceptions to be expected everywhere," blacks and other "major and minor ethnic groups" in Iowa City "have not felt the hurt of discrimination and segregation. Where they have, they have seen hopeful possibilities for easeful acceptance and integration."[37] Gilgun and Barba exemplify the students, staff, and faculty who saw UI as a cosmopolitan jewel in the quiet Midwest. The contrast between their views and Harper's reflections on his time at UI reinforces the fact that he saw a different world when he surveyed the town. While his peers regarded Iowa City as a creative utopia, Harper judged it a hypocritical purgatory. He initially enrolled "as a midyear student" who "was out of sequence . . . and insecure."[38] His atypical entry paralleled his distinctive point of view.

Harper came to Iowa from Los Angeles, and he arrived in January 1961. When he mentioned that he was looking for a place to stay, Paul Engle, the director of the workshop, recommended that he meet Helen Lemme, a local black property-owner who rented rooms to black students. Harper ignored

Engle's advice and thus commenced his education on race relations in Iowa. In a 1976 letter, he ruminated over his rooming situation while he studied at the workshop: "I had much difficulty living off campus, in any kind of private housing."[39] His descriptions of these difficulties never include a specific catalog of affronts; instead, they give a generalized yet pervasive impression of spiritual wounding. Consequently, Harper presents his year in the heartland as emotionally arduous. This is not to say that he experienced the workshop as unabated misery; rather, it is to frame his presence through the isolating lens of race. Where the picketers in front of an Iowa City Woolworth's struck white workshoppers as forward-looking, for Harper their demonstrations epitomized the belated nature of the civil rights struggle in Iowa City. He described "Iowa" as "an immersion in another kind of segregation," and he found that such separation reigned not only in housing but also in workshop classrooms.[40]

Henri Coulette, Wirt Williams, and Christopher Isherwood, a trio of workshop alumni, all taught Harper during his undergraduate days at Los Angeles State College, and each of them recommended him when he sought admission to the workshop. Although this marshaling of Iowa's much-mentioned networking power got him into the institution, the actual space that the workshop gave Harper for developing his talent proves difficult to gauge. Upon arriving at Iowa, Harper "was interested in the speech patterns of innovators who were telegraphing a special vernacular, a melding of speech and decorum" that he "felt unique to the American tongue."[41] His instructors — Philip Roth, Paul Engle, and Don Justice — proved inept in advancing his command of his creative experiments. While their ineptitude was shared, each imbued it with a different quality. Roth vexed Harper by alleging that he plagiarized a paper about William Golding and by asking him whether he knew James Baldwin, a man fourteen years Harper's senior who had grown up in Harlem rather than Harper's native Brooklyn. These irksome habits led Harper to "war" with Roth, and his relationships with Engle and Justice were even more complicated.[42]

Engle, in Harper's eyes, was the man who "kept things afloat" at the workshop.[43] Since his administrative prowess enabled midyear enrollment, Harper respected Engle's diligent ingenuity. This respect, however, did not translate into a fertile instructional relationship. Harper arrived at Iowa filled with an urge to experiment with "open" poetic "forms," but he sensed that Engle and Justice wanted to make sure that his brand of creativity did not get "much worksheet attention."[44] Even so, Harper regarded his teachers as "helpful" and "generous"— they just could not grasp the engine of his art.[45] These blind spots clarify the difference between his and his peers' workshop training.[46] When Lewis Turco, one of Harper's contemporaries in the poetry section of the workshop, praised the inspirational "effect" that Justice "has on the minds of many of his students," he testified to the vocational progress that the workshop sometimes produced.[47] Merging sublimity and technique, faculty members could prod workshoppers toward a "religiously serious" outlook on writing as a "calling."[48] This nearly sublime rallying to discipleship was conspicuously absent from Harper's matriculation, and his unfulfilled spirit tempered his sense of the workshop's significance.

Harper stressed that his teachers were tone-deaf regarding his creative ambitions; however, he also acknowledged that his surliness made the job of advising him all the more difficult. His sensitivity to what he earlier termed his "insecurity" reveals another aspect of the minority student's negotiation of a majority environment. Whether because of ignorance, arrogance, or perceptiveness, Harper, dubbing himself "incorrigible," refused to "listen" to his instructors.[49] This disdain showed his character, but the workshop's reaction to it reveals its calculated tolerance. Harper understood that rigid prescription may have warped his artistic will, so the workshop's willingness to grant him the right of repudiation earned the institution his measured gratitude. He avers that Iowa permitted him the "opportunity" to "[blunder] in [his] own way."[50] Through this permission, the workshop fueled his artistry even as aspects of its formal program were counterproductive. One facet that revealed this informal efficacy was his friendships with such writers as Lawson Inada, Vern Rutsala, and Bob Berner. Just as Herb Nipson counted James Hall, Joseph Langland, and Gene Brzenk among the peers who helped him hone his style, Harper saw his interactions with Inada, Rutsala, and Berner as edifying. In contrast to Nipson, who mentioned editing sessions where writers explicitly discussed one another's work, Harper stressed the ways in which Inada's love of jazz and Rutsula's intelligence on workshop politics eased his movement through a space defined by alien aesthetic impulses and disorienting cultural assumptions. Inada, Rutsala, and Berner existed as life preservers within the white sea of workshop creativity, but Harper found sustaining forces in his interactions within Iowa's black community. At UI, this community linked artists and athletes in unexpected ways.

As Richard Breaux argues elsewhere in this volume, athletes — especially male ones — have long comprised a significant portion of the black undergraduate population at the University of Iowa. White workshoppers were not oblivious to this cohort. On Saturdays, they would cheer on the football team, and more blue-collar attendees such as Philip Levine struck up friendships with individuals including the soon to be three-time All-American Calvin Jones.[51] Harper, however, established solidarity with African American sportsmen through more enduring relationships. He "spent most of" his "downtime with black athletes" because whether consciously or unconsciously the white writers in the workshop made him feel marginalized.[52] Conversely, the atmosphere at 20 West Harrison Street, a house that the athletic department rented for black players, made him feel connected to a vibrant community. Harper befriended men such as Frank Davis, who was struggling to balance academic ambition, rambunctious carousing, and an august family legacy. Davis afforded Harper a catbird seat for lessons on the consequences of Iowa's accumulated impact on a black male psyche. Al Hinton embellished the curriculum by confiding that the combination of being a football player and a painter led to a situation where "no one took him seriously as an artist."[53] The opportunity to wrestle with these issues with fellow black male students made 20 West Harrison a crucial site of Harper's Iowa City education.

Of course, his interactions with black male students were not confined to the athletic house. Harper found a fellow creative artist in Oliver Jackson, a graduate student who was studying for an MFA in painting. The two men frequently attended the free movies shown on campus and visited the art library to "peruse the oversized art books of the masters." In Jackson, Harper found a peer whose attention to craft and whose blend of influences held much in common with his own. Their friendship provided Harper a unique sounding board for his experiments with authoritative creative expression. He stressed the value of this discovery in his description of Jackson: "He was an inspiration because he validated what I knew about black men and ambition, and we discussed what never got touched in seminars, our sense of aesthetics."[54] By identifying Jackson as an interlocutor in aesthetic mediation, Harper confirmed what many workshoppers said about the benefits of having sharp-minded peers.[55] He also reveals that there were vigorous incubations of black expressivity taking place in spots aside from those commonly associated with the flowering of creativity known as the black arts movement.

As I have explained elsewhere, the terrain of 1960s black literature flows as a tributary between the banks of Ralph Ellison on the one hand and the black aesthetic on the other.[56] Harper celebrates Ellison as a standard-bearing expositor of "rhetoric and democratic values," yet his insistence that figures such as jazz saxophonist John Coltrane exemplify a serious grappling with such imaginative conundrums marks a point of departure from an elder statesman whom he venerated.[57] Harper's ability to fold the influences of Ellison and Coltrane into his poetic voice captures what I term "communion without consensus."[58] Two cultural titans such as Ellison and Coltrane may embody the most impressive examples of divergent aesthetic impulses that influenced his work, and Harper discovered the viability of appealing to both in the cauldron of the Iowa Writers' Workshop. Indeed, his negotiation of a space that featured white expertise unfitted to his needs alongside buoyant black experimentation that he found inspiring impelled Harper to produce his thesis, "Blues and Laughter." With this work, he sowed the seeds of what some critics call the New Breed in black literature.[59]

"Blues and Laughter" features poems that examine evocative combinations. In "The Primal Chair," this combining occurs when a Puerto Rican woman wants a son by a black man. The woman, "a white Puerto Rican," embraces black as "her favorite color";[60] however, on a subway platform, she talks to a black man who has a "brown" baby with a lady "like" her. He confesses, "I am a father. I feel good," yet before jumping in front of a moving train, he laments, "It is too bad . . . I cannot see him."[61] Stressing the challenges that attend encounters across cultures, this poem contains a fusion of intimacy and alienation that recurs in Harper's texts. He portrays such sentiments in varied situations. From a jazz club to a morgue in "Phoenix or All the Things You Are," he maps saxophonist Charlie Parker's straddling of social realities. "African Woman on a Bicycle" probes cultural conflict in an office through choices about the hanging of a photograph. Perhaps most tellingly, "The Blonde Liberal" muses on an American who "fled to Venice" and depicts the work's namesake as holding "Kerouac under one arm" and *Ebony* under the other."[62] Within such unexpected conflations, Harper identifies the wide range of emotions that must be managed in a nation defined by pluralistic values. His aesthetic approach, although still in formation, clearly displays angles of vision that he acquired in Iowa City.

After he left the workshop, Harper concluded that the Midwest familiarized him with the "schizophrenic society" of the United States, and he implies that the heartland "toughened" him as he searched for democracy's possibilities.[63] For instance, when white Iowans claimed common cause with the Greensboro sit-in movement and the sentiments animating the Freedom Riders, onlookers such as Barba extolled the decency and fair play that prompted their actions. Harper similarly acknowledged their deeds, yet he saw them within broader structural and social contexts. He observed, "I remember refusing to hold hands with Iowa students while they sang 'We Shall Overcome.' I thought this was hypocrisy, their political action clubs, and a covenant of gerrymandering, and worse, tormentors in cars, yelling obscenities as black students walked up the hill from the library, or downtown to window shop."[64] The friction between Harper and the white protestors unveils the tension at the heart of the freedom struggle as it unfolded across the country. White Americans often felt moved to participate in high-profile protests, but this did not always affect their daily interactions with black citizens. Harper refused to overlook the tacit demand that black Americans yield space "in a world that had been a true test to them." Since the inducements to yielding were so pervasive, the remedy even as one gained access to white institutions was to be astutely "attuned to" one's "ancestry."[65] As John Edgar Wideman, a workshop attendee in the 1966–1967 school year, would later declare, the admonitions toward that sort of black consciousness were rarely heard in such mainstream spaces as the workshop.[66]

Harper believed in the guild-like energy that a label such as "the Workshop" connoted. As Loren Glass has suggested, the term *workshop* evoked "concepts of discipline and craft" that "provide[d] a teachable element as well as a work ethic to temper the leisurely lifestyle of the bohemian community."[67] Harper showed up at the University of Iowa convinced that he would benefit from such training; he thought that he was entering a space where his writing would gain "the tradition and context" that would allow him to "find [his] own voice."[68] Instead of encountering master craftsmen who could initiate him into a creative freemasonry, he was thrust into a space where his lessons came from "psychic window peeping" and "nascent" "voyeurism."[69] This confounding of his expectations became the unintended yet endlessly stimulating foundation of Harper's Iowa interlude. Through these hidden curricula, he discovered routes to artistic power and the peculiar dynamo of interracial collaboration. That discovery proved the most profound revelation that he could gain about blackness and access to majority institutions. In contrast to his age-group peers in the black arts movement who scorned any semblance of tokenism that sought to pass as genuine exertions on behalf of democracy, Harper advocated for a more nuanced approach to racial progress via artistic production. In an inimitably gruff manner, he has always noted the workshop's role in speeding him along that trail.

Intriguingly, Michael Harper is the only African American included in Robert Dana's praise-song *A Community of Writers: Paul Engle and the Iowa Writers' Workshop* (1999). Although many factors may explain his distinction, Harper clearly did not gain entrance into this published community by ignoring the contradictory nature of his workshop sojourn. With his memories of Iowa awash with references to well-known athletes such as Calvin Jones, Emlen Tunnell, and Connie Hawkins or more obscure figures such as Dayton Perry and Joe Williams, Harper colors his heartland training as akin to athletic striving. The Big Ten and the broader world of sporting competition struck him as apt metaphors for his struggle to claim control of black performativity in a white context. As such scholars as Jewel Prestage make clear, the existential fellowship between black students across campus offered immense consolation to black Hawkeyes in a range of programs and departments. In the final analysis of his Iowa days, Harper determines, "I wasn't damaged much by the experience."[70] His sentiment resonates with Margaret Walker's assessment of her Iowa years.

Margaret Walker's People: Radical Folk

Consisting of two epochs separated by more than twenty years, Margaret Walker's studies at the Iowa Writers' Workshop provide chronological bookends for this chapter. She first attended Iowa from 1939 to 1940, seven years before Herbert Nipson enrolled. After briefly revisiting campus in summer 1961, she began her PhD studies during fall 1962, a mere eight months after Michael Harper left town. Walker's status as a figure who frames Nipson and Harper provides a helpful image of the changing contours of the workshop. While Wilbur Schramm, the first head of the workshop, pegs its birth in 1936, Stephen Wilbers, the most thoroughgoing historian of the Iowa institution, identifies the summer of 1939 as the moment when the entire enterprise coalesced into its modern form. No records of black students in the precursor English department courses from which the workshop germinated exist, and since Walker began her studies in the summer of 1939, she is perhaps the first black individual to ever study in the Iowa Writers' Workshop. This racial first may have been neglected by history, but Walker's centrality to the post–Harlem Renaissance, pre-naturalist-realist school of black writing has not been overlooked. Despite such recognition, most — if not all — critical analyses of Walker have ignored how her Iowa years fit into her artistic gestation. This oversight is ironic given that the two most heralded literary products in Walker's corpus, *For My People* (1942) and *Jubilee* (1966), were produced during moments when she was either attending or enrolled in the workshop. While many commentators have quoted Paul Engle's assertion that the workshop did not "pretend to have produced" its successful writers, the paradox of what the institution did to "the genes rattling in ancestral closets" surfaces starkly in the career of Margaret Walker.[71]

The aesthetic sensibility Walker brought to the workshop was shaped by her southern childhood and midwestern undergraduate education. She was born on July 7, 1915, in Alabama, and she grew up in New Orleans. Even though she lived in the segregated South, she had direct interactions with the black American writers who anticipated and anchored the Harlem Renaissance. Walker's parents prized learning and exposed her to myriad cultural activities. During her teenage years, they took her to readings by James Weldon Johnson and Langston Hughes. These events not only exposed her to these writers' art but also, in the case of Hughes, they afforded her chances for conversation. From these conversations, Walker gleaned lessons regarding reading widely and writing regularly. She put these instructions into practice. Through the works of Countee Cullen and Claude McKay, she expanded her already rich sense of poetry's possibilities. As her talents shone more conspicuously, her parents recalled Hughes's recommendation that they educate Walker outside of Jim Crow Dixie. Heeding that advice, Walker's family enrolled her at Northwestern University in 1932. Her stay in the Windy City provided a leftist sociocultural critique and a broader access to folk materials that would influence her formal impulses after she arrived at Iowa. In many ways, the source of both of these provisions was Richard Wright. Walker states that Wright "had a concept of the problems of being a black person in this country, and he could tell you and show you what we do not have." Listening to these explanations, Walker experienced an artistic shift. She moved away from "a very romantic and sentimental type of poetry to a very realistic and factual" style. Far from coincidence, she claims that she "was very conscious of making that change."[72] Walker's stylistic evolution also led to a heightened appreciation of the folk language and culture that had peppered her childhood and that she was exposed to anew in her work with the Illinois Writers' Project (IWP).

Walker heard stories about slavery from her maternal grandmother. While these stories defined one part of her interest in communal memory, her work on the IWP also showed her how literature could use black folk culture. As a southerner, she was aware of black striving in an agricultural context; the IWP gave her a chance to see urban realities. Specifically, she witnessed the struggle for individual dignity that occurred when blacks confronted a modern city. Although she agreed that radical ideologies accurately diagnosed the problems of African Americans in the 1930s, Walker felt that the remedy was not class warfare. Instead, she believed in cultural reservoirs such as black stoicism, an attitude that fueled earlier generations' ability to overcome huge obstacles.[73] Walker's focus on candid accounts of hardships overcome with the aid of old-fashioned values of progress predicted the prevailing literary mood of the post–civil rights era. Remarkably, she developed this forward-looking creative posture as a result of her transition from Chicago to Iowa City. In the span between the South Side Writers Group and the Iowa Writers' Workshop seminars, she honed her commitment to transcendent black cultural particularity. The literary currents that surround each of her transitions to the workshop clarify how her artistic development reflects her grappling with the possibilities of Iowa. From 1939 to 1965, she refines those possibilities in ways that make her a singular trailblazer in African American letters.

Walker did not arrive at the workshop as a household name, but she did come in as a published writer. The circumstances surrounding that publication are illustrative. After hearing a lecture in Chicago by W. E. B. DuBois, Walker, then an undergraduate, told the scholar that she wrote poetry. He asked her to send some poems to *Crisis*, the magazine of the National Association for the Advancement of Colored People (NAACP), and in 1934, he published "I Want to Write," a short poem written by Walker. By 1939, the workshop already had seen graduates such as George Abbe and Herb Krause publish books, but few students entered with the kind of training and connections that Walker boasted. Her attitude differed starkly from students such as Olga Opfell, a workshop attendee from 1942 to 1943, who admitted, "I was just out of college and felt terribly insecure in the company of older and more seasoned writers."[74] Opfell thought of faculty including Marguerite Young and Paul Engle as remote, intimidating sages, while Walker saw these instructors as sounding boards who might help her publish a book. Her confidence stemmed from her interactions with not only DuBois and Hughes but also Richard Wright and Ralph Ellison. By 1939, Walker had already been working with accomplished writers including Sterling Brown and Arna Bontemps. Although she did not deem herself the equal of these men in accomplishment, she linked herself with them in terms of writing ambition. Her experiences in the South Side Writers Group in Chicago reinforced this outlook. Their meetings allowed her to interact with writers including Fenton Johnson, Frank Marshall Davis, and Fern Gayden. Her exposure to veteran authors and seminar style discussions identified Walker as the kind of young, talented student who could burnish the Iowa Writers' Workshop's reputation. The fact that she was a black woman made Iowa's ability to enroll her even more of a coup for the institution.

Notwithstanding the ways in which her gender, race, and rarefied writing experiences would have made her conspicuous, Walker does not seem to penetrate the awareness of her peers. She is absent from their letters about the workshop, some of which run to as many as twenty pages. Yet Walker's remarks about her time at Iowa in 1939–1940 suggest that like Harper, she grew in the workshop environment because of productive tension. Walker attended workshop classes with Kimon Friar, Leonard Unger, Theobald K. Shattuck, and Joseph Langland, and she concluded that their cohort was a "strange group of people." She also noted the presence of "a very young and catalytic" teacher, Paul Engle.[75] Her praise of Engle as a classroom instructor rather than as an administrator deviates from the usual image of the workshop head. Engle did in fact teach Walker to appreciate the poetic possibilities of the ballad form, and for that instruction, she was thankful. She also fondly remembers his classes: "We had great fun, great and memorable sessions." Interestingly, that fun was defined by how much the teacher and the student "fussed and fought over [her] poetry and outrage."[76] Indeed, this oppositional instructional posture captures a more pervasive characteristic that seems crucial to understanding the training black students received at predominantly white schools.

Engle counseled Walker to use the folk ballad form as she developed her poetic voice. His recommendations echoed the perspective of Nick Aaron Ford, a black critic who had completed his master's in English at Iowa in the mid-1930s. Engle's advice also revealed his willingness to engage in a bit of fussing and fighting as well as his sometimes backward aesthetic notions. Walker recalls that Engle asked her to write some ballads that he then critiqued: "Your stuff is too bitter. You're just too bitter. You need to write some funny ballads about a good ole Negro preacher." Perceiving this as a request for black stereotypes, she quipped, "I don't think that would be funny. My father is a preacher, and my grandfather was a preacher. And I don't think they are funny." Walker's umbrage at Engle's suggestion reflects her disdain for his glib repudiation of her work's biting tone as well as her sense that he was demanding that she turn her artistic ambitions into quasi-minstrel antics. Commenting on how such a demand would strike Walker, Maryemma Graham observed, "In her mind, it was necessary to refute [demeaning images of blacks]....There's always this grounding in a different reality, in correcting the distortions of the past."[77] This convergence of technically astute yet culturally insensitive advice highlights the challenges that Walker confronted in using the workshop to reach her goals. Between her first and second stints, the ratio of these elements in her experience shifted fairly dramatically; however, in 1940, she bristled at her instructors' prescriptions regarding content even as she heeded their guidance in terms of form. The poems that she produced reflected this precarious balancing.

The thesis that Walker submitted for her master's degree was entitled "For My People," and with few exceptions, it was identical to the collection of the same name that won the 1942 Yale Younger Poets prize. The works in Walker's thesis take the ballad form and mold it to the ironies of black experience. Although the title poem "For My People" has commanded considerable scholarly attention, other works capture Walker's position as a black artist honing her voice in the workshop. In "Sorrow Home," her speaker proclaims, "My roots are deep in southern life."[78] "Delta" echoes this sentiment when it states, "I am a child of this valley. Mud and muck and misery of lowlands are on thin tracks of my feet."[79] If these poems confirm southern blackness as an orienting experience for Walker, then "Address to America" confirms how Walker sees other regions of the United States, especially "Middle America."[80] Her vision perceives midwesterners "washing your lives with pity, smoothing your ways with vague apologies."[81] Through a fused regional awareness, Walker not only expressed her suspension between the South and the Midwest but also captured a more general midcentury mood in a nation where "a union of two strange worlds must be."[82] Walker's reflections on that situation arrested the eyes of the judges for the Yale Younger Poets award. Since the judge for that contest was Stephen Vincent Benét, a frequent visitor to the workshop, one must consider whether it was Walker's talent that brought acclaim to the workshop or the workshop's network that brought honor to Walker.[83] Regardless, seven years before Gwendolyn Brooks won the Pulitzer Prize, Iowa could boast an attachment to arguably the most decorated black female poet in the United States. As Stephen Wilbers points out, Walker becomes a part of a group of first-guard workshop alumni whose publications and awards "helped to draw nation-wide attention" to the enterprise.[84]

Despite her success, Walker's first trip through the Iowa Writers' Workshop left bruises that reflected more than Paul Engle's buffeting. Where Nipson and Harper identify housing as the litmus of the lacerating racial reality in Iowa City, Walker endured depression and romantic frustration as constant companions. This viewpoint surfaces in her journals where she writes of "defeating" herself "through negative attitudes" and of despairing over her wardrobe, her health, and her inability to find a "mate."[85] These may seem like trivial matters to some observers, but their impact on her participation in the workshop suggests otherwise. In a journal entry for November 19, 1939, Walker states that "coming to Iowa was a definite and what I felt positive and constructive effort to keep emotionally balanced and sane. My mental growth far surpasses all others — still I am not a scholar nor diligent student."[86] Because she treats graduate creative writing as a kind of psychoanalysis, Walker's encounters with the workshop acquire a heightened significance. She not only identifies the space as a writing lab but also as a therapist's couch. While this therapy did not preclude socialization, it centered on making her "work and career" a launching pad for "prestige and public standing."[87] Her success in this enterprise is best glimpsed through the lens of her return to the workshop in 1962.

After her first workshop stint, Walker achieved nationwide recognition for her poetry; however, she had not intended to focus on verse when she enrolled at Iowa. During her undergraduate days at Northwestern, she had begun a draft of a novel, and she wanted to work on this book as she pursued her graduate studies. This project was tabled when she showed promise as a poet. Her shift from one genre not only defined the early part of her career; it also determined the teachers under whom she studied. In 1939, the workshop was not as rigidly divided between poets and fiction writers as it would soon become; however, the division did exist. Since Engle handled most if not all of the poetry instruction, Walker's first tenure at the workshop bears deep imprints of encounters with him. Although he also played a key role in her second workshop sojourn, her renewed interest in completing a novel meant that she spent most of her time interacting with fiction instructors.

Her interactions with Verlin Cassill were the most sustained. Walker did not establish a residence in the workshop until summer 1962, but during summer 1961, she studied under Cassill in an eight-week summer session. Alerting her to the fact that she was "telling and not showing" in her fiction, Cassill taught Walker how to "do close critical reading and how to make character charts, establish relationships, and control the language more powerfully and effectively."[88] Cassill's solutions to the technical flaws in Walker's writing recall the impact of the New Criticism not only in analyzing but also in writing literature. Beyond this reflection of an interpretive style, Cassill's reactions differed from Engle's in that he did not dismiss the topic of her writing (slavery) or the tone of her prose (edgy). This encouragement proved a crucial complication in Walker's second tour through the workshop.

Walker's return to Iowa City occurred against the backdrop of a dry span as far as her literary productivity was concerned. While the desires, professional and romantic, that dominated her first stay blossomed into an award-winning poetry collection and a family including a husband and four children, in the intervening decades her publications stagnated because of teaching obligations, health issues, and domestic duties. She thus sought in the 1960s workshop a space where she could rekindle her creativity, and through her interactions with Cassill, she discovered a catalyzing spark. This inspiration sustained her through a five-year journey that ended in a doctoral degree, a prestigious fellowship, and the publication of a best-selling novel. If the credential marked Walker as a scholar-writer who joined such other workshop alums as Wallace Stegner and Joseph Langland, then her unique balancing at an intersection of acclaim and social consciousness branded Iowa's creative writing program as an unlikely training site.

Walker's 1962 return to this site followed her path through different colleges and universities between 1942 and 1948. But in 1949, she began what would be a long-term association with Jackson State, a historically black college in Jackson, Mississippi. Like many of the black graduate students analyzed in this volume, Walker knew that one option for making her livelihood would be finding employment at an HBCU. The intellectual recognition connected to such jobs differed mightily from the reality of taking such work. Walker quickly discovered that her teaching demands at Jackson State left little time for writing. Because of her goals, this situation distressed her. She explains, "As much as I love [teaching] I have always rationalized that it was only a means to an end, since the chief goal of my life was to be a writer."[89] Because her circumstances — both professional and personal — distracted her from writing, after receiving a Rosenwald Fellowship (1944) and a Ford Fellowship (1954), Walker determined that a prolonged stay at the workshop might be the creative prod she needed. Her decision to retrace her steps to Iowa City reflects a fascinating symmetry. When Walker studied at the workshop in 1939–1940, she took not only graduate-level poetry seminars but also classes in American civilization that addressed her interest in slavery. These classes propelled her along a research path that preoccupied her for the next two decades of her life. As she was rounding out these studies in the late 1950s, she felt that returning to Iowa — the place where she began her systematic exploration of US history — would be reassuring and efficacious. Her decision, as well as her work with Cassill and other white instructors, epitomizes an interracial experiment that comes to signify the collaborative possibilities between the black student and the white institution.

Walker's decision to return to a site of interracial instruction is not surprising. Throughout her career, she gained access to a dizzying array of both private and governmentally subsidized inducements for the creative writer. On both occasions when she arrived at the Iowa Writers' Workshop, she had already applied for and received help from white organizations that supported writing. Her track record set the foundation for an assimilationist outlook, and without a doubt, Walker was an integrationist. That being said, she viewed black institutions as crucial repositories, and because of that, she not only embraced a folk aesthetic in her writing but also sought to make academia responsive to the ever-complicating contours of the civil rights struggle. Her suturing of a technically adept style of folk fiction and intellectual activism thus became the nucleus of a coherent aesthetic philosophy, and Walker's second stay facilitated her careful molding of its significance. In the midst of the civil rights movement and the rise of a forceful militancy, Walker used her time at the workshop to hone an independent creative approach to her writing. Thus, even as her presence at the workshop reflects her connectedness to its charismatic leader and her status as an establishment writer, she ably exemplifies the emerging trend of black writers learning to redeem crucial educational opportunities without submitting to the tyranny of mainstream expectations. The content and the tone of Walker's dissertation eloquently illustrate the ways in which she sought to honor Cassill's craft critiques without sacrificing the integrity of her imagination.

Walker's example anticipates the sort of negotiation that is at the center of Larry Neal's wrestling with Ralph Ellison. On the one hand, Walker and her Iowa interactions seem unrelated to the transgenerational wrangling that sees Neal go from hating to loving Ellison. Yet a closer look reveals that as they decide whether and how blackness and democratic pluralism might be compatible, Walker and Neal must square their allegiance to black culture and experience with their ambivalence toward white collaborators who might aid in the renovation of such rich reservoirs. Where for Neal this was an indirect meditation on Ellison's candid commendation of what Henry James, T. S. Eliot, and James Joyce taught him about the use of folk materials, Walker's experiences involve an assessment of what Paul Engle and Verlin Cassill might contribute to making "For My People" and *Jubilee* the paeans to black survival that anchored her artistic legacy. She concludes that however imperfect Iowa's instructions might have been, they were key beacons in her creative development. Although it would take the black arts movement and black feminism a decade to grasp the fullness of her declaration, Walker unabashedly acknowledged the impact of her training in the Iowa Writers' Workshop. Her deeply principled and highly respected corpus and career proved that blackness without apology could be cultivated even amid the misguided pressure of white progressivism. Through this proving, she embodied the university's strenuous struggling with the nation's creeds. Perhaps, the most telling evidence of Iowa's baffling perspective is its failure to capitalize on this episode even from the standpoint of marketing. That failure brings us full circle in making meaning out of this early trio of black workshoppers.

The Paradox of Iowa City:
I Only Meant to Wet My Feet

In some ways, Herbert Nipson, Michael Harper, and Margaret Walker are prototypical Iowa Writers' Workshop graduates. Nipson spends his entire career working at one of the foremost publications in the United States, and Harper and Walker teach at universities while they continue to publish their own creative work. In the midst of long and distinguished service, they all garner some of the highest recognitions that their professions offer. Their stories sound like yet another press release from the annals of a storied creative writing program except that for some reason, the University of Iowa has never marketed this constellation of writers. Undoubtedly, the official explanation for this will be that the workshop does not keep track of its writers' race: it merely seeks to educate its writers. This line of thinking squares with a twenty-first-century fantasy of postracial prose, but from 1939 to 1965, the harsh reality of segregation and the unique challenges of the civil rights movement meant that race was not inconsequential; rather, it was determinative. This was true for students and for the university as it strove to settle on a consensus self-portrait. On the one hand, Iowa was the spot that graduated the first black law student. Alternately, it was the university that "permitted discriminatory practices with no basis in formal policy."[90] Like the other university units analyzed in this book, the workshop through its participation in this self-study can best be gauged in examining the experiences of its black students. Nipson, Harper, and Walker are thus representative of Iowa's complicated identity; like the student-chauffeur in *Invisible Man*, they must tell the university its fate. By looking at each writer's creative work, we glimpse their testimonies as well as Iowa's character.

Nipson, Harper, and Walker all envisioned a stylish blackness that smoothed the path toward a fuller realization of American democracy. Although they attended the Iowa Writers' Workshop in different eras and under distinct historical realities, they saw their presence as an actualization of both professional opportunity and social change. Their range of postures in pursuing these twin goals becomes the advance scouting for black bourgeois self-definition in the post–civil rights era. In simple terms, this trio expresses various options for performing racial pride and artistic integrity within the majority white, higher educational context. Their trailblazing yields two vivid lessons. First, by ignoring the teacher-to-student and peer-to-peer exchanges that their experiences reveal, scholars have promoted a narrative of abrupt integration that conceals too much preparatory labor. Nipson, Harper, and Walker not only expand our understanding of the program era but also complicate narratives that focus on the autodidactic black writer. The next truth that these black alumni reveal is the ladder of support that enabled black matriculation at the workshop. The trio stretches across twenty-five years, and by 1990, their harvest produced an even larger cohort of black graduates. Their legacy also claims a permanent faculty member in James Alan McPherson and a host of black visiting writers. To comprehend the true significance of these students' accomplishments, the workshop should not content itself with boosting its bibliography; it must acknowledge that its moral wrangling extended to race as well as aesthetics. Within such acknowledgment, it will both reclaim and refine its tradition.

* * *

GOING THE DISTANCE

* * *

came to the University of Iowa because of its reputation as the most liberal school in the country regarding black people; I also came because I was a distance runner. Back then, height and race dictated whether people thought that you could run distance. These assumptions stemmed from the Germans' purist belief that for physiological and psychological reasons, only white Western-cultured individuals could be distance runners. In the 1950s, nowhere in the world had blacks run distance; nevertheless, I did. I stood six foot three and ranked number two nationally in both the two-mile and the mile. Schools offered me scholarships, but most of them did so before they found out I was black. Upon learning about my race, they withdrew their offers. After having been rejected at many other universities, I enrolled at UI because just like the black authors in the Writers' Workshop, I thought that I would receive instruction and have the opportunity to develop. My thinking proved correct.

Just before the Big Ten meet at Evanston in 1950, Francis Cretzmeyer, the head track coach, contacted me about attending Iowa. He was a remarkable gentleman. Since he had just taken the job and didn't have a lot of good athletes, he tried something different. He recruited blacks. Where other coaches conformed to prejudice, Cretzmeyer possessed a color-blind commitment to talent. He fielded more black athletes at UI than any other school in the conference and perhaps the country. Since track and field rarely achieved high visibility, his actions did not make national news. Still, before football and basketball ever attracted high percentages of black players, UI track and field boasted significant numbers of black athletes. The popular sports programs eventually became 33 and then 50 percent black, but the trend toward having bunches of black athletes on a UI team started with track and field. I committed to running for Cretzmeyer at Iowa because he allowed such trends to grow.

I got into running as a teenager. After dropping out of high school, I visited Illinois in August. I walked along the canal in Evanston on McCormick Street, and some youngsters from the high school cross-country team passed me. As a joke, I started jogging behind them. They ended up at their high school, and their coach convinced me to return to school. My track-and-field career started with that simple conversation. I became good very quickly, and around the nation, people recognized me as a phenom of sorts. Although my sports career took off immediately, my academic odyssey took longer to gain momentum. My high school journey featured many twists and turns. In Evanston, I attended one of the best high schools in Illinois. Since I had missed a year of school, I found my first semester back very difficult. The school presented challenges, but I knew it provided the right fit for me. In order to get myself prepared, I went to a school in Johnstown, Pennsylvania, and worked quite hard. I stayed in Johnstown for one semester, and then I spent my junior and senior years at Evanston. There, I discovered the uniqueness of being a runner. The environment on Evanston's North Shore differed from Pennsylvania or from Georgia, where I grew up. Because I did something unique — run — people in Evanston took an interest in me. This motivated me. I had been ignored for many years, and after struggling academically and socially, I found that by running I could get admiration and dignity. This made it pretty easy for me to say, "This is where I want to be." It also gave me the chance to earn a spot at Iowa.

When I went to UI, there must have been fifteen or fewer undergraduate black men and almost no black women. In effect, no social life existed. Mrs. [Bettye] Tate and Mrs. [Helen] Lemme, two outstanding women who kept houses where black students could board, made these difficulties easier to bear. Of the two, Mrs. Tate exhibited a little more austerity. She was a very proud, disciplined woman, who did almost no socializing with the people who lived with her. Although I didn't stay there, I got to know her by visiting my friends, the black football and black basketball players, who rented from her. Mrs. Lemme behaved differently. With her ears attuned to campus happenings, she kept tabs on the black students. She always knew what you were doing, if you stepped out of line, and if you were doing well. At least two or three times a year, she made sure that every black student went to dinner. When Duke Ellington came to town, he would play at Mrs. Lemme's. We would all go down there and listen to Duke until the sun came up. Mrs. Lemme nourished us, and she turned a negative into a positive. Without segregation, there would not be either a Tate or a Lemme, but in difficult times, they made great contributions to humanity by making it possible for black students to be more comfortable.

In 1950, Amera Saunders and I lived in South Quad. Before that, out-of-state blacks had not been permitted in the dorms. By 1946, in-state blacks could stay on campus, but the university funneled out-of-state students to private homes like Mother Ferg's [Mrs. Estella Ferguson's], Mrs. Lemme, or Mrs. Tate's. Amera and I were among the first exceptions to that practice. Unlike today when housing staff often assign black students to live with one another, my roommate was white, a guy from Ottumwa, Iowa. Overall, living with him turned out positively. There is a certain level of paranoia that exists for blacks in all-white environments, and we know when there's a real wake-up call. If there is racism, black people pick that up very quickly. In my first semester, I had none of those troubles. Part of the serenity, I think, stemmed from being an athlete of color. While racism existed at UI as it does in other places, I noticed it less because of my associations with white faculty members and my white dorm director, Mrs. Spencer. I experienced quite good fortune because other than the inability to date interracially, I did not deal directly with racism on campus. In fact, I encountered different reactions.

As a black guy at Iowa, I got a lot of attention from people who felt that they should reach out to a person who was less fortunate than them. These white people may have been trying to make up for some of their intolerant peers. Whatever the case, I — like many athletes — benefited from their generosity. Some of these people want to associate with you because you're a jock, but another set want to see you do something besides throw the football or run around the track. These folks gave me a chance to have social experiences and to develop certain intellectual processes. As a black athlete, I got access to rich opportunities that allowed me to lead a meaningful life. This mixture of athletic and scholastic rewards represents the best gift that a school can give their sports competitors. The reasons for this are simple. Once an athlete, especially a track one, has sweated for the black and gold and finished their career in sports, there was no bridge program that would allow them to make a living. I formed my opinion about these things based on how my college career unfolded.

After completing my freshman year in 1950–1951 — a year when I couldn't run — I was drafted in 1951 and was out of college for two years. In the army, for some reason, they let me — a guy in boot camp — become the track coach. One of the men I coached was a sergeant named Gastro Lee Finch. Finch was a nice guy, so after being around him a few weeks, I said, "You're going to go to the University of Iowa." He said, "What do you mean?" I said, "I am going to make you good enough as a quarter-miler to get a scholarship." After he had trained with me for a few months, I called Coach Cretzmeyer and told him, "I want you to take somebody." He said, "Well, how good is he?" I said, "You'll make him good, just take him." Between October and April, I convinced him to go, and Finch left that summer to come to UI. I joined him later, and we ran on teams together. Throughout my career, I enjoyed helping out my team-mates. During my senior year, we had a special team. It was so special that even though I was on scholarship, I gave up my funding for my teammates. That gave me more pleasure than anything else. Since I had the power to survive financially, I knew that sacrificing my scholarship would help the team. No one told me to do that or talked about how that was going to happen, but it made sense to me. On another occasion, I gave every team member a wristwatch, whether they won or not. Performing these deeds cultivated my character. In considering my undergraduate days, I relish this kind of growth. Every year at UI contributed to my overall development; still, if I look at all my years there, there wouldn't be a competition regarding which one I liked the most.

After I went undefeated in 1956, my senior year, I made the United States Olympic Team and competed in Australia. My Olympic experience trans-formed me. Athletic competition plays one part in the Olympic Games, but by the time I traveled to Melbourne, I had lived in a small mining town in Pennsylvania, in a rural area of the segregated South, and gone through the army. Because in each place I saw how divided people were, I developed an idea that athletics could bring people together. I tried out this theory in Mel-bourne. When I went to the Olympics, the competitors were together from August 'til December in this country [the United States] and then from Sep-tember to December [in Australia]. I discovered that when you stayed in the same village with people for that long, you got a fantastic education just from socializing with them. The vision of being successful on the track almost became secondary. Even though I trained with Merv Lincoln, an Australian, who was the best in the world, I found myself more interested in the human interests of the scene than in the sporting contest. I didn't get the medals finishing seventh, and Merv took home a silver for second. Although my result was disappointing, my overall experiences — going to church with Italians; seeing Kenyans, East Africans, and West Africans — were revelatory. The Olympic Games afforded me a taste of what the world could offer. The experience of traveling and meeting people broadened me, enabling me to digest my life better. By providing me a better understanding, it let me look forward to appreciating the history and the cultures of other peoples.

The Olympics most likely led me to coaching. I didn't coach because I wanted to develop champions. I coached because I was a person who had come from zero. Since running had gotten me out of that situation, I thought that it might help others. When I think about Sergeant Finch, whose son graduated from law school, I know that being around to offer individuals a chance to pick themselves up is what's most important. The University of Iowa helped me along the path to understanding race relations in America, and it taught me about the ways that athletics could grant you chances that you might never get otherwise. To this day, I credit UI with helping me recognize that athletics is not only about competition but also about helping people.

"TIRELESS PARTNERS AND SKILLED COMPETITORS"

Seeing UI's Black Male Athletes, 1934—1960

In July 1999, as the women's softball complex at the University of Iowa (UI) neared completion, the director of Women's Intercollegiate Athletics announced that with the receipt of a $150,000 gift from the George H. Scanlon Foundation, the women's softball field would be named Bob Pearl Softball Field "in honor of Pearl, the first black baseball player at the UI."[1] Robert L. Pearl pitched for the UI baseball team from 1958 to 1960. He graduated in 1960 and then served as president of the Letterman's Club and a member of the club's board.[2] A number of campus and local publications, including the *Daily Iowan*, the *Iowa City Press Citizen*, and *Spectator*, reprinted information from an apparent press release noting the field's new name. Publically, no one disclosed the motivating factor behind naming the women's softball field for Robert Pearl. While a student at the University, Pearl lived with the Scanlon family for a time and maintained a relationship with the Scanlon's grandchildren.[3] These grandchildren wanted to honor Pearl. Grateful to receive the donation and quick to release this information to the press without fact-checking, UI administrators immediately recognized Pearl for his historic achievement. There was only one problem — Pearl was not, as the Scanlon family remembered, the first African American to play baseball for UI.

Why, then, did Pearl receive this honor? Perhaps the Scanlon family believed Pearl was the first African American baseball player at Iowa because he was the only African American student they knew. Possibly Jackie Robinson's recent retirement in 1956, ten years after he desegregated Major League Baseball and reintegrated professional baseball, prompted the Scanlons to believe that Iowa could not be any more or less racially progressive than the majors. The tension between a blind belief in Iowa's enlightened racial politics and a reality at odds with this conviction reveals the peculiar position black athletes occupied at UI during the mid-twentieth century. In truth, at least three other African American men preceded Pearl on the University of Iowa varsity baseball team. The failure of both the Scanlon family and UI administrators to possess knowledge of this history speaks to the social invisibility of African American athletes in particular and African American students in general. The collision of black students' highly acclaimed performances in sports at a historically white university unprepared to welcome African Americans fully into campus and local life often meant black male athletes were physically, academically, and athletically present but unseen by the wider social and civic mainstream consciousness.

Pearl represents one of many African American male athletes rendered hypervisible in a city where his race simultaneously obscured his full humanity. As a result of a generous donation, the donor's request, and faulty memory, the field was named for Robert Pearl on October 2, 1999. In the end, "The field [was] not being named because of Bob Pearl's athletic accomplishments," wrote the associate director of Women's Intercollegiate Athletics, "but rather because" the donors requested the name.[4] According to historian David R. McMahon, this was feel-good history gone terribly wrong: "one minority was as good as another." [5] Despite reservations from people on the fund-raising committee about naming the field for a man rather than a woman — and a letter and supporting documents from a UI graduate student disproving the historical claim made about Pearl — one minority was, indeed, as good as another.

The presence of Chicago-born Robin Crawford on the 1919 Hawkeye team clearly demonstrates that there were black baseball players at UI forty years before Pearl. Crawford and other black baseball players at UI before 1955 eluded historians with limited knowledge of black life at the University of Iowa for at least two reasons. First, freshmen men's and women's athletic association sports are almost always totally ignored by college sports historians, who tend to focus on African American firsts or star athletes on varsity track, baseball, football, and basketball teams. Second, historians often grant lighter-skinned athletes the benefit of the doubt with regard to whiteness because it perpetuates the notion that Jim Crow was not a porous institution. The fair-skinned Crawford played at least three regular-season varsity games against Michigan,

Notre Dame, and Iowa State, had a season batting average of .500, and led the Hawkeye nine to a 5–3 season. Crawford may have continued to be rendered invisible had it not been for a single photograph of him sliding into home base in the 1921 *Hawkeye* yearbook. Sadly, Crawford died of pneumonia the next winter and nearly disappeared from the annals of Iowa history. Following Crawford, Isaac G. Hill played varsity baseball in 1921, and three other African Americans, including John Kenneth Titus, suited up for the freshmen baseball team before 1934. Their races are confirmed by their membership in Kappa Alpha Psi (a fraternity in the Greek system with a predominantly African American membership) and the organization's group picture in the 1921 *Hawkeye*. By 1955 and 1956, Henry Berry of Chicago reopened the door to black baseball players at UI as an occasional center fielder and regular pinch hitter. Berry, who dated and later married the first African American Miss SUI, Dora Martin (see her testimonial in this volume), was also one of three African American men, which included McKinley "Deacon" Davis and Carl Cain, on the varsity basketball team in 1954.

One of the major problems with feel-good portrayals of the athletic history of the University of Iowa is its piecemeal treatment of African American athletes. The story of African American athletes at UI cannot be separated from that of all other African Americans at UI. Despite the publication of at least one book chapter on African American athletes in the state of Iowa and a chapter on African Americans in UI sports literature by David R. McMahon, the stories of African American athletes at the university remain invisible.[6] Their position at UI recalls the proclamation of Ralph Ellison's unnamed protagonist who declares his social, political, and cultural invisibility because US society refuses to see his humanity. Likening himself to the "bodiless heads" thrill-seeking and curious gawkers come to catch a glimpse of at circus or carnival sideshows, *Invisible Man* proclaims, "I am a man of substance, of flesh and bone, fiber and liquids — and I might even be said to possess a mind."[7] Like Ellison's protagonist, African American male athletes at UI between 1934 and 1960 lived simultaneously visible and invisible social and academic lives complicated by concurrently expressed racial acceptance, tolerance, and discrimination. Most thrived because they worked to create fully developed academic, cultural, and social spaces that affirmed the complexities of their blackness and their humanity. Some experienced racism but never graduated. Others were marginalized but graduated and are counted among the University of Iowa's well-known alumni. Regardless of their trajectory,

African American athletes at UI helped challenge racial discrimination on campus and off as their very presence impacted the broader course of the US civil rights struggle.

Indeed, their public performance both in the classroom and on the field defied the late nineteenth- and early twentieth-century myth of African American physical and intellectual inferiority. As these students strove to overcome the stereotypes that provided the foundation for the more contemporary stereotype of the dumb, mindless jock — or the naturally gifted super spade — they broke down barriers for other minority students.[8] Although some scholars deem college athletes a separate caste that perpetuates male privilege, more recent sports literature suggests that black athletes resemble those in Ellison's battle royal scene: they are used as pawns in sports dominated by white owners and coaches who profit off the bodies and labor of mostly black and brown men.[9] Sports reporting, and sports history and historiography, usually follow at least one of these trajectories.

This chapter takes a different approach to tell a different story. It explores African American male athletes' lives on and off the field at the University of Iowa from 1934 to 1960. Along the way, it uncovers the failed promise of racial equality at the University of Iowa and in the Midwest despite significant moves toward racial desegregation by the university and its sports teams. Rather than provide an analysis of the inclusion or exclusion of African American male athletes in existing UI sports histories, this chapter draws on Ralph Ellison's idea of invisibility to argue that African American men's gendered lives at UI have been presented through "mirrors of hard, distorting glass."[10] These mirrors have rendered the social, personal, and academic lives of African American male athletes at UI invisible. Yet they, like other African American athletes on predominantly white teams, lived under the proverbial microscope. They were expected to be hyperdisciplined while quietly enduring racism and appearing grateful for the privilege of attending college at all. As sportswriter William C. Rhoden points out, "Black athletes have symbolically carried a race's eternal burden of proof; their performances [and their ability to endure or confront racism] were among the most visible evidences that blacks, as a community, were good enough, smart enough, strong enough, brave enough — indeed human enough — to share in the fruits of this nation with full citizenship and humanity."[11] Even as these men strived against the reality of Jim Crow policies, their athletic performances and work beyond athletic arenas signaled their pivotal role in the civil rights struggle roiling the US heartland.

By drawing on African American publications such as the Iowa *Bystander*, the *Minneapolis Spokesman*, the *Crisis*, *Opportunity*, the *Kappa Alpha Psi Journal*, and the Alpha Phi Alpha *Sphinx* in addition to mainstream sources, the complex and multidimensional lives of African American male Hawkeyes emerge from the shadows of a forgotten history. Their stories prove that UI, like other midwestern institutions, was neither wholly friendly nor unbearably hostile. All Big Ten schools, for example, barred African Americans from campus housing. An unquantifiable but documented number of professors never gave African Americans, no matter how academically accomplished they were, a grade higher than a C. Campus eateries Jim-Crowed black students, and some local restaurants barred them completely. Even some sports and academic departments restricted or excluded African Americans from intercollegiate participation and majors. These were common experiences for African American students at Big Ten universities regardless of where they enrolled and whether they were athletes or not.

When considering athletes in particular, we can divide their experiences into two eras after 1924: first, the period before 1947, when UI openly sanctioned racism and barred all African Americans from campus housing and eateries, excluded black students from most varsity sports, and left African American students dependent on black Greek-letter organizations for every aspect of their social lives in college; and second, the period from 1947 to 1960, when the university dismantled institutional racism, saw its social institutions become more accepting of African American students, and continued to accept the remnants of the Jim Crow era with regard to fair housing and service in barbershops, stores, and restaurants in town. Examining black male athletes' experiences during these two periods brings into sharp relief the difficult reality of being a visible man at UI.

Where to Eat and Live:
African American Fraternities and Athletes in Iowa City

Although many African American athletes were recruited to UI and seen as proof of the university's racially progressive politics, these black male students often arrived at an institution that barred them from living on its campus.

Indeed, housing remained a critical issue for African Americans even beyond 1960. The demand for housing increased in the 1910s as the number of African American students enrolled at the university surpassed forty and the university established an unwritten policy to bar black women and later black men from campus housing. Only a brief period during World War I proved an exception. While the Iowa Federation of Colored Women's Clubs bought and operated a home for African American women from 1919 to 1950 at 942 Iowa Avenue, black men were forced to seek other alternatives.

Even as housing policies changed throughout this period, African Americans were not totally segregated in Iowa City since the black population never exceeded two hundred persons. The racial housing crisis arose as white landlords prevented African American faculty, graduate students, and undergraduates from purchasing homes or renting homes and rooms across the city. Those from outside the state often had to walk the streets until they found a room to rent from one of the local black families in town. By the late 1930s and early 1940s, African American students and alumni collaborated to develop a referral and greeting service for newly enrolled black students. Newcomers to Iowa City were met at the train station and existing students drove new arrivals around town to assist in finding a place to rent, offered room in their places of residence, or relied on such local residents as Haywood Short on South Madison, Allyn and Helen Lemme at 15 East Prentiss and later at 603 South Capital, Carl and Frances Culberson at 713 South Capital, Bettye and Junious Tate at 914 South Dubuque Street, Steve and Estella Ferguson at 213½ South Clinton, or Roy and Wilda Hester at 8 South Capital. After African American student Philip G. Hubbard received his bachelor's degree in 1947, he and his wife, Wynonna, offered space in their first home at 209 South Madison Street, continuing the tradition adopted by the Short and Lemme families in the 1920s and 1930s. All these locations happened to be within fairly short walking distance to the university, so African American students had quick and easy access to campus even when barred from campus housing. Although Iowa City was not a wholly segregated town, persons familiar with Iowa City most assuredly notice that almost all these homes were located on Iowa City's south side just east of the Iowa River.

While the challenges posed by segregated living spaces forced black students to form intimate connections with local African Americans, black male athletes also sought communal spaces with African American students on campus. In an effort to create community and to combat racial discrimination

in housing, African American students established their own fraternal organizations as early as 1910. First, students founded a local organization, Tau Ipsilon Tsest in 1910, the Euclid Club in 1913, and then local chapters of national
black Greek-letter organizations. Varsity football player Archie Alexander and
intramural basketball player James W. Crump along with five other African
American students established Tau Ipsilon Tsest to provide academic study
and social opportunities to African American male students. Crump became
a charter member of the local chapter of Kappa Alpha Psi fraternity and Alexander later served as head of the national organization, bearing the epithet
of Grand Polemarch.

These organizations helped alleviate pressures related to finding student
housing from the 1910s to the 1930s. Kappa Alpha Psi's Gamma chapter,
founded in 1914, and Alpha Phi Alpha's Alpha Theta chapter, chartered in
1922, maintained houses at 301 South Dubuque and 818 South Dubuque in
the 1930s when student-athletes including Ozzie and Don Simmons arrived
from Fort Worth, Texas, in 1933 and demanded an opportunity to try out
for the football team. After tryouts, Simmons secured a spot on the varsity
team his sophomore year. Coach Ossie Solem, aware of the policy against
blacks in university dorms, asked that the Simmons brothers be allowed to
stay at the Alpha house. During the spring of their first year, Don and Ozzie
pledged Alpha Phi Alpha. African American fraternities flourished on many
midwestern campuses including Indiana University and the Universities of
Illinois, Kansas, Minnesota, and Michigan for similar reasons, thereby making
the heartland a surprising leader of chapter formation in these organizations.

Notwithstanding the positive aspects of African American student initiative in response to housing segregation on campus, the policy was a blot
on the university's reputation for being racially progressive. By the 1930s the
University of Iowa' s practice of barring African American students from
college dormitories but having them as athletes on its varsity football and
track teams was well known in African American communities across the
United States. In 1930 and 1931, W. E. B. Du Bois failed to list the University
of Iowa with twenty-one other institutions that admitted African Americans
but refused them residence in campus dormitories, but those blacks in Iowa,
Missouri, Illinois, and other states who received the Iowa *Bystander* newspaper
already knew black students were barred from housing at the university. In
1937, an anonymous UI administrator claimed on a survey of racial climate at
midwestern institutions that blacks had the same academic but not the same

social privileges as white students on campus. Two black graduate students, G. Victor Cools in 1918 and Herbert Jenkins in 1933, had extensively documented the dynamic nature of racism and Jim Crow at University of Iowa.[12]

Locating a place to dine out in Iowa City and on campus proved as difficult for black male athletes as securing a residence. Restaurants often served one or two African American students at a time but never a group of black students. On a whim, any employee could refuse African American students service of any kind, and the Iowa Memorial Union mirrored this policy. During the 1930s, approximately thirty to forty restaurants and lunchrooms operated in Iowa City. None of these eateries — the College Inn, the Princess Café, Reich's Café, the Hamburg Inn #1, Maid-Rite, or Savoy Café — attracted even small groups of African American students, but one or two black Hawkeyes and particularly African American athletes might grab a snack at one of these places. Black athletes, on occasion, enjoyed slightly greater privileges when they were well-known football players.

Most African American male students ate meals at the Kappa Alpha Psi fraternity house at 301 South Dubuque Street or at Alpha Phi Alpha fraternity house at 818 South Dubuque Street. As the number of African American students decreased as a result of the Great Depression, the Alphas maintained their house, but Kappa Alpha Psi members moved to a number of places, including Steve and Estella "Ma" Ferguson's at 213 South Clinton and the so-called Girls' Home operated by the Iowa Federation of Colored Women's Clubs at 942 Iowa Avenue. Football players such as Don and Ozzie Simmons regularly took their meals at the Alpha house. Others, including Iowa's first African American football captain Homer Harris and sprinter Eugene Skinner, found room and board with the Fergusons. When the Fergusons moved to 116 East Burlington, members and future members of Kappa Alpha Psi moved with them, including Jim "Iron Man" Walker and track team member Lee Farmer, who shared a room with Hubbard.

Other black male students took regular meals at their places of employment, while black women rarely went out until Vivian Trent, an African American alumna of the University, opened Vivian's Chicken Shack in 1937.[13] University administrators took little notice of where black men or women dined. Although administrators did not believe it was their responsibility to "solve the race problem," an undisclosed restaurant — most likely Smith's Café — pulled UI president Virgil Hancher into a white-town-black-gown conflict when it refused to serve an African American athlete in the spring of 1942.[14] After a meeting between Hancher, a university committee, and the local restaurant, the group came to an agreement. But this was not before members of the Negro Forum, a student group established in 1925, sent pairs of students, one black and one white, into every restaurant in Iowa City to see if they would be refused service. Their activism spotlighted the Jim Crow policies that persisted in Iowa City. Only one restaurant — Smith's Café — refused to serve the students.

A number of African Americans at UI in the 1930s and 1940s remember Smith's Café, and to a lesser extent Whetstone's Pharmacy, as places whose employees were the most openly racist in their refusal to serve African Americans. After he relocated from Clear Lake, Iowa, Roland Smith established Smith's Café in Iowa City in the 1910s, and it operated continuously until 1943. White and black students protested Smith's Café and believed they helped shut down the small lunchroom when it failed to open the following winter. However, Smith's reemerged a few years later and remained open through the 1960s. Despite the longevity of Smith's Café, African American students noticed a significant change in how restaurants treated them after World War II. Some athletes recognized that restaurant owners and employees treated them differently and others attributed these privileges to their status as athletes.

By the 1940s, Iowa City had thirty restaurants and lunchrooms. Richard "Dick" Culberson, who became the first African American to play varsity basketball for the Hawkeyes, recalled a somewhat different experience at local eateries. Culberson's parents had moved to Iowa City to help support his maternal aunt Lulu Merle Johnson while she pursued graduate work at UI. As a result, Culberson spent his formative years in Iowa City before he left to attend Virginia Union University for two years. When he returned home to attend UI in 1944, Culberson suggested that his hometown roots and familiarity with local businesspeople made restaurant owners open to allowing him and a friend or two to dine where most African American students were not welcome. Perhaps Culberson indirectly played a role in broader changes. Still, neither he nor other African American athletes enjoyed the freedom to eat wherever they wanted. Having pledged Alpha Phi Alpha at Virginia Union, Culberson recalled that at UI, he and most of the members of his fraternity ate lunch and dinner at his parents' home. Nevertheless, as the university, and to a lesser extent Iowa City, became more accessible to African Americans, the overt and covert influence of high-profile African American athletics on and off campus cannot be understated.

The realities of war also contributed to changing longtime practices. With the wartime shortage of men on campus, local businesses and UI suffered financial losses that combined with evolving racial attitudes to engender a significant shift in the unwritten policies held by the university and local businesses. Betty Jean Arnett, a resident of Clarinda, Iowa, desegregated the dormitories in 1945 when she was moved into Currier Hall on an experimental basis. The following fall, five African American women officially desegregated Currier, and by 1948, eighteen men had desegregated various dorms on campus. University officials first limited campus housing for African Americans to Iowa residents, but by 1950 they abandoned the residency requirement. Access to on-campus housing also meant open access to meals in dining halls and the Iowa Memorial Union. Unfortunately, the opening of campus housing and dining did not mark the end of problems for African American athletes and students.

Black students remained segregated with regard to room assignments, so while they were permitted to live in UI dormitories after 1950, African Americans had to live alone or with other black students. Rarely, if ever, did African American students room with white students. Both the Quadrangle and Hillcrest served as the main residence halls for men beginning in 1920 and 1939, respectively, yet the University of Iowa barred African American men from these halls until the 1946–1947 school year. Hawkeye football player and Des Moines resident John M. Estes and Davenport native Robert Wright were among the group of eighteen men to officially desegregate the Quadrangle and Hillcrest. Estes lived in Quad Cottage 22 from the fall of 1946 until 1948. Wright lived in the Quadrangle.[15] Those African American athletes barred from campus housing in the 1930s and 1940s read like a who's who of African American sports personalities at UI and included track and field members Roy Eugene Bradshaw, Eugene Freels, Leon Bland, Richard Washington, and Robert Turner, and football players Jim Walker, Otis Finney, Earl Banks, and Emlen Tunnell.

After 1950, African American athletes rarely ran into trouble with housing since as undergraduates they could live on campus regardless of whether they were state residents. If they chose to live off campus, however, there were problems. For instance, a recently honorably discharged African American student named Eugene Peniston and his wife, Nellie, reported that they could find no white landlord willing to rent to them in Iowa City. In 1955, Peniston, after a two-year stint overseas as a US Army lieutenant, claimed he and his wife would have to commute because there was no place in town willing to rent to an African American couple. Born in Osceola, Iowa, Peniston and his wife found white Iowa City residents particularly hostile: "I didn't know people in Iowa could have such as repugnant attitude towards minority people, even though I lived in Iowa all my life."[16] While a number of black and white students with families moved into Quonset huts, temporary barracks, and trailers that remained on campus after World War II, families with children gained preference in the scramble for decent and affordable housing in the 1950s. The Penistons had no children, so they were wait-listed for family housing and were forced to commute from the Quad Cities (a distance of fifty to sixty miles) despite the promise of assistance and change to come by members of the Iowa City Chamber of Commerce.

Upset by reports of racism in Iowa City, one student wrote, "The north should clean its own house before raving about southern racial discrimination."[17] Still other students offered a list of offenses by whites toward blacks in Iowa City which included the following: (1) an African American student forced out of an apartment because he could find no roommates to assist with the rent in off-campus housing; (2) restrictive covenants signed by white Iowa citizens to prevent blacks from buying in certain neighborhoods; (3) whites-only membership in Inter-Fraternity Council and Panhellenic Council fraternities and sororities; (4) barbershops and beauty salons that would not dress or cut African Americans' hair; and (5) employment discrimination in city employment. These students urged chamber of commerce intervention in employment, business, and housing discrimination in Iowa City; student government involvement in eliminating racism in Greek life; and an organized body of students, administrators, and local church leaders to apply the same strategies that were used to end discrimination in local restaurants.[18] The application of such a strategy meant that force and power beyond that wielded by African American athletes was necessary to create change. In hindsight, we know these students were correct.

Even as athletes made small progress in certain areas, the struggle for equal housing in Iowa City and at the University of Iowa dragged on for years with only marginal support from local chapters of national civil rights organizations. African American law student Edwin Taylor solicited the help of James Weldon Johnson of the National Association of Colored People (NAACP) as early as 1920, when he believed a local Ku Klux Klan sought to bar African Americans from renting certain properties in Iowa City. Johnson offered

no resources to students, and he deferred to the Des Moines branch of the
NAACP to take up the matter. Although students established the Negro
Forum as a local civil rights organization to fight racism in local restaurants
and housing, the group lacked regional or national support of groups like the
NAACP. The next efforts came in 1950 and 1955. But with the dorms technically desegregated, the students and local residents who formed local chapters
of the NAACP enjoyed little success.[19]

By 1960, the local chapter of the Congress of Racial Equality (CORE) in
conjunction with the UI Student Council worked to create a policy by which
landlords guilty of racial discrimination had their rental properties or rooms
removed from a list of university-approved housing and could not rent to any
student for at least two semesters after the incident.[20] CORE was an interracial
civil rights organization founded in Chicago in 1942 to confront racial injustice
through nonviolent, direct actions of civil disobedience. It had some fifty local
chapters across the United States, including one in Iowa City. In December
1960, eight out of fifteen randomly surveyed landlords opposed this policy
based on the belief that property owners have the right to rent to whomever
they wish. Some white landlords argued that the "Student Council was pushing integration too fast."[21] Other landlords replied that they had rented to
African Americans previously with no problem, and still others argued that
they would not rent to African Americans again because black students threw
loud and wild parties. There may have been an element of truth to the charge
of spirited parties, but it is unlikely that black student parties proved more
boisterous than gatherings hosted by white students. Their get-togethers did,
however, go a long way toward ameliorating black students' experiences in the
challenging space of midcentury Iowa City.

One of the most difficult aspects of being an African American athlete
during the Jim Crow era was negotiating the adulation received on the field
compared to the isolation often experienced in daily existence at UI. For many
African American men who sought female companionship to mitigate this
contradictory reality, courtship could prove challenging. The relatively low
enrollment of African American women during the Jim Crow era meant that
either they courted one of the few African American women on campus or
they dated African American women who attended other Big Ten campuses
or other Iowa colleges and universities, or they had hometown sweethearts.
For example, Frederick "Duke" Slater dated Iowa Wesleyan College student
Etta J. Searcey. After three years at Iowa Wesleyan, Searcey transferred to UI.

She and Slater were married in 1926.[22] Another African American UI athlete, Charles Brookins, seems to have passed for white on campus. He married Zula Mae Mechler of Des Moines, who was presumably white, only to cheat on her and lose his job after a scandalous divorce.[23] Ironman Jim Walker dated and then married fellow African American Hawkeye Sammye Mae Sadler, a graduate student from Muskogee, Oklahoma, who before their marriage lived with nine other women including Elizabeth Catlett (see chapter 2) at 942 Iowa Avenue.[24]

By the 1940s, African American male athletes occasionally crossed the color line to date white female students, but their doing so caused dangerous tension. Sherman Howard played on the football team in 1946 and recalled being unable to get haircuts in Iowa City, being prohibited from living in dormitories, and seeing white female students harassed and called "Nigger lover" if they even talked to African American male athletes outside class. The combination of all these things convinced Howard to leave after one year.[25] By contrast, Don Tucker remembered having a very different social life in the mid-1950s. He and other African American players dated black and white women. Leisure time might be spent playing cards or eating in the Iowa Memorial Union, in dormitory rooms, or on short drives to clubs in Cedar Rapids. Tucker recalled dating fellow students and townswomen. He was hit on by male professors and had affairs with female instructors. While he struggled to adjust academically, his social experiences, although not free from prejudice, were a far cry from those of black student athletes in the 1920s, 1930s, and 1940s.[26]

But even as some aspects of black athletes' social lives changed, the role of African American fraternities and sororities remained the same: they were the source of many weekend parties and social events available to black students. Almost any time there was a home game, some African American alumni from Des Moines, Waterloo, Fort Madison, Cedar Rapids, Davenport, or Chicago traveled to Iowa City and paid a visit to members of Kappa Alpha Psi, Delta Sigma Theta, Alpha Kappa Alpha, or Alpha Phi Alpha. Homecoming weekend was especially eventful because a host of African American alumni returned to Iowa City for the festivities. Hawkeye football and Kappa Alpha Psi alumni Archie Alexander and Frederick "Duke" Slater were among those who were popular and present at many homecoming games and weekend dinners, dances, and gatherings among African Americans and the football team in the 1930s, 1940s, and 1950s. Slater, by that time a judge in Cook County,

Illinois, made it a point to encourage younger gridiron players including Don and Ozzie Simmons, Homer Harris, Emlen Tunnell, and Calvin Jones. A host of nonathletes including Dr. Lee B. Furgerson and Lily Williams-Furgerson, Dr. Harry D. Harper and Lillie Harper also regularly attended homecoming and encouraged their children and grandchildren to attend UI.[27] While at UI and long after leaving Iowa City, many of these alumni continued the work of making individual and collective civil rights gains for themselves and for future generations of African American Hawkeyes. Their social gatherings served a much greater purpose than simple college revelry: they used these parties to continue their push toward claiming their rightful and equal place at UI and in American society.

At Home and Away:
African American Hawkeyes on the
Court, Field, Course, and Track

Given their activist work to survive in Iowa City, it is not surprising that black male athletes often found their treatment at their home institution better than when they traveled with the team. The University of Iowa maintained a hot-and-cold attitude toward African American athletes but ultimately proved more committed to racial fairness in sporting events in Iowa City than those on the road. Jim Crow ruled at away games, and even if African American players could compete against opposing teams, hotels in Bloomington, Indiana; Champaign, Illinois; Madison, Wisconsin; Minneapolis, Minnesota; Ann Arbor, Michigan, and other cities refused black Hawkeyes even one or two nights' stay.

During the university's early years, the track and field and football teams were most likely to be open to one, two, and later a handful of African Americans in any given year. Starting with Frank K. Holbrook in 1896, African Americans appeared on Hawkeye track and field teams as well as freshman and varsity football squads, with the caveat that no more than two African Americans were on the field at once. Racist opponents rioted, requested black players' removal from games, and demanded that black players get left behind for games outside Iowa City. Baseball remained wholly segregated until after World War I, desegregated, and then resegregated in all but its freshman teams through the 1930s, totally resegregated again, and finally desegregated in 1955 and remains so today. Wrestling and basketball had the most restrictive rules regarding African American male students. Surprisingly, despite segregated physical education swimming activities, a single African American male participated on the swim team. Individual black athletes also belonged to the rifle club and golf team. Louis B. White, a member of Alpha Phi Alpha, became the first African American on the Hawkeye varsity soccer team around 1928. In his junior year, classmates elected White to Phi Beta Kappa, making him the second black student at UI and the first black UI athlete to earn such an award.[28]

These statistics regarding black participation in sports placed the University of Iowa on par with or slightly ahead of other teams in the Western or later Big Ten conference, which earned UI the reputation of being racially progressive. Incidents such as the infamous University of Missouri riot at Columbia, where Missouri fans and players in 1896 wielded clubs, sticks, and ropes as they shouted racial epithets and threats at African American Hawkeye junior Frank K. Holbrook, have been discussed by a number of scholars and sports historians. Yet other incidents reflect less glowingly on UI. Iowa's policy to play black players at home but bow to the request of racist opponents on the road began with Archie Alexander. From 1909 to 1911, Alexander thrilled fans as a member of UI's football team. Opposing teams refused to play against Alexander as they had Holbrook, thereby resurrecting the difficult issue of addressing racism at sporting events.

Alexander had transferred to UI from Highland Park College in Des Moines "due to the fact that Highland Park College changed their policy of admitting Negro students in the fall of 1908."[29] Upon his arrival in Iowa City, Alexander worked as a janitor to pay for school. According to historian Raymond A. Smith Jr., Alexander sat out three games because opposing teams refused to play against a black player.[30] One of these teams, the infamously racist University of Missouri, refused to play against Alexander for two consecutive seasons, 1909 and 1910. In 1910, UI president George MacLean struck a deal with University of Missouri president A. Ross Hill that UI would not play black players against the University of Missouri when the games were scheduled in Columbia, but regardless of an opponent's protests, black players would be allowed to play in games in Iowa City. Soon after, UI no longer scheduled games against Missouri.[31]

The other school determined to keep Alexander off the field, Washington University in Saint Louis, forced UI to bench Alexander for the 1910 season finale in Saint Louis. The *Hawkeye* yearbooks confirm Smith's assertion.

These books include lists of players and the games in which they played.[32] The 1913 *Hawkeye* noted:

> Archie A. Alexander — Another All-State man for three years is Alexander, the great colored tackle. No one feared the opponent's plays when they were directed at his position and few gains were made through him. His ability to open holes in the opposing line was one of his strongest points and added many yards to Iowa's gains. Attempts on the part of institutions to bar him from competing, in most cases, no doubt, were for reasons other than his race.[33]

Black and white folks from all over the state could not make any sense of such openly blatant racism. A Davenport, Iowa, man wrote to George MacLean to establish whether reports from Saint Louis were accurate. A story in the *Davenport Times* noted that Archie Alexander had been barred from the game against Washington University in Saint Louis and from the hotel where the team had reservations. Hawkeye football coaches and players yielded to Washington University's and the hotel's demands. Davenport resident W. N. Romidy questioned the wisdom of such a compromise and demanded to know why people representing UI caved to such outrageous prejudice. He challenged MacLean with the question of whether a desire to win a game trumped "the honor of acting as citizens worthy of the name free men."[34] While there were some reports of George Washington University's bar of Wallace and Dickerson in 1932, it received far less attention than earlier instances because this was an away game and Iowa's policy of capitulating in contests outside Iowa City was twenty years old. Black UI athletes continued to be removed from games as late as 1932, when Herbert Jenkins reported that "if, however, opposing teams object to the presence of Negro players it is the practice of the coach to keep the protested members on the bench."[35] Both Wilbur Wallace and Voris Dickerson suffered the humiliation of watching from the sidelines when UI faced George Washington University in Washington, DC. The nation's capital remained a segregated city into the 1950s.[36]

In spite of the Jim Crow compromises and concessions made by UI at away games, the regional and national black press combined with the power of word-of-mouth testimony to garner the university a reputation for being a school that gave black athletes a fair shot. Before 1934, the University of Iowa claimed approximately twenty-six African American athletes. Seventeen played on freshmen or varsity teams, and eight played class, major, or academic discipline–specific teams. In the early 1930s, the National Urban League's *Opportunity* noted that African Americans "who possess superior athletic ability have turned their faces toward the Middle West, where the state universities by law must accept them as citizens and where moderate tuition fees are not prohibitive to students of slender means."[37] African American publications such as the Des Moines–published *Iowa Bystander* and the *Minneapolis Spokesman* featured stories on African American students at the Universities of Iowa and Minnesota. For example, in 1932 the *Bystander* noted that George Washington University sidelined UI's two African American football lettermen, Voris Dickerson and Wilbur "Windy" Wallace, during their Capital City showdown. Dickerson and Wallace did not even suit up for the game; however, black George Washington University fans and supporters stood in solidarity with Dickerson and Wallace and boycotted the game.[38] These newspapers especially focused on the football rivalries, caravans of black students and alumni going to either Iowa City or the Twin Cities when the two schools faced off, and the African American players on each team.[39]

Magazines such as the NAACP's *Crisis* had been somewhat partial to stories about Iowa collegians since 1914, perhaps because its editor, W. E .B. DuBois, married a Cedar Rapids native in 1895. The *Crisis* had long recorded stories about the establishment of the university's local Kappa Alpha Psi chapter in 1914, the founding of an African American alumni organization in 1917, and coverage of football stars Archie A. Alexander and Frederick "Duke" Slater. In an annual college graduation issue, African American involvement and achievement at Iowa's flagship university signaled to many African Americans that black Hawkeyes were serious, were organized, and possessed the strong work ethic associated with midwesterners. Readers appreciated that UI at least allowed most black students to flourish academically and play certain sports. The *Crisis* November 1934 issue featured a photograph of the University of Iowa's Ozzie Simmons on its front cover with the caption "Iowa's Simmons (As Great as Grange? – see page 329)." The story reported Simmons's exploits in his first varsity game against Northwestern and cited Northwestern University football coach Dick Hanley's comment that Simmons was among the best right halfbacks he had ever played against or seen. The Hawkeyes had hammered Northwestern, 20–7, and Simmons rushed for 175 yards. It was his first varsity game and already he was being compared to the former

Illinois and Chicago Bears great Edward "Red" Grange.[40] As the national black press saw it, Simmons's accomplishments on the field might translate into civil rights gains off the field.

Unfortunately, his stellar debut made Simmons the prime target of opposing teams. Marked for late hits, illegal blocks, piling on, and racial taunts on the field while forced to face heightened media attention, opponents' rage, everyday racism, and an ongoing struggle to earn decent grades off the field, Simmons was pushed to the breaking point. The University of Minnesota Golden Gophers became particularly well known for their rough play and abuse of Simmons. In their first meeting, Simmons accused Minnesota defenders of unsportsmanlike and illegal plays which forced Simmons to leave the game several times in Iowa's 48–12 loss. Hawkeye fans proved to be so infuriated by the unsportsmanlike conduct that they swore to fight back themselves if the treatment resumed in the next year's game. The war of words between teams and fans spilled over into regional politics and prompted Iowa's governor Clyde Herring to issue a statement all but endorsing fan violence when the showdown moved to Iowa City in 1935. Black and white Hawkeyes alike prepared to settle the score.

The Iowa–Minnesota football game was memorable and historic for numerous reasons, not least of which was the Golden Gophers' 51–0 trampling of the Hawkeyes. The regional black press, however, focused on other aspects of the game. Reporters noted that black Iowans and Minnesotans attended this contest in large numbers because a total of five African American players (two for Minnesota, Horace Bell and Dwight Reed, and three for Iowa, the Simmons brothers and Harris) played in this game. The November 6, 1936, issue of the black-owned *Minneapolis Spokesman* noted that "400 brown-skinned Iowans" were among the thousands of Iowans expected to descend on the Twin Cities for this matchup and other activities related to game weekend. Moreover, local chapters of Kappa Alpha Psi, Alpha Phi Alpha, Omega Psi Phi, and Alpha Kappa Alpha scheduled postgame gatherings and dinner parties for their respective members, and a jointly sponsored dance at the Saint Paul auditorium followed these activities.[41] "Thousands braved the severe cold weather and snow" to partake in the tradition of African American students and alumni who caravanned between states and universities to attend big conference games and student–alumni gatherings.[42] The growing number of black male athletes on the field often directly impacted the social opportunities for the larger African American midwestern population.

Its status as one of the most lopsided games in Big Ten history together with Ozzie Simmons's subsequent temporary walkout also made the Iowa–Minnesota classic memorable. University of Minnesota alumnus and future NAACP executive secretary Roy Wilkins attributed the publicity — as well as the comparison to Grange so early in Simmons's career by W. E. B. Du-Bois — to Simmons's problems with teammates and coaches. Wilkins noted that after Minnesota's 51–0 blowout of Iowa, Simmons quit the team for a day in protest. Perhaps, Wilkins quipped, Iowa's reputation for being a place where Simmons "heard there was no prejudice at the university" was not altogether accurate.[43] In the same article, Wilkins added information about Ozzie's older brother Don Simmons, who played end and was stacked behind starting right end Homer Harris, an African American player from Seattle, Washington. Perhaps Wilkins's criticism of Ozzie Simmons and UI's race relations stemmed from objective observation, but Roy Wilkins was also a University of Minnesota alumnus.

Homer Harris, like Ozzie Simmons, came to UI because he thought he would get a fair shake. His on-field accomplishments would forever change the history of Iowa football. In high school, he played football and basketball and ran track, but he knew coming to UI meant he would have to forgo basketball. When Harris arrived at the train station in Iowa City, he was met by football coach Ossie Solem. The coach drove him around until he found a place to live with Steve and Estella Ferguson. He did not join a fraternity in exchange for housing; in fact, he did not pledge Kappa Alpha Psi until his senior year. Harris recalled that he enjoyed no privileges as an athlete, but he knew there were places in town he could rent a room or eat. He soon attained special status on the team. At the football team's annual banquet just months after the Simmons walkout incident, the UI team elected Harris captain for the 1937 season. Harris recalled that he had no idea he was being considered until that day. When ballots were circulated at the banquet, he admitted that he naturally voted for himself. Coach Solem and UI officials made this important event even sweeter for the 6-foot, 2-inch, 200-pound right guard when the team announced that its first game for the coming season would be against the University of Washington Huskies. This meant Harris could play in front of his family and friends back home in Seattle.[44] Assuming a leadership role on the team and performing before African American supporters outside of Iowa positioned Harris to represent the racially progressive face of the University of Iowa.

Even as African American athletes such as Harris played an important role in breaking down racial barriers in some sports and on campus, life was not so good for the embattled Coach Solem. While he remained silent on the matter of Simmons's walkout, the season record jeopardized Solem's coaching job. Around the same time Harris was elected captain of the football team, Solem lost his jobs as coach and athletic director despite announcements to the contrary made by the UI Athletic Board. Solem could only claim winning seasons in 1933 and 1935, and his overall record at UI of 15–21–4 doomed his tenure as a Hawkeye. Neither the public reconciliation with Simmons nor the selection of the first black captain could salvage his career.

Toward the end of the season that Homer Harris captained the football team and the same week that Ozzie Simmons quit and rejoined the Hawkeye football team, the UI track team named African American distance and cross-country runner Robert "Bob" Nelson captain of the team. Like UI's first African American track captain and UI's first African American Olympian, Charles R. Brookins, Bob Nelson came to the university from Oskaloosa, Iowa.[45] Nelson became the second African American track captain at the University of Iowa and undoubtedly added to the university's racially liberal reputation among black athletes. The selection of cocaptains for track was a common practice and was not a racial slight, although certainly one may question the timing of the announcement, which coincided with the Simmons–Solem controversy. In the end, historians just don't know exactly why Simmons walked off the team for a day in protest. Both Simmons and Solem refused to speak publically about the controversy even years later. We do know that as a young African American man from Texas, Simmons had probably heard, if not witnessed and experienced, white challenges to his blackness, manhood, and personhood. While some of Simmons's teammates and critics saw him as an overconfident showboat, the fact that he was willing to risk his education and protested so publically complicates this picture. His actions almost certainly impacted the wider environment for black athletes at UI.

The track team, for example, continued to make progress in welcoming black athletes. Robert Nelson ran the half-mile, mile, and two-mile runs. He had three other black teammates on the varsity track team, which included Lamar Smith, Eugene Skinner, and Wilson Briggs in 1937, but he was the lone black runner on the cross-country track team.[46] Nelson proved through training, conditioning, and practice that despite the prevailing racist science, blacks could make strides in distance running events.[47] Although some historians mistakenly believe Theodore "Ted" Wheeler was the Hawkeyes' first black distance runner and African American track coach, Charles Brookins worked as an assistant track coach under coach George T. Bresnahan from 1927 to 1931 and in 1934. It is Bresnahan who can be credited with breaking down the color line in coaching and distance events when he hired Brookins in 1927 after the Olympics and allowed Eugene Mallory to compete in freshman and varsity distance running events from 1929 to 1931.[48] It was also Bresnahan who allowed black distance runners and then coached and groomed teammates Bob Nelson and Francis Cretzmeyer. His example shaped Cretzmeyer's well-publicized liberal attitudes about African American distance runners such as Wheeler and Deacon Jones.

Notwithstanding these impressive strides in football and track, for the first half of the twentieth century, blacks remained absent from Big Ten wrestling. Although UI had a black heavyweight boxing champion in 1933, Big Ten wrestling did not desegregate until the 147-pound wrestler Simon Roberts broke the color barrier at UI in 1957. Roberts, a native of Davenport and the first African American state high school wrestling champion, also became the first African American to win an NCAA wrestling title in the same year.[49] Ironically, in the case of UI, which had campus or intramural boxing teams, at least two black students participated in campus boxing matches in the early 1930s.[50] Sources do not reveal the reason that white UI athletic administrators permitted black students to box against white students but not wrestle. The protocol for boxing, an intramural sport, like the freshmen baseball team's rules concerning black players, was more elastic and arbitrary than wrestling. Black and white newspapers celebrated Roberts's achivements and his role as a pioneer who altered the trajectory of UI's history of wrestling.

The University of Iowa's racial progressiveness in allowing African Americans to play certain sports neither translated to an active effort to break all athletic racial barriers nor achieved an absence of racism on Hawkeye sports teams. The presence of black players normalized racially desegregated spaces and exemplified the possibility of interracial progress and cooperation, yet it was commonplace for athletic coaches to direct racial epithets toward African American players on opposing teams. In 1944, one of Iowa's assistant football coaches ordered his team to injure African American guard J. C. Coffee because Coffee's blocks allowed the Hoosier halfback to rush for 74 yards and two touchdowns in the Hoosiers' 32–0 crushing of the Hawkeyes.[51] The

University of Iowa's 180-pound African American letterman, Joseph Howard from Des Moines, demanded that the coach apologize to Coffee. When the coach refused, Howard walked off the team, ending his football career at Iowa at season's end. This incident highlights the inconsistent nature of racially progressive attitudes among UI coaches and the difficult task black male athletes faced in the day-to-day reality of their respective sports.

A later example further highlights the inconsistency black male athletes endured. Five African American Hawkeyes made history during a nonconference game in 1950 against the University of Miami Hurricanes. Although it was a publicly funded stadium, no African American had ever played in the Orange Bowl Stadium or the annual Orange Bowl game. Bernard Bennett, Mike Riley, Delmar Corbin, Harold Bradley, and Don Commack all played for the Hawkeye football team. According to the November 25, 1950, *Daily Iowan*:

> The game marked the first time Negroes ever played against whites in the historic Orange Bowl. Iowa had five Negroes on the traveling squad and all of them saw action. *Iowa's lone touchdown was scored by Bernard Bennett, Negro halfback from Mason City. When he scored, Negro spectators in the east half of the end zone gave him a tremendous cheer.* (emphasis in original)[52]

Often reports in the *Daily Iowan* failed to capture the full complexity and irony of games where African American Hawkeyes appeared. On the one hand, black Iowa players were the first African Americans to play in Miami's Orange Bowl stadium and compete with and against white players, yet at the same time Jim Crow and racism in Miami relegated African American spectators to a roped-off section of the eastern end zone. Furthermore, while white Hawkeyes spent the night in hotels, African American Hawkeyes, barred from these same hotels, had to sleep in private black homes.

Jim Crow policies and laws in southern states and in many southern and northern hotels prohibited African Americans from sleeping or eating on their premises through the 1960s. On occasion African American players traveling with predominantly white teams roomed, ate, and enjoyed local attractions and entertainment with their teammates, but before 1954 they were just as likely to face hotel, restaurant, and cinema Jim Crow policy. When Iowa played in the 1955 NCAA Men's Basketball Tournament, McKinley "Deacon" Davis and Carl Cain faced racism in Kansas City's Continental Hotel, local restaurants, and movie houses. The Missouri side of Kansas City, where the tournament was held, was the worst. Whites pushed Deacon Davis off the hotel elevators, whites refused to let Carl Cain board elevators by claiming there was no room, and white waitstaff "threw food in their faces" and made them wait for their food until whites who were seated after them were served.

Other tournament teams with African American players reported similar experiences, including the star African American players for the 1955 NCAA champion San Francisco Dons, Bill Russell.[53] One year later, African American Simon Roberts faced similar discrimination while he attended the national championships in Stillwater, Oklahoma, with the UI wrestling team. In a 2007 interview, Roberts recalled:

> The only time I can remember any open discrimination was Stillwater [Oklahoma], at the nationals. The Iowa team went downtown for our post weigh-in meal. They seated the entire team, about a dozen of us, including me. But the waitress brought glasses of water for everyone but me. Barron Bremner [his teammate] seemed to notice it right away, didn't say anything to me, but got up and went over to talk to the waitress. She motioned toward the kitchen, so Barron went through the doors into the kitchen. He was there a few minutes, came out, then the manager or owner motioned to the waitress. They talked a bit, then she brought a glass of water to me. That was the end of it. I was served my meal with the rest of the team without any incident. And we didn't discuss it either.[54]

No matter how famous or recognizable they had become, African American athletes, like African American celebrities, seemed only acceptable to whites in the role of entertainers. Many whites believed no matter how famous or wealthy, African American celebrities and athletes needed to remain in the place of social subordination. The inconstant policy practiced by UI coaches and administrators before 1960 often forced black male athletes to negotiate this difficult reality alone.

Representing a Nation:
Black UI Olympians

As African American Hawkeyes excelled on the local, conference, and world stage between 1934 and 1960, some white Americans began to accept the possibility of blacks as equals. African American athletes proved they would put their best foot forward in representing their country and the state of Iowa; yet the residue of racism persisted even after African American athletes successfully and respectfully represented the United States in several Olympic Games. As was the case with returning African American soldiers, black Olympic athletes found themselves entangled in the paradox of serving a country that did not necessarily and equally serve them. Nevertheless, black UI Olympians from the 1930s through the 1960s were inspired by the likes of Charles R. Brookins and Ed Gordon, earlier black UI athletes who competed in the Summer Olympics in 1924, 1928, and 1932. At the 1924 Paris games, Brookins won the silver medal in the 400-meter hurdles, but he was disqualified for stepping outside his lane. The selection of Brookins as track-and-field team captain marked the first recorded time an African American student led a Hawkeye team. Brookins, who earned an NCAA championship and set a new world's record in the 200-meter low hurdles in 1923, was clocked at about 53 seconds at the Paris Olympics. The 1925 *Hawkeye* noted, "For the first time in its history, Iowa produced a world record breaker in track. Charlie's feat of reducing the low hurdle record to 23 1–5 seconds was one of the outstanding performances of the year. As captain-elect he ought to have another successful season." [55]

The previously unresolved question of Charles R. Brookins's racial background can finally be laid to rest. Most sources contemporary to Brookins's Olympic appearance never mention his race, and only a handful of black newspapers at the time laid claim to him being African American. All *Hawkeye* yearbook pictures show that he was lighter-skinned, and his employment as the freshmen track coach for the five years after he graduated suggests he likely lived as a white person. Brookins's passport contains witness statement affirming his birth in Oskaloosa, his picture, and his reason for seeking a passport as the Olympic Games, but this confirms only his nationality as racial classification did not and does not appear on US passports. The 1910 and 1920 US Census, however, lists the widow, Sarah Brookins of Oskaloosa, Iowa, and her two sons, William L. and Charles R. Brookins, as mulatto. She and her late husband were born in Charlottesville, Virginia.[56] Given their presence among a host of African American families in Oskaloosa during this period, it should come as no surprise that Philip Hubbard, contemporary black news editors, and others placed Brookins among Iowa's early black Olympians.[57]

Four years after the Paris Olympic Games, UI long jumper Ed Gordon, born in Mississippi but raised in Indiana, tied for sixth place with a best distance of

7.32 meters in the preliminaries. Unfortunately, a poor second jump pushed him out of top six qualifiers in the Amsterdam games. As a student Gordon captured an unmatched number of long jump titles, including Big Ten and Drake Relays titles in three consecutive years: 1929, 1930, and 1931. By 1932 and closer to home, Gordon won the gold medal in Los Angeles, jumping just over 25 feet, or 7.64 meters.[58] Gordon became the last African American Hawkeye to compete in the Olympics for a twenty-four-year span. Despite all his achievements on the field, Gordon never managed to earn a degree from the University of Iowa. He joined the ranks of numerous early black athletes who were "prized performers, but frequently overlooked students."[59]

No black Iowans competed in the now famous 1936 Berlin Olympics, and World War II forced the cancellation of the 1940 and 1944 summer games. In 1956, UI sent three African Americans to the Melbourne, Australia, Olympics: Carl "Sugar" Cain, Charles "Deacon" Jones, and Theodore "Ted" Wheeler (see Wheeler testimonial in this volume). Cain starred on the 1956 gold-medal-winning basketball squad along with the University of San Francisco's African American players Bill Russell and K. C. Jones and his white fellow Hawkeye Charles Darling. Wheeler and Deacon Jones were the first documented African Americans to compete in the distance-running events. Wheeler tied for eighteenth overall in the 1,500-meter run, or metric-mile, thus missing the 1,500-meter finals. Jones bested his slightly older teammate's performance when he placed ninth in the 3,000-meter steeplechase in 1956 and seventh in the same event at the 1960 Rome Olympics.

In recognition of UI's three black Olympians — and the importance of their position as trailblazers for midwestern racial progress — 1936 African American gold medalist Jesse Owens visited and spoke at UI in 1957.[60] Owens, of course, had become a symbol of the Berlin games when his four gold-medal performances shattered Adolf Hitler's idea of an Aryan master race. Wheeler and Jones disproved Hitler's revised notion that people of African descent were only good at jumping and short-distance running events. But like Cassius Clay from Louisville, Kentucky, the UI athletes competed as African American Olympians who could not choose to live where they wanted in the towns from which they traveled to compete in the Olympics. While African Americans could live in University of Iowa dormitories by the 1950s, they still could not live wherever they wanted in Iowa City.[61]

As the 1950s came to a close, African American Hawkeyes could look back over the past thirty years and give testimony to the fact that much had changed in slightly over a generation's time. African American students could live in on-campus dormitories, they overwhelmingly ate their meals in campus dining halls and the Iowa Memorial Union, and they participated in nearly every collegiate athletic team or individual sport they wished.[62] There were still battles to be fought for social and academic support on campus for African American students and against individual acts of racism committed by students, staff, and faculty.

Although Martin Luther King Jr. spoke at the University on October 22, 1958, and again on November 11, 1959, phase one of the modern civil rights movement arrived in Iowa City and at UI in 1960. Black and white students began a campaign against racially segregated fraternities on campus. Students charged Sigma Nu, Sigma Chi, Pi Kappa Alpha, and Alpha Tau Omega with barring African Americans from membership. Two years later, the campaign continued and a small but vocal group of students unsuccessfully called on UI to boycott its December 17, 1962, basketball game against Clemson University. Clemson was in the midst of a protracted legal battle to bar twenty-year-old Harvey B. Gantt admission, and instead the South Carolina regional education board paid his tuition for a year to attend Iowa State University in Ames.[63] By 1969, a new phase of the struggle for civil rights and racial equality would force sixteen African American athletes (members of the Black Athletes Union) at UI to walk out of spring practice with demands for "adequate, specialized academic counselors provided for athletes; the extension of financial aid until graduation . . . ; a five-year scholarship plan for those athletes who cannot complete their requirement for graduation in four years; more autonomy in the athlete's personal, political, and social life, and the acceptance of a $15 a month allowance by the Big Ten."[64] Nevertheless, race no longer barred African American students from certain departments or areas of study. Although the Greek-letter fraternity and sorority system remained segregated, black students — including some of UI's best-known male athletes — established their own organizations and created a well-developed social life that included formal dinners and balls, informal house parties, visits by renowned African American literary figures, and concerts that featured the likes of Duke Ellington and Louis Armstrong. While Ellington and Armstrong entertained largely white albeit racially desegregated gatherings of students, these giants of American jazz also played afterparties at the homes of Betty and Junious Tate and Helen Lemme. Anytime Ellington's band was in Iowa City, which it was in 1949, 1951, 1953, and twice in 1957, the band made it a priority to eat a home-cooked meal, hang out, and entertain African American Hawkeyes.[65] The band made similar stops in Waterloo at the home of black UI alumni Lee and Lily Furgerson when it played in Waterloo or Cedar Falls, the latter town the site of Iowa State Teachers College, Iowa's third state university, now called the University of Northern Iowa.[66] Similarly, when Louis Armstrong and His All Stars visited Iowa City to play campus events in 1948, 1957, and 1958, he and the band stopped in at the Tates' or Lemmes'. In 1958, Armstrong closed his set on a cold February night at the Iowa Memorial Union with an old Thomas "Fats" Waller tune that perhaps best captured the struggle of African American Hawkeye athletes for racial equality from the time Waller composed the song through the thirty-year period that Armstrong made it famous. The song's chorus poses a seemingly simple question and is referenced in the opening of Ralph Ellison's *Invisible Man*. It asks, "What Did I Do, To Be So Black and Blue?" As black Hawkeyes delivered performances that left their mark on the local, national, and international athletic stage, this is a question that continued to reverberate both on and off their fields of competition.

THE TWO-EDGED SWORD

. . .

n 1955, I was watching Iowa's football team play another Big Ten school on television. Something astonishing happened during that game. Calvin Jones, Frank Gilliam, Eddie Vincent (the Steubenville, Ohio, trio), John Burroughs, and Mike Hagler — five Black football players — were a major part of the Iowa team, and they were all on the field at the same time. I counted them and couldn't believe it. Iowa's coach, Forrest Evasheski, was playing the best players regardless of color. No other Big Ten team, at that time, had put that many Black football players on the field at the same time during any football game. That was the moment I knew where I wanted my future to be headed. "Self, this is the school for you!"[1]

After graduating from Tilden Technical High School, in Chicago, in 1956, I got a football scholarship to the University of Iowa. This was the first time I'd lived away from home, and Iowa would be one of the most fantastic experiences of my young life.

I drove to Iowa City, home of the university, with another Black football recruit, a very good player, from Dunbar High School on the south side of Chicago. When we arrived, we were told to go to the Administration building to take an admission test. I passed the test, but my friend didn't. He was not allowed to enroll at Iowa and was obviously disappointed. I saw him after we got our grades; we shook hands and wished each other luck. He told me he'd be back to take the test again, but I knew he didn't really believe this. He left Iowa, and I never saw him again. I knew he would have to face the dangerous, uncertain future of surviving in Chicago.

Iowa had very good football teams, and during my stay, I was proud to be a part of them. I also wrestled and was on the track team. My roommate, Dan Jones, was from Ohio. He'd come to Iowa as the first Black quarterback recruited by Iowa. Dan had been legendary in high school and showed a lot of promise at Iowa until he was injured. Afterward, he was never able to show the abilities expected of him. He remained at Iowa, however, until his scholarship expired.

Dan was a few years older than me and was considered the Black guru on campus. Everything seemed to run through him. Most of the card and craps games were generated in our room. Because of his age, he was also one of the few students who could go to the state liquor store and buy bottles of whiskey. Iowa was a dry state at the time, and the state liquor store required all customers to sign a ledger after each purchase to buy hard booze. Beer was sold at the local taverns. The liquor bottle had a number on it to coincide with the purchaser. Dan would scratch off the number on every bottle or had me do it.

One of Dan's best friends was Calvin Jones, all-American and probably one of the best linemen ever to play college football. Calvin once stopped by our room, prior to leaving Iowa to play in an all-star football game. He was a lock to make the pros, and I remember him promising to bring me a trinket from the game. Calvin was killed in an airplane crash soon after leaving our room.

I didn't get a lot of sleep rooming with Dan because there was something going on every night; it was the meeting place. I didn't have enough sense to get sleep or develop study habits because I was in such awe. The classes I signed up for were very difficult for me; I wasn't smart enough to ask for help in selecting my major, so I had chosen business administration so I could learn to manage all the money I would eventually make as a professional football player. HORRIBLE CHOICE. WRONG MAJOR! DUMB ASSUMPTION!

High school hadn't prepared me for the difficult course work. If I'd chosen simpler classes and a different major at the outset, possibly I would have been able to keep up with the rest of the students. After the first year, I had to leave because I was flunking out. . . . Even though my grades were poor, I was doing very well on the football team and had high hopes, knowing I could play at that level. Unfortunately, I didn't realize that to be really successful, I had to be a student first and get a degree, just in case! I wasn't mentally prepared for this, and I paid the price. I left school and worked at Spiegel's Catalog Warehouse on Thirty-fifth Street in Chicago, Illinois.

Somehow, with the money I'd made and with my mom and dad borrowing more, I finally went back to Iowa in the fall of 1957. I had to write a letter to the dean of students telling him how sorry I was, how I had let my family down, had let my university down, and was a disappointment to my race (I thought this would be a good touch). I admitted to not applying myself to schoolwork, begged for a second chance to show how I would be a credit to Iowa, myself, and my family. I really poured it on. Most of it, even I believed.

The dean allowed me to reenter Iowa, but I was put on scholastic probation. Could I make it this time? My mom would always say, "The proof is in the pudding." I really applied myself, developed strong study habits, and realized that when I studied, the classes were much easier (a no brainer). . . .The amazing thing was, I did it on my own with very little help. So many kids, from the poor areas, grow up with some basic smarts, but because of our culture, this ability remains dormant and never cultivated.

Literature, criminology, and psychology classes were my favorites. I also got excellent grades in my communication classes. One of my communication instructors was gay. Once I saw him in a pub near campus and walked to where he was sitting with other professors, to say hello. He obviously had had too much to drink. I felt him rub his hand up my leg and whisper, "If you let me get my hands on you, you won't want to be with another woman." He scared me, so much, I became homophobic for a long time. My literature instructor was another story.

I was having a relationship with another student, and the literature instructor talked to me about how she thought I was too experienced for the student and would only hurt her. I initially thought, *What business did she have, getting involved in my dating choices*? During class, the instructor would sit on a high stool in front of me and continually cross and uncross her legs. She was aware of every move she made. This was even before Sharon Stone in *Basic Instinct*. She gave me a book to read called *Lady Chatterley's Lover*. It was a very sexy book. And so was the affair. I would sometimes meet her late in her office. We tried every sexual position she had ever read about. . . .The affair lasted until I left her class. She refused to give me an A, stating that she wasn't paying for my services. I got a B and was very happy with that grade. I honestly believed I deserved an A because I really enjoyed the class and did well on the tests.

Iowa's football team won the Big Ten Championship in 1958 and went to the Rose Bowl in 1959. For a kid from the ghetto, getting on a plane in Iowa City, Iowa, where it was 18 degrees, and landing in Pasadena, California, at

75 degrees and with palm trees, was like dying and going to heaven. It was a memorable time in my life, and we won the game. My two good friends, Willie Fleming and Bob Jeter, both Black, had a spectacular game. Jeter was named MVP [most valuable player] for the game and broke the Rose Bowl rushing record. Fleming eventually dropped out of school and went on to be one of the best running backs the Canadian Football League had ever seen. Jeter left school and became an outstanding defensive back with the Green Bay Packers and won Super Bowl rings.

I only weighed 160 pounds dripping wet; I would try not to be the smallest guy on the football squad, and on weigh-in day, I drank a lot of water and did as little as possible. When Coach Evasheski didn't like the quality of the practices, he would shout, "Button your chin straps, this is live!" We would then have a spirited practice knocking heads. I always played very hard and gave it all I had. Afterwards — you guessed it — I weighed in as the smallest guy on the team. The one thing I did learn was the fact that only about 80 percent of the football players actually received a degree. Only a small percentage of football players make it to the professional level. Having a backup plan, that includes a degree, is very important for future life and success. So many athletes fail this important qualification. In my last year, in spring practice, I moved up to the top running back at my halfback position. I had high hopes for the fall season but got hurt and didn't recover.

For about two years, I wrestled at Iowa for Coach [David] McCuskey. When I wrestled, I could beat our 175-pounder with my quickness but would tie the 154-pounder, who eventually became an Olympic champion. The 175-pounders on the other teams were too big and too strong for me, although I did win a few matches. When I took off my robe prior to a match, we looked like a muscular combination of Mutt and Jeff. The 175-pounders would normally weigh about 200 pounds, but would lose weight during wrestling season. I wrestled a guy from the University of Minnesota who was a linebacker on the football team. I had played against him during the previous season. I knew I was in trouble when we locked up head-to-head. After locking up with this guy, I couldn't move my head from the strength of his grip. Experienced wrestlers will tell you when you see the lights, you are being pinned. The only time I saw the lights was while wrestling during this match.

I enjoyed the experience of being on the team and traveling to different Big Ten schools in vans and station wagons. Wrestling teams didn't have the budget to travel expensively. After two years, I busted my hip and quit wrestling to concentrate on football. One Black Iowa wrestler, Sy [Simon] Roberts, became the first Black to win the NCAA championship in his weight class. I always admired and respected him for the way he carried himself — not flashy but confident!

Some outstanding athletes were at Iowa at that time, and pickup games with basketball players and football players were classic. Don Nelson, who played pro ball with the Boston Celtics, and Connie Hawkins, another star pro player, used to have some classic confrontations during those pickup games. Hawkins was a legendary high school player. He and Nelson were in the same freshman class. Hawkins, from New York, got caught up in a basketball scandal and had to leave school. He was later found innocent. I would have given anything to watch him and Nelson play on the same team for Iowa. Can you say Big Ten Championship? Nolden Gentry, Bobby Washington, and others were also on the Iowa basketball squad.

Deacon Jones was on the Iowa track team and was my look-alike. He was a US Olympic distance runner. People would mistake me for him and would pat me on the back after Deacon won a track race. It felt good, so I just went with it. We later became good friends and would laugh at those Iowa days. I told him if I did anything wrong, my name would be Deacon. It did help with the ladies.

During my last year at Iowa, my friend Peanuts (Eugene Mosley) and I lived in an apartment off campus. In the building across a courtyard from us, a woman in one of the apartments would leave her shades up and would walk through her apartment naked. She knew we were watching her but seemed to enjoy flashing two sexually hungry college guys. We tried to get her attention, but then she would pull down the shades. Night after night she would do the same thing: no acknowledgment, yet still naked . . .

On one occasion, I was at a party with other football players and several attractive college girls. An off-duty officer was going after the same girl I had my eyes on. One thing led to another, we got into a fight, and I had to deck him. My route on the way home from school took me past the police station, and several times, I took back alleys to avoid the officer. One night he almost trapped me when I was in a Hamburger Inn restaurant and saw him in his police car. He was obviously waiting for me to leave, but I stayed in the Inn until closing. When he had to return to the station for a shift change, it was my chance to run home. My football speed came in handy. He never was able to get me in a confrontational situation.

In my final year, I had to go to summer school to graduate. I was no longer on scholarship and my parents didn't have much money. I put in a call to my mom and thanked her for all she'd done for me. "I've run out of time and I can't graduate," I told her slowly, holding my breath. "How much will it cost for you to go to summer school to take those nine hours you need?" she asked immediately. That's my Mama Easter, always two steps ahead of me. I knew she didn't have that kind of money. When I told her the tuition fee, she ordered, "Duck, register for summer school. I'll get the money somehow." "There's a second problem, Mom," another deep breath. "I need a 3.5 GPA [grade point average] in order to graduate." Although I'd become a much better student, I didn't think I was that good. But my mom did, although she had no idea what a GPA was. Again, without skipping a beat, she replied, "Duck, I have faith in you, and I know you can do it. I want you to study as hard as you can and bring me that diploma. I'll send you the money." There are times when someone makes an inspiring statement that will guide you for the rest of your life. My mother's statement still makes my eyes moist every time I think of it. She never told me how she got the money.

Prior to getting my final grades, I knew I hadn't made it. Giving it all I had just wasn't good enough. I got two Bs and two As. One B+ was in my criminology class; I thought I'd gotten a better grade. I went to see my criminology professor, Dr. [Robert G.] Caldwell, who had also written a crime book, and we had a long talk. He told me I had done an excellent job in the class but because the school was grading on the curve, he could only give two As. We talked about my career plans, my mom, my family, and the neighborhood I came from. I told him I had an offer to work for the Federal Bureau of Narcotics in Chicago, a job that I was offered after my backfield coach at Iowa, Jerry Burns, introduced me to George Belk, the agent in charge of the Chicago FBN. . . . Dr. Caldwell . . . had worked with Eliot Ness in New Orleans. We continued to talk, and I'll never forget his final words: "Donald, there isn't much of a difference between a B+ and an A– . . . is there??" I left his office after giving him a big hug, and thinking my mom was there with me. I got my 3.5 GPA, walked with my class at graduation, and took my degree home to my mom.

＊ ＊ ＊

Iowa gave me a chance to become successful and provided me with the knowledge that serves me today. THANK YOU IOWA!!

CONCLUSION

MICHAEL D. HILL

. . .

AN INDIVISIBLE LEGACY

Iowa and the Conscience of Democracy

. . .

Between 1934 and 1965, the experiences of black students at the University of Iowa featured a blend of obstacles and opportunities. This messy mixture launched careers that impacted American higher education, molded debates regarding art, and shaped the global reputation of the Midwest. Despite such profound effects, the university's attitude toward its mid-twentieth-century black students remains puzzling. Official histories of UI include such individuals as Elizabeth Catlett, Simon Estes, Margaret Walker, Calvin Jones, and Ted Wheeler, and these authorized narratives suggest pride regarding the school's interracial legacy. Yet this record also raises the question of why people such as Herbert Nipson, Eddie Robinson, and Dianna Penny fail to claim sustained attention in accounts of the university's development. *Invisible Hawkeyes* thus far has addressed these issues through an introduction, chapters, and testimonials that present and analyze the Iowa school days of several black performing arts students and athletes. By offering these treatments, the editors and contributors argue that documenting the black presence in American institutions of higher learning constitutes a first step toward understanding a specific instance of democratic striving. These portraits move beyond the explosive threshold experiences that define so many narratives about American civil rights. By looking at what happened after blacks gained access to whites' spaces, this book has stressed localized exchanges even as it occasionally notes the national and international effects of UI black alumni's accomplishments. With this foundation in place, we can conclude by dwelling on the collective meaning of both the struggle these graduates faced and the altered landscape they left in their wake. Their footprints created a path on the flat geography of the heartland that primed it to play a leading role for a nation seeking direction and cultural understanding.

But to comprehend the University of Iowa's place in larger discourses on civil rights, we must confront deeply entrenched ideas of white rescue and black agency. In a recent book on race in film, Matthew Hughey states that interracial interaction often is represented through such tropes as "the white savior narrative," a plot wherein a white character or characters delivers a minority character from his or her dilemma.[1] David Sirota says that such stories "insinuate that people of color have no ability to rescue themselves. This both makes [whites] feel good about themselves by portraying them as benevolent messiahs (rather than hegemonic conquerors), and also depicts people of color as helpless weaklings."[2] Hughey and Sirota discuss films; however, their observations also explain historical realities, especially those related to blacks attending white universities. The dynamic in these spaces rarely followed the popular script that cast African Americans as victims in need of white redeemers.

In fact, Iowa emerges as an apt refutation of this myth. When Phil Hubbard suggested that UI manifested benign neglect toward its black students up until the 1960s, he acknowledges a common mind-set at the flagship institution. Many individuals felt the mere presence of a black student within a white school represented a benefit that should trump any indignity students might encounter. At the core of this reasoning rests a belief that the white institution of higher learning claimed an intrinsic value that inevitably redeemed blackness once students physically accessed the campus. Admitting black students was enough. If the white institution proved its progressiveness by admitting the black student, black students proved their victim mentality by complaining about the prejudicial dimensions of the white institution. According to this logic, the only valid response for a black student permitted to attend a white school was thankfulness. Thus, there was little need for the white savior in the midwestern plains.

The story midcentury black UI graduates tell is more complicated. For Cal Jones, Iowa was a place that "treated [him] like a white man."[3] Nevertheless, when his unequivocal endorsement of the university's decency is placed beside Ted Wheeler's claim that he could not date because there were few to no black women and the white coeds were off-limits, the tensions of UI as a multiracial community become clear. Such tensions were not assuaged by the midcentury institutional belief that it embodied a generous if imperfect saving spot for black students. For African Americans who enrolled at UI during the period of our study, the arduous task of succeeding amid difficulties with finding housing, enduring cultural alienation, or suffering insults instilled within them the strength of character crucial to the success of the civil rights movement. As a result of their presence and comportment, when the 1960s stirred widespread questioning of the redemptive role whites played within the drama of integration, the University of Iowa was a step ahead of its peers. We celebrate that vanguard position by checking the impulse toward concealing the interracial struggle that is part and parcel of its history. By refusing to treat blacks who attended UI from the 1930s through the 1960s as mute pioneers who signaled institutional goodwill and personal fortitude, this conclusion meditates on the unruly negotiations that define routes to racial togetherness. Our collection allows black Hawkeyes' stories to emerge as dynamic case studies that spotlight the strenuous exertions demanded by the work necessary to achieve democratic pluralism. Their experiences thus recovered give the lie to the notion of white deliverance and black impotence and replace it with a model of pragmatic collaboration. Thus, the textured legacy of UI's history of integration represents an opportunity to applaud its progress even as we acknowledge its failures.

James Alan McPherson, one of Iowa's most famous African American graduates in the arts, provocatively captures the variegated past that links midcentury black student struggles with the seeds of promise they sow in the Iowa heartland. McPherson enrolled at UI after earning a bachelor's degree from Morris Brown College in Atlanta, Georgia, and a law degree from Harvard University. Bridging the segregated South and the Ivy League Northeast, his educational odyssey adds a new twist to the pipelines that shaped black journeys to Iowa. Where earlier students came to UI seeking to gain the credentials that would confirm their legitimacy for the larger world, McPherson arrived at the university with his talent and his intelligence securely validated.[4] He had already published in such leading magazines as *Atlantic Monthly*, and while he studied at the Iowa Writers' Workshop, he traveled between Iowa City and Chicago to work on journalistic assignments for prestigious New York periodicals. He also taught at the University of California–Santa Cruz. On the one hand, McPherson epitomized the top-notch talents who burnished the workshop's reputation as one of the foremost creative writing programs in the world. On the other hand, he emerges as an unlikely midwestern votary proffering the most eloquent defense of the land of the Hawkeyes since the halcyon days of regionalists such as Grant Wood and John Towner Frederick. McPherson's veneration of Iowa City, however, proves distinct in that unlike his white predecessors, he ruminates on Iowa City's racial realities to reach his earnest conclusions.

Interestingly, McPherson's eloquently rendered perception of Iowa began taking shape at the same time he came to know Ralph Ellison. McPherson's 1968 arrival as a student in the Iowa Writers' Workshop coincided with the blossoming of his friendship with Ellison. The history of their exchanges captured in letters and interviews over a twenty-year span highlights the irony underpinning their respective relations to UI and Iowa City: the space that suggested but failed to corroborate the country's democratic ideals for Fanny and Ralph became a fertile field for McPherson's contemplation of US pluralistic possibility. In McPherson's long 1969 interview of Ellison that was eventually published as "Indivisible Man," we see the outlines of how his conversations with the author of *Invisible Man* helped him negotiate the thorny reality left by midcentury UI black students. In a 1970 letter, McPherson admits that he seeks Ellison's guidance because the years encasing his workshop experience prove artistically and culturally lonely: "I have no one here with whom I can talk and, possibly, sharpen and get a better grasp of my mental wanderings. . . . I think that I am thinking; but there is no one here who shares my special interest in . . . how it is possible to create good literature out of the black American experience."[5] Ellison fills the gap that brings our contemplation of black student experiences in the arts and athletic performance at UI full circle. The coincidental convergence between McPherson's Iowa years and his relationship with Ellison — and the fact that Ellison's refusal to join the workshop faculty cleared the way for McPherson to become the first African American permanent faculty member in 1981 — make his experiences in and perceptions of the place a poignant bookend for *Invisible Hawkeye*'s explorations.

Interracial Exchange in the Heartland: Won't You Be My Neighbor?

In his 1998 memoir, *Crabcakes*, McPherson stated, "Life in Iowa, with its daily reminders of the ritual sacredness of natural rhythms, has been very kind to me. It has provided me with the time and quiet to *re-collect*, to harvest, the scattered shadows of" my past.[6] This remark sounds nothing like Cal Jones's endorsement of UI, yet at its core, it venerates the same midwestern generosity that prompted him to become a Hawkeye. Through a concept called "neighboring," McPherson captures the nuances of his adopted home's giving. He explains:

> I learned here in Iowa City the local meaning of the term "neighboring." It evolved out of the frontier tradition of the rural landscape: If a neighboring farmer could not take care of his planting or his harvest, or could not manage heavy rain or snow on his own, it became tradition for people living nearby to step in and offer assistance. Soon the word was abstracted from agriculture and employed to describe absolutely any helpful human gestures. In places like Iowa City, such "neighboring" gestures are normative.[7]

McPherson wrote these words in 2008, and he described an Iowa that had been devastated by a flood and was coping with the devastation through a fidelity to its foundational values. His observations affirmed the twenty-first-century practice of selflessness and communal obligation and summoned a legacy in Iowa City broadly and at UI specifically that manifested similar scenes of support. Here, McPherson trumpets sentiments shared by black graduates who decided to call Iowa home after graduating from the university. Although the musings of alumnae such as Dianna Penny and Lois Eichaker rarely receive top billing in UI histories, their views of Iowa, like McPherson's, uncover the benefits and bedevilments of pluralistic community. Just as a black administrator like Phil Hubbard prods the university bureaucracy to discover its better self, McPherson probes the deep roots of black and white Iowa neighbors that originated in university experiences but flourished in the years that follow.

The line McPherson draws from his student days to his tenure as a university professor is not always easy to trace. Yet following this thread gives powerful voice to the democratic work shouldered by black graduates who decided to call Iowa home. In a speech that he gave in Tokyo on June 20, 1990, McPherson compared the unrest that rocked New York after the murder of Yusef Hawkins to the "peace and quiet and absence of extreme tensions in [his] home state of Iowa."[8] He suggested that the ethnic composition of the two venues might explain the difference in mood, yet he felt that the distinctions also stemmed from Iowans' "openness to . . . new people, or at least a *determination* to be open."[9] Though his example of Iowa's openness is a neighbor's naturalization ceremony, his reference to escalating black–white antipathy in Bensonhurst is telling. McPherson presents a predominantly white Iowa that defines itself in neighborly encounters with minorities. If his portrait clarifies his fondness for Iowa, then it also raises questions about who performs the work of democracy. Classical historiography endorses a hierarchy of sources that makes white men the most visible actors in American history.

McPherson's discussions with Ellison suggest he formed a different view. In answer to McPherson's question regarding black cultural contributions that strengthen African Americans and the country, Ellison responded, "As for those charges of white paternalism, part of this business is a way of relating, which becomes offensive because it's presumptuous." Notwithstanding such attitudes, he explains, "our kids are going to have to learn what their fore-fathers learned; that there is a certain forbearance, and a certain acceptance of our own maturity, our own human maturity. And in some ways Negroes are much more mature; we damn well should be because we've had a harder time."[10] McPherson clearly understands this maturity as embodied by black UI graduates even as he lives through the epochal shifts that occurred in the 1960s. Midcentury students hauntingly imbricate McPherson's sentiments, and in revealing his sensitivity to the wrestling at the heart of progress, they capture the challenging sincerity of his witness.

When McPherson reached Iowa City in 1968, he brought with him vivid impressions of southern racism and keen awareness of Eastern pretension. His mind-set thus detected in the white midwestern ethos a morally vigilant decency that could tutor a nation. By linking his convictions to the experiences of the black students who preceded him at UI, I want to suggest that McPherson's views of white Iowa's post–civil rights era moral resolve reflect not only a set of regional values that predate a significant black presence in the state but also some hard-won realizations about pluralistic community that directly result from interracial exchanges between the 1930s and the 1950s. UI and its midcentury black students are exemplars of rapidly catalyzing demo-cratic processes. Whereas the time lines of the civil rights movement opt for convenient signposts to mark phases of such changes, McPherson, guided by Ellison, senses that in Iowa City the activity of democratizing human experi-ence was already under way. The irony of such realizations, of course, is the riddle of incompleteness. While a progressive university should and does look different from a repressive one, UI — as the bulk of this book shows — was by no means consistent in its progressive racial consciousness. Its concomitant forward-thinking attitude and backward actions become the junction at which McPherson and prior black Hawkeyes are best met.

McPherson's introduction to the complexity of UI character commenced when he attended the school from 1968 to 1971 and deepened when he began teaching there in 1981. In simple terms, McPherson found UI and Iowa City humanizing. Yet he differed from most black graduates who deemed UI a proving ground where credentials could be claimed to enable the performance of civic obligations by returning to black communities and institutions. Though this trajectory unquestionably represents one tutorial in effective citizenship, McPherson suggests another possibility. By using calculations about the United States that he borrowed from Ralph Ellison, McPherson reveals his view of Iowa as a space that had both imbued and been imbued with scenes of democratic labor. Writing to Ellison in 1970, he muses:

> You said once that the Negro cultural experience is the only one, in the American pluralistic pattern, rich enough to forge a cultural metaphor that could explain, or suggest, the broader American cultural reality. I have been considering this, and I have concluded that my generation, perhaps more than any other, has gained the experiences and insights necessary for the exploration of this idea in fiction. . . . Last year I concluded that the best place to be, for whatever insights were available, was . . . the university; and the best course to teach, for my own benefit and as a way of gaining access to the thinking of young Negro students and young white students, was a course in the Negro cultural experience.[11]

The indivisible legacy he probes, then, eventually unfolds in the late twentieth-century and early twenty-first-century classrooms of the University of Iowa. He expresses this revelation in the fullest voice within a 2011 essay, "Pursuit of the Pneuma."

The Labor of Democratic Union and Belated Recognition

Recounting conversations that he had with Phil Jones, a former UI vice president for student services, McPherson writes in his essay that through these dialogues, he had begun to glimpse how "a muscular bureaucratic structure . . . during the 1960s, 1970s, and 1980s" testified to "Iowa's institutional receptivity to non-white students, especially black Americans."[12] His observation is remarkable both because it offers his most explicit commentary on black student experience at UI and because it provides a supremely ironic yet ideologically consistent portrait of Jones. Jones, a black man and UI graduate who was suing the university for wrongful termination, stands in for the opportunities and trials that Iowa presented to an earlier generation of black students. Alternately, though, McPherson makes him an emblem of a cohort of blacks that includes Ted Wheeler, Phil Hubbard, and Lois Eichaker, alumni who made UI and Iowa City their home. Between the itinerant residency of those black students who visited and departed UI and Iowa City and those who embraced exile in the "rural landscape of the state" and the "small-town intimacy" of the city, there are lessons about the ultimate implications of blackness, higher education, and specific probing of pluralistic democracy.

When McPherson states that Jones reveals his "affectionate relationships . . . with his colleagues and peers" at UI, he is not smoothing over friction — after all, he does candidly state that Jones is suing the institution for unjustly terminating him; rather, he is shifting the terms by which we should understand both conflict and intimacy.[13] A problem with a family member carries equally combustible consequences, yet it also is subject to the conditioning of earlier shared experiences. By referencing Iowa, Iowa City, and UI as spots where an earlier conditioning mediated any subsequent controversies, McPherson not only casts Jones's lawsuit in an alternate light but also suggests a way of seeing the ambivalent experiences of midcentury black Hawkeyes as coterminous with his own rather different days in Iowa. What makes his contention all the more fascinating is the way that he makes blackness an attribute that does not disqualify one from Iowa insider status. Jones makes this point notwithstanding the fact that he has been fired, and McPherson himself, who continues to be employed by the university, highlights that in the heartland, he has found a home. This discovery returns us to Ellison's theories of racial chaos and democracy.

In his acceptance speech for the National Book Award, Ellison stated, "The way home we seek is that condition of man's being at home in the world, which is called love, and which we term democracy. Our task then is always to challenge the apparent forms of reality — that is the fixed manners and values of the few, and to struggle with it until it reveals its mad, vari-implicated chaos, its false faces, and on until it surrenders its insight, its truth."[14] McPherson detected in his Iowa sojourn the practical adjuncts to his mentor's lofty rhetoric.

Where UI has heretofore often blanched at the aggregated accounts of its midcentury black students, we recognize such aggregation as elucidating the "chaos against which" the university's muscular morality refined itself.[15] Such elucidations err when they cast either a black individual or a white institutional agent as a singular determinative actor in scenes of interracial reckoning. Using Ellison's metaphor of democracy as a refining struggle, we see that the university defines itself in a sequence of admissions, matriculations, and graduations of black students. What McPherson tells us is that the UI interludes were not preparations for later integrative activities; rather, they were in themselves occasions of participatory democracy. Iowa's disposition toward artistic talent made it uniquely suited to provide the site for such democratic labor, and black students willingly took up the gauntlet.

The individual essays in this collection prove the impressive abilities showcased by midcentury black students, and their convergence upon UI is not coincidental. A final turn to McPherson's letter to Ellison underscores his awareness of this point. As he wraps up his extended rumination on the position of the black artist, McPherson quotes Ellison's words from "The World and the Jug" at length. He declares:

> Some of the bravest words ever written by an artist are these: "But there is also an American Negro tradition which teaches one to deflect racial provocation and to master and contain the pain. It is a tradition which abhors as obscene any trading on one's own anguish for gain or sympathy; which springs not from a desire to deny the harshness of existence but from a will to deal with it as men at their best have always done. It takes fortitude to be a man and no less to be an artist. Perhaps it takes even more if the black man would be an artist."[16]

McPherson ponders the difficult path that makes his current Iowa experience possible. But beyond his individual experience, he implicitly recognizes how the larger cohort of trailblazing black graduates of UI arts programs participates in the democratic struggle. This is not a matter of identifying singular agents who act heroically in the service of a democratic agenda; rather, it is a case of what Richard Breaux calls "tireless partners and skilled competitors" who glimpse a worthy end and see no distraction in pursuing it.

In some ways, this elevation in perception defines the arc from Fanny Ellison to James Alan McPherson, the earliest and the latest black Hawkeyes that this book treats. When McPherson received the first annual Paul Engle award in 2011, he was feted by, among others, Michael Harper, a poet who had attended the Iowa Writers' Workshop almost a decade before him. Harper's tribute signaled the sort of collectivity that Jewel Prestage suggested was so vital to black students' survival at Iowa. Yet McPherson's reconstructions of UI rarely dwell on these intraracial support structures. What do we make of these explicit silences? On the one hand, McPherson's silence on the inter-locutors who hurtled UI along its pathway to being a better self may be mod-esty since McPherson himself is a key player in such a cohort. Alternately, McPherson may have failed to chronicle black student contributions to UI because he was not aware of the details comprising their legacies. An irony most arch would be that the alumnus of a historically black college or uni-versity (HBCU) would arrive at a midwestern utopia that had been created in part by earlier voluntary exiles whose experiences he understood only in the abstract terms he discusses with Ellison. If this is the case, McPherson is not alone in his unfamiliarity with the details of Iowa's remarkable history.

Obama's Midwestern Road to the Presidency

In 2008, several months after the Iowa state primary, Ta-Nehisi Coates, a black writer at the *Atlantic* and 2015 recipient of the MacArthur Fellows Program "Genius Grant," offered a pregnant confession: "I was stunned by [Barack Obama's] victory in Iowa."[17] Elsewhere, he elaborated, "We can talk about White Racism all day, but I'm still grappling with the idea that this dude won primaries and caucuses in states that a lot of us presumed were off limits to black folks. I know that Appalachia explains a lot, but still, it didn't explain it two years ago. No one thought this was going to happen."[18] Coates's quote epitomizes Iowa's enigmatic place in the contemporary imagination. On the one hand, the state heralds the plausibility of an African American president. On the other hand, it remains a heartland Appalachia, a space where unremit-ting whiteness prevails. This anomaly exists as early as the American Civil War, but after a flood and two hotly contested presidential elections, Iowa City and the University of Iowa have become conspicuous, if inconsistent, weather vanes in contemporary debates about American identity.

Considering this publication environment, James Alan McPherson's "Pur-suit of the Pneuma" joins a host of twenty-first-century accounts that examine Iowa, Iowa City, and UI's place in imagining the United States. While the most acerbic commentary might be Stephen Bloom's "Observations from 20 Years of Iowa Life" (2011), Iowa's connections to national moods can also be seen in Sean Lewis's play *Mayberry* (2012), Joe Blair's memoir *By the Iowa Sea* (2012), Marybeth Slonneger's collection *The Burg* (2012), and Eric Bennett's article "How Iowa Flattened Literature" (2014).[19] In terms of mood, McPherson's essay treads an intriguing middle ground. It does not uncritically venerate Iowa City's soul by way of celebrating Midwestern communitas, yet it also refuses to lampoon myths of small-town wholesomeness. McPherson engages racial realities and suggests that lessons in the difficult work and accomplishment of cultural exchange and understanding might be the town's most underappreciated legacy. I want to propose that the sudden fashionability of many of his peers' assessments celebrates an effect without adequately accounting for its antecedents.

Barack Obama's presidential campaign and subsequent visits made the legibility of race and regional reality a matter of national commentary in the first decade of the twenty-first century. While pundits like Coates plunge into cogitations regarding black candidates and a white electorate, their explanations neglect a history of interracial contact that goes back to the nineteenth century. From those early roots, the Iowa version of pluralistic collaboration has been quieter but no less meaningful than the headline-grabbing episodes elsewhere. These subtler exchanges suggest that for more than a hundred years, the truth has marched on unabated in Iowa. A thick description of integration at UI provides indispensable intervention in a debate that risks playing to and getting distorted by irrelevant agendas. By concentrating on buried encounters, *Invisible Hawkeyes* brings UI black students from the 1930s to the 1960s back into the continuum that includes Obama's triumph. The longitudinal focus on interracial attempts to shape a shared community at Iowa clarifies the circulations of what Ellison called "the fixed manners and values of the few."[20] In this regard, the fetishistic embrace of Obama as a marker of Iowa's progressivism is yet another uninformed evasion. The responsible action in the face of such sidestepping is contextualizing confrontation. This is the work *Invisible Hawkeyes* willingly undertakes.

During fall 2011, when UI hosted "Iowa and *Invisible Man*: Making Blackness Visible," the collaborative residency that helped develop the world-premiere stage adaptation of Ralph Ellison's canonical novel, it revealed the intricate interconnections between contemporary civic endeavors and an earlier history of how UI's arts programs mirrored evolutions in American racial possibilities. Validating Ellison's persistent claims that the Midwest forecasted democracy, this residency prompted the editors of this volume to heed these contentions by attending to the new textures that emerge in the national conversation regarding democratic pluralism when the heartland venue changes to Iowa and the institutional index shifts to the white public university. By focusing on an overlooked space of democratic exchange, this book reminds readers that the desire of the United States to be a diverse republic demands a persistent commitment to strenuous reexaminations. This is the closing word of *Invisible Hawkeyes*. As revisionist historiographers alerted us to the lapses lurking in embracing a "great man" theory of history, the hitherto unexamined labor of UI black students from the 1930s to the 1960s holds treasures that, like *Invisible Man*'s zoot suit, may lead us to untapped democratic resources. This is the indivisible legacy we celebrate.

Dora Martin Berry worked for twenty-nine years as a licensed social worker in a school district just outside of Princeton, New Jersey. After that experience, she took a position in a small, private mental health agency. In 2013, she retired from social work, and since her retirement, she has volunteered with women who are transitioning from addictions.

Richard M. Breaux is an assistant professor of ethnic and racial studies at the University of Wisconsin–La Crosse. His work has appeared in the *Journal of African American History* and the *History of Education Quarterly*.

Kathleen A. Edwards is senior curator of the University of Iowa Museum of Art. She has curated more than eighty exhibitions, including *Lil Picard and Counterculture New York* (2010) and *New Forms: The Avant-Garde Meets the American Scene, 1934–1949* (2013).

Lois Eichaker served as executive director of the Southeast Iowa Community Action Board, and in recognition of her lifelong work for the community, the organization named its Fort Madison branch the Eichaker Community Action Center. She was a 1994 inductee into the Iowa Women's Hall of Fame, and in 2014, the African American Museum of Iowa honored her at its History Makers Gala.

Brian Hallstoos is assistant professor of history at the University of Dubuque. He is curator and editor of the exhibition and catalog *Racing Past the Color Line: Sol Butler and Paul Robeson in Collegiate Sports* (2014) and *Ahead of the Curve: The First Century of African American Experiences* (2015). He is also author and producer of the one-act play *Sol and Paul* (2014).

Lena M. Hill is associate professor of English and African American studies at the University of Iowa. She is the author of *Visualizing Blackness and the Creation of the African American Literary Tradition* (2014) and the coauthor of *Ralph Ellison's Invisible Man: A Reference Guide* (2008).

Michael D. Hill is associate professor of English and African American studies at the University of Iowa. He is the author of *The Ethics of Swagger: Prizewinning African American Novels, 1977–1993* (2013) and the coauthor of *Ralph Ellison's Invisible Man: A Reference Guide* (2008).

Dianna Penny has retired from her full-time position at the University of Iowa's Medical School; however, she still works there on a part-time basis. Away from campus, she finds plenty to keep her busy. In additon to playing the piano and the organ at Bethel AME

Church, she also shares her painting talents at fairs, festivals, and exhibitions through-out Iowa. Her essay "One Christmas Eve" appeared in the *Iowa City Press-Citizen* on December 25, 2014.

Donald W. Tucker has had a long and distinguished law enforcement career. After work-ing with the United States Secret Service for almost twenty-five years, he spent time in the US Marshals Service and as the chief of Court Security for the Administrative Office of the United States Courts. Drawing on his experiences in these jobs, he has written two novels, *The Two-Edged Sword* (2010) and *The Complex* (2011).

Theodore "Ted" Wheeler coached the University of Iowa track team from 1972 to 1996. After his retirement, he became a major fund-raising force behind what are now known as the Ted Wheeler Scholarships. Through these awards, he continues to mentor and support University of Iowa students. This support reinforces his belief that individuals should have both a fit body and a fit mind.

Introduction

1. Arnold Rampersad, *Ralph Ellison: A Biography* (New York: Knopf, 2007), 176.

2. Michael Harper writes, "It was Fanny who would not allow Ellison to teach at Iowa in the workshop, so bitter were her memories of discrimination." In Robert Dana, ed., *A Community of Writers: Paul Engle and the Iowa Writers' Workshop* (Iowa City: University of Iowa Press, 1999), 86.

3. For information on UI's black enrollment, see Herbert C. Jenkins, "The Negro Student at the University of Iowa: A Sociological Study" (master's thesis, University of Iowa, 1933), and Leola Nelson Bergmann, *Studies in Iowa History: The Negro In Iowa* (Iowa City: State Historical Society of Iowa, 1969). Philip G. Hubbard, *New Dawns: A 150-Year Look at Human Rights at the University of Iowa* (Iowa City: Sesquicentennial Committee, University of Iowa, 1996) also touches on the numbers of black students.

4. Alexander G. Clark Jr., received his LLB degree from the University of Iowa (then called the State University of Iowa) in 1879, and in so doing he became the first black man to receive a law degree from a college west of the Mississippi River. Clark's father, Alexander Clark Sr., took his law degree from Iowa in 1884. See J. Clay Smith, *Emancipation: The Making of the Black Lawyer, 1844–1944* (Philadelphia: University of Pennsylvania Press, 1993); Bill Silag, ed., *Outside In: African American History in Iowa, 1838–2000* (Des Moines: State Historical Society of Iowa, 2001).

5. Cases such as *Missouri ex rel Gaines v. Canada* (1938), *Sipuel v. Board of Regents* (1948), and *Sweatt v. Painter* (1950) legendarily granted black defendants access to law schools at white public universities. For fuller accounts of the NAACP Legal Defense Fund's challenges to segregation, see Richard Kluger, *Simple Justice: The History of Brown v. Board and Black America's Struggle for Racial Equality* (New York: Vintage, 1975); Juan Williams, *Thurgood Marshall: American Revolutionary* (New York: Three Rivers Press, 1998); Michael Klarman, *From Jim Crow to Civil Rights: The Supreme Court and the Struggle for Racial Equality* (Oxford: Oxford University Press, 2006).

6. James Meredith was an African American air force veteran who famously integrated the University of Mississippi in 1962.

7. Hubbard, *New Dawns*, 22.

8. Ibid.

9. Ibid., 23.

10. Ralph Ellison, "The World and the Jug," in *The Collected Essays* (New York: Random House, 2003), 163, 164.

11. Madgetta Dungy, "African American Graduate School Experiences at the University of Iowa, 1937–1959: An Oral History" (PhD thesis, University of Iowa, 1997), 21.

12. Ibid., 23, 24.

13. Ibid., 28.

14. "Minutes State Teachers' Association — Beaumont Meeting," *Texas Standard* 11, no. 4 (March 1938): 4. Jimmie Lewis Franklin, *Journey Toward Hope: A History of Blacks in Oklahoma* (Norman: University of Oklahoma Press, 1982), 73, 75.

15. Leola Bergmann, *The Negro in Iowa* (Iowa City: State Historical Society of Iowa, 1969), 71.

16. Ibid., 134–35.

17. Hubbard, *New Dawns*, 14.

18. Quoted in Ellison, *Collected Essays*, 744.

19. Ibid., 757.

20. Ibid., 758.

21. Quotation in Peter Gillette, e-mail message to Lena M. Hill, May 22, 2013.

22. Jewel Prestage, interview by Michael D. Hill, Summer 2013.

23. Thomas Pawley, interview by Lena M. Hill, August 6, 2014.

24. James Melvin Washington, *Conversations with God: Two Centuries of Prayers by African Americans* (New York: HarperCollins, 1994), xlvi.

Chapter One

1. Philip G. Clapp to Albert W. Dent, 24 April 1942, Papers of Philip G. Clapp, University of Iowa Libraries, Iowa City (hereafter cited as Clapp Papers); Harry Washington Greene, *Holders of Doctorates among American Negroes: An Educational and Social Study of Negroes Who Have Earned Doctoral Degrees in Course, 1876–1943* (Boston: Meador, 1946), 121.

2. Clapp to Dent.

3. Steven Houser, "O. Anderson Fuller, the First Black Doctor of Philosophy in Music in America, and His Development of the Music Education Curriculum at Lincoln University" (PhD thesis, Lincoln University, Jefferson City, Missouri, 1982), 34; George Overall Caldwell student records, Office of the Registrar, University of Iowa.

4. Mitchell B. Southall to Philip G. Clapp, 21 August 1950, in Clapp Papers.

5. Dungy, "African American Graduate School Experiences," 99; William Oscar Smith, *Sideman: The Long Gig of W. O. Smith: A Memoir* (Nashville, TN: Rutledge Hill Press, 1991), 215.

6. Dungy, "African American Graduate School Experiences," 97–98.

7. Smith, *Sideman*, 215.

8. Greene, *Holders of Doctorates among American Negroes*, 18, 25. As Oscar Fuller noted in his master's thesis, "the ranking of teachers has received more serious consideration in recent years due to efforts to meet accrediting." O. A. Fuller, "The Teaching of Music in the Leading Negro Colleges" (MA thesis, University of Iowa, June 1934), 35.

9. Dungy, "African American Graduate School Experiences," 22–32.

10. By 1937 Maryland, Missouri, Oklahoma, Tennessee, Virginia, and West Virginia helped fund African Americans for out-of-state professional schooling, largely in response to the acute need for black doctors, dentists, and pharmacists. "Minutes State Teachers' Association — Beaumont Meeting," 4; Dungy, "African American Graduate School Experiences," 178–79.

11. Franklin, *Journey Toward Hope*, 73, 75.

12. *Session Laws of 1935* (Oklahoma City, OK: Harlow, 1935), 138–39; Thanks to Ellen L. Jones, reference librarian at the University of Iowa Law Library, for providing invaluable information on Oklahoma and Texas legislation regarding stipends for out-of-state study and related NAACP correspondence.

13. Franklin, *Journey toward Hope*, 72–73.

14. Zella J. Black Patterson, *Langston University: A History* (Norman: University of Oklahoma, 1979), 147.

15. Richard T. Hamilton to Charles Houston, 12 May 1937, NAACP Papers.

16. Ibid. See also H. Y. Benedict (president of University of Texas) to R. T. Hamilton, 27 February 1937, NAACP Papers.

17. R. T. Hamilton to Charles Houston, 4 June 1947 [sic]; R. T. Hamilton to James V. Allred, 27 May 1937; James V. Allred to Richard T. Hamilton, 28 May 1937, NAACP Papers; "Minutes State Teachers' Association — Beaumont Meeting," 4; Ellie Alma Walls, "Negro Student Aid Bill," *Texas Standard* 12, no. 1 (November 1938): 16–17.

18. According to the state legislation, the scholarship aid was for "qualified Negro students who have been residents of Texas more than eight years for graduate and professional study in approved colleges or universities outside of Texas; schools and students to be selected by a committee composed of the Dean of the graduate schools of A. & M. College, University of Texas, and the Dean of Sam Houston State Teachers College." *Forty-Sixth Legislature — Regular Session of Texas* (Austin, 1939), 359.

19. Lois Towles McNeely, "The History of Music Education at Wiley University" (MA thesis, University of Iowa, 1942), 8.

20. Franklin, *Journey toward Hope*, 75.

21. Gary M. Lavergne, *Before Brown: Heman Marion Sweatt, Thurgood Marshall, and the Long Road to Justice* (Austin: University of Texas Press, 2010), 37–38.

22. This ruling presumably led Oklahoma and several other states to pass their bills that funded out-of-state graduate and professional training. The irony is that the Maryland Supreme Court rejected the argument that out-of-state scholarships could satisfy the equal protection requirement.

23. Lavergne, *Before Brown*, 42. Lloyd Gaines was never found. He has since been honored by the University of Missouri as well as the state.

24. Ada Lois Sipuel Fisher, *A Matter of Black and White: The Autobiography of Ada Lois Sipuel Fisher* (Norman: University of Oklahoma Press, 1996), 81–85.

25. Melvin C. Hall, "Fisher, Ada Lois Sipuel (1924–1995)," in *Encyclopedia of Oklahoma History and Culture*, accessed September 21, 2014, http://digital.library.okstate.edu.

26. Fisher, *Matter of Black and White*, 145–46, 148.

27. Alfred L. Brody, "McLaurin v. Oklahoma State Regents (1950)," in *Encyclopedia of*

Oklahoma History and Culture, accessed September 6, 2014, http://digital.library.okstate .edu.

28. Werdner Page Keeton, "Sweatt v. Painter," *Handbook of Texas Online*, June 15, 2010, accessed March 3, 2016, https://tshaonline.org/handbook/online/articles/jrs01; Larry R. Faulkner and John R. Durbin, "In Memoriam: W. Page Keeton," updated August 15, 2013, accessed March 3, 2016, http://www.utexas.edu/faculty/council/1999-2000/memorials /Keeton/keeton.html.

29. Lavergne, *Before Brown*, 257.

30. Charles Houston to A. Maceo Smith, 8 October 1937; Charles Houston to R. T. Hamilton, 14 June 1937, NAACP Papers.

31. Thanks to Sarah Harris, senior associate registrar at the University of Iowa, for making registration records available to the author.

32. At the University of Iowa, Southall completed his MA in 1947 (nine years after a segregated University of Oklahoma first awarded this degree), MFA in 1948, and PhD in 1949. Mitchell Bernard Southall student records, Office of the Registrar, University of Iowa; *Acts of the Fifteenth Legislature* (Oklahoma), 138; Jan Russell (office assistant, School of Music, University of Oklahoma), e-mail message to Brian Hallstoos, July 6, 2015.

33. Herbert C. Harris student records, Office of the Registrar, University of Iowa.

34. Edison Holmes Anderson and Oscar Anderson Fuller student records, Office of the Registrar, University of Iowa. Unfortunately, information on where transcripts were sent is unavailable for several music graduate students due to recent digitization of records.

35. Lois Towles McNeely student records, Office of the Registrar, University of Iowa.

36. North Texas Teachers College (now University of North Texas) first offered a PhD in musicology, composition, or theory in 1950. The University of Texas at Austin followed in 1953 with a PhD in musicology. Joel Wiley (administrative specialist for Admissions and Scholarships, University of North Texas), telephone conversation with Brian Hallstoos, June 30, 2015; Brian Hallstoos, e-mail correspondence with Cely Smart, assistant registrar, University of Texas–Austin, and Clifton Evans, graduate advisor, University of Texas–Arlington, June 2015.

37. The National Association of Schools of Music first approved the North Texas Teachers College for graduate study of music in 1941; the school began to offer a performance-oriented MA of music and thesis-oriented MA of arts. If these were the first graduate offerings of music in Texas, then any state stipends Edison Anderson and Oscar Fuller may have received for out-of-state study represented a similar reversal in privilege as that enjoyed by McNeely. Wiley telephone conversation.

38. Franklin, *Journey toward Hope*, 73, 75; Ellen L. Jones (reference librarian, University of Iowa Law Library), e-mail correspondence with Brian Hallstoos, July–August 2014.

39. Edison Holmes Anderson, "An Interpretive Analysis of Fourteen Songs by Samuel Coleridge-Taylor" (MA thesis, University of Iowa, 1941), acknowledgments.

40. According to school records, Anderson entered in the summer of 1940 and Fuller shortly thereafter at the start of fall semester. The Prairie View newsletter of May 1940, however, noted that Fuller had just returned to the college for the summer after having

been away for his studies. This evidence suggests that Fuller, perhaps with Anderson in tow, may have started in January 1940.

41. Gloria Edwards Anderson, *Just to Shake His Hand* (printed by author, 1997), 1–17; the author self-published this biography on her spouse, Edison Holmes Anderson.

42. Ibid., 13, 17.

43. Ibid., 16.

44. Ibid.

45. The University of Oklahoma awarded its first PhD in music education in 1966. Russell e-mail.

46. Charles Edward Calmer, "Philip Greeley Clapp: The Early Years (1888–1909)" (MA thesis, University of Iowa, 1981); Charles Edward Calmer, "Philip Greeley Clapp: The Later Years (1909–54)" (PhD thesis, University of Iowa, 1992); Dorrance Stinchfield White, "A Biography of Dr. Philip Greeley Clapp, Director of Music at the State University of Iowa, 1919–1954" (University of Iowa Special Collections, 1960).

47. Calmer, "Clapp: Later Years," 95, 170–71, 354; see also Calmer, "Clapp: Early Years," 4.

48. "Into Boston Newly Troop the Basques," unidentified journal or newspaper clipping, April 17, 1919, Clapp Papers.

49. "Latent American Music," manuscript, n.d., box 14, Clapp Papers.

50. George Overall Caldwell student records, Office of the Registrar, University of Iowa; Houser, "O. Anderson Fuller," 37; Edwin Homer Bayliss, "The Negro Student at the State University of Iowa, His Preparation, Interests, and Achievements" (MA thesis, University of Iowa, 1935), 29.

51. "Alumni Briefs," *Daily Iowan,* April 13, 1929, 4.

52. Steven Houser, "O. Anderson Fuller, The First Black Doctor of Philosophy in Music in America, and His Development of the Music Education Curriculum at Lincoln University" (PhD thesis, University of Missouri–Columbia, 1982), 34.

53. Oscar A. Fuller, "The Creation: An Oratorio" (PhD thesis, University of Iowa, 1942).

54. Clapp to Dent. Concerning Clapp's high regard for Fuller's skill as a composer, see Philip Clapp to Oscar Fuller, 9 March 1942, Clapp Papers.

55. Houser, "O. Anderson Fuller," 32–33.

56. "Florence Beatrice Smith Price (1887–1953)," in *The Encyclopedia of Arkansas History and Culture,* last updated September 16, 2013, accessed March 3, 2016, http://www .encyclopediaofarkansas.net/encyclopedia/entry-detail.aspx?search=1&entryID=1742; "William Grant Still (1895–1978)," in *The Encyclopedia of Arkansas History and Culture,* last updated September 19, 2013, accessed March 3, 2016, http://www.encyclopediaof arkansas.net/encyclopedia/entry-detail.aspx?entryID=1775.

57. Houser, "O. Anderson Fuller," 33.

58. "Between 1929–1942 at Prairie View, Dr. Fuller studied at Iowa several summers and during the academic years when leave from Prairie View was permitted." Houser, "O. Anderson Fuller," 34.

59. "1928" folder, box 6, Clapp Papers.

60. Houser, "O. Anderson Fuller," 35; "WSUI Program," *Daily Iowan*, February 13, 1934, 5; March 6, 1934, 3; March 20, 1934, 5.

61. A June 1934 Prairie View College newsletter noted, "Mr. Fuller at Iowa University will return in time to join us in Summer School work." Prairie View Archives. Thanks to library assistant Terrell Chase for researching and sending materials on Dr. Fuller and Prairie View's ties with the University of Iowa.

62. "Three Music Students Will Give Recital," *Daily Iowan*, May 15, 1934, 5.

63. O. A. Fuller, "The Teaching of Music in the Leading Negro Colleges" (MA thesis, University of Iowa, June 1934).

64. Ibid., 32.

65. For example, 316 African Americans earned a PhD from 1930 to 1943, which was more than six times the 51 earned before this period. Greene, *African American Holders of Doctorates*, 23–24.

66. According to the document from the late 1930s, the other leading producers of degrees among faculty at Prairie View included Tuskegee Institute (eight), Cornell University (six), Columbia (five), University of Michigan (five), Ohio State (four), University of Southern California (four), and University of Wisconsin (four). The document from 1935 lists seven from Iowa State, five from University of Iowa, along with five each from University of California, Columbia University, and Cornell University. "Institutions from which 165 Prairie View College Employees Received Their Highest Degrees or Highest Training," n.d., and untitled document, 1935, Prairie View Archives.

67. The Prairie View faculty trained at the University of Iowa include Edison Holmes Anderson (music), Elizabeth Catlett (art), C. E. Carpenter, Frank Greene Davis (economics), T. P. Dooley (biology), Oscar Fuller (music), Alana Glass (Home Economics), A. C. Lamb (Theatre), M. Levealle (Home Economics), Thomas Pawley (Theatre), Rufus P. Perry (chemistry), and A. M. Randall. See Prairie View newsletters dated June 1934, June 1937, June 1938, August 1938, September 1938, August 1939, and June 1940, Prairie View Archives.

68. Prairie View newsletter, August 1939, Prairie View Archives.

69. Rampersad, *Ralph Ellison*, 37, 41–47, 52–59, 67–74, 79–80.

70. Anderson, *Just to Shake*, 19, 21.

71. Dungy, "African American Graduate School Experiences," 115–33.

72. Ibid., 142.

73. Ibid., 104–14, 121, 142–45.

74. Clapp to Dent.

75. The alumni whom Dungy interviewed for her doctoral thesis understood the correlation between the number of African American students and levels of racism. In explaining the lack of overt departmental racism, she wrote that the "prevailing thought was that this may have been due to [the black students'] small numbers. As one respondent put it, 'Where Black people are concerned when you are in small numbers things tend to work out a little better. It's when you get more than three [Black] people that you begin to have problems.'" Dungy, "African American Graduate School Experiences," 144.

76. According to a list compiled by Dr. Philip G. Hubbard on African American graduates who ended up teaching at HBCUs, thirty-four African Americans earned an MA between 1937 and 1950, and twenty-three earned a PhD between 1939 and 1950. Nineteen of the MA degrees and thirteen of the PhD degrees were earned *before* 1943. Hubbard, *New Dawns*, 127–37.

77. Clapp to Dent.

78. Hubbard, *New Dawns*, 22.

79. Smith, *Sideman*, 219, 222, 224.

80. Ibid., 227–28.

81. Lois Towles McNeely, "The History of Music Education at Wiley University" (MA thesis, University of Iowa, 1942).

82. Dale Wright, "The Pianist Who Captured Paris," *Jet* 5 (December 10, 1953): 58–60; David Park, "Caesar, Lois Towles," *Handbook of Texas Online*, June 12, 2013, accessed June 30, 2015, https://tshaonline.org/handbook/online/articles/fcaeu.

83. H. Franklin Mells, "Symphony Number Two, B Minor 'Burdened Chile'" (PhD thesis, University of Iowa, 1944).

84. H. F. Mells to P. G. Clapp, 10 October 1944; P. G. Clapp to H. F. Mells, 17 October 1944, Clapp Papers.

85. Calmer, "Clapp: Later Years," 82.

86. Anderson recalled Clapp's six-page letter — sent more than six decades earlier — that responded to his postcard inquiry regarding the graduate program and "encouraged me to come to Iowa." Clapp died shortly before Anderson moved to Iowa to work on his PhD. Thomas Jefferson Anderson, telephone conversation with Brian Hallstoos, June 30, 2015; Thomas Jefferson Anderson, e-mail message to Brian Hallstoos, August 17, 2014.

87. Dungy, "African American Graduate School Experiences," 120; Robert V. Morris, *Tradition and Valor: A Family Journey* (Manhattan, KS: Sunflower University Press, 1999): 69, 74, 109.

88. Calmer, "Clapp: Later Years," 352–68.

89. Houser, "O. Anderson Fuller," 30, 38–39.

90. Edison Holmes Anderson Sr., "The Historical Development of Music in the Negro Secondary Schools of Oklahoma and at Langston University" (PhD diss., State University of Iowa, 1957), 196.

91. Anderson, *Just to Shake*, 7.

92. Clapp wrote, "I honestly think that you would find a position in which you enter as Dr. Southall, trained first at Langston and then at the State University of Iowa, would give you a better chance to stand on your own feet and even put your best foot foremost, than to be trying to get full recognition in your own Alma Mater where people can remember you when you were younger and less developed, and where besides there is already another alumnus with similar training to yours who has seniority over you in being appointed to the faculty." Philip G. Clapp to Mitchell B. Southall, 30 January 1953; Mitchell B. Southall to Philip G. Clapp, 24 January 1953, both in University of Iowa Special Collections.

93. Obituary, *Black Perspective in Music* 8, no. 1/2 (1990): 221.

94. Helen Day Caldwell, *Color Ebony* (New York: Sheed and Ward, 1951), 4; Hubbard,

New Dawns, 127–37; Subject Files Administration, University Committee on Cooperation with a Negro College, 1963–1964, University of Iowa Special Collections.

95. Smith, *Sideman*, 201, 206–8.

96. Ibid., 219.

Chapter Two

1. Elizabeth Catlett, interview by Melanie Herzog, June 14, 1991, Cuernavaca, Mexico, audiotape.

2. Harry Stinson, the School of Fine Arts sculpture instructor, was also awarded an MFA that year. Stinson completed a thesis paper, "A Sculptured Figure in Cast Stone," and an exhibition, but he was not a matriculated student. The third MFA was awarded to Jewel Petersen in music. According to University of Iowa Archives pamphlets, "Candidates for the Degrees of Master of Fine Arts, Master of Arts, and Master of Science," for June 1940 and August 1940, in June 1940 an MA in sculpture was awarded to Catlett's close friend Shirley Briggs, and MA degrees in sculpture were awarded to Allen Downs and Carl Heeschen in August. At the time, MFA degrees with different requirements were also awarded at Yale and Princeton universities.

3. Melanie Anne Herzog, *Elizabeth Catlett: An American Artist in Mexico* (Seattle: University of Washington Press, 2000), 16.

4. Julie L. McGee, *David C. Driskill, Artist and Scholar* (Petaluma, CA: Pomegranate, 2006), 16.

5. Michael Brenson and Lowery Stokes Sims, *Elizabeth Catlett Sculpture: A Fifty-Year Retrospective*, ed. Lucinda H. Gedeon (Purchase, NY: Neuberger Museum of Art, 1998), 33.

6. Richard J. Powell, "Herein Lie Buried Many Things, Screens, Entryway, and Cabinets in Twentieth-Century Black Visual Discourse," in *African American Art: Harlem Renaissance, Civil Rights Era and Beyond*, by Richard J. Powell and Virginia M. Mecklenburg (Washington, DC: Smithsonian Art Museum, 2012), 150.

7. Brenson and Sims, *Elizabeth Catlett Sculpture*, 33.

8. Jane Gail Abbott, "The Barnett Aden Gallery: A Home for Diversity in a Segregated City" (PhD diss., Pennsylvania State University, State College, 2008).

9. Catlett, interview by Herzog.

10. Stacy I. Morgan, *Rethinking Social Realism: African American Art and Literature, 1930–1953* (Athens: University of Georgia Press, 2004), 15.

11. See Federal Writer's Project of the Works Progress Administration for the State of Iowa, *Iowa: A Guide to the Hawkeye State* (New York: Viking, 1938), 140–48.

12. See a reproduction of this work on the Iowa State University Museums website at http://umsm003.its.iastate.edu/view/objects/asitem/search@/3/title-asc?t:state:flow =353313d7-4d86-48be-acb3-21976085d3d7.

13. Joni L. Kinsey, "Modernism Ascendant, The Contested History of Modern Art at the University of Iowa," in *New Forms: The Avant-Garde Meets the American Scene, 1934–1949*, ed. Kathleen A. Edwards (Iowa City: University of Iowa Museum of Art, 2013), 20.

14. Ibid., 21.

15. Summary of the Faculty Meeting on Curriculum, September 21, 1938, 4, Subject Vertical File collection, Art category, curricula, 1938–1974, University of Iowa Archives, Iowa City, Iowa.

16. Catlett interview by Herzog, quoted in Herzog, *Elizabeth Catlett*, 14.

17. Elizabeth Catlett and Francisco Mora, interviews by Dr. Clifton H. Johnson, 1984, box 3, folder 24, audiotape cassettes, Amistad Research Center, Tulane University, New Orleans.

18. Catlett, interview by Herzog.

19. Kathleen A. Edwards correspondence with Bronwyn Solyom, curator, Jean Charlot Collection, University of Hawaii at Manoa Library, Honolulu, July 11, 2013.

20. See Peter Morse, *Jean Charlot's Prints: A Catalogue Raisonné* (Honolulu: University Press of Hawaii, 1975), 402, 403, 443, 444.

21. "Grant Wood to Lecture, Charlot Exhibit to Be Gallery Talk Topic," *Iowa Press Citizen*, November 11, 1939.

22. In Mexico City Catlett studied wood carving with José L. Ruiz and ceramic sculpture with Francisco Zúñiga, at the Escuela de Pintura y Escultura, Esmeralda, and worked in the community printshop Taller Gráphica de Popular.

23. Quoted in Herzog, *Elizabeth Catlett*, 19.

24. Catlett and Mora interviews by Johnson.

25. Ibid.

26. Quoted in Herzog, *Elizabeth Catlett*, 20.

27. Catlett interview by Herzog.

28. Grant Wood to Archie F. Winter (with a copy to Reeves Lewenthal), 27 December 1938, quoted in Sylvan Cole Jr., *Grant Wood: The Lithographs* (New York: Associated American Artists, 1986), 6.

29. Ibid.

30. Subject Vertical File collection, Art exhibitions, 1938–1940, University of Iowa Archives.

31. Elizabeth Catlett, questionnaire from Richard Breaux for his dissertation research, January 16, 1999.

32. In 1992 Catlett created a portfolio of six prints titled in honor of Walker and her poem "For My People." Since 2000, the University of Iowa Museum of Art has acquired thirty prints (including the *For My People* portfolio) by Catlett, and in 2006, the University of Iowa Art in State Buildings acquired the sculpture *Stepping Out* (2000) for the Iowa Memorial Union. I visited Catlett in her home in August 2004 to select the prints for the museum. In 2006, Catlett created an endowed Elizabeth Catlett Mora Scholarship to benefit deserving undergraduate or graduate UI art students in printmaking who are African American or Latino.

33. Johnson, quoted in Herzog, *Elizabeth Catlett*, 19.

34. See Richard Melvin Breaux, "A Comparative Study of African American Students' Experiences at White Colleges: Nineteenth Century to the Pioneers Who Desegregated the Southern Flagship Schools" (PhD thesis, University of Iowa, 1998); John R. Crist,

"The Negro of Iowa City, Iowa: A Study in Negro Leadership and Racial Accommodation" (PhD thesis, State University of Iowa, 1945); Dungy, "African American Graduate School Experiences."

35. "Elizabeth Catlett, National Visionary," National Visionary Leadership Project, accessed March 2, 2016, http://www.visionaryproject.org/catlettelizabeth/.

36. Catlett, Breaux questionnaire.

37. Catlett and Mora interviews by Johnson.

38. Derived by Melanie Herzog from interviews conducted by Glory Van Scott (1981), Clifton Johnson (1984), Camille Billops (1989), and Herzog (1991 and 1993) in the Elizabeth Catlett Papers, Amistad Research Center, Tulane University, New Orleans, Louisiana, and quoted in Herzog, *Elizabeth Catlett*, 13.

39. Elizabeth Catlett, "Sculpture in Stone: Negro Mother and Child" (MFA thesis, State University of Iowa, Iowa City, June 1940), 1.

40. Catlett interview with Herzog.

41. Catlett, "Sculpture in Stone," 3.

42. Ibid., 2.

43. Ibid.

44. Ibid., 5.

45. *Official Program and Guide Book, American Negro Exposition* (Chicago: Chicago Coliseum, July 4–September 2, 1940), 28.

46. Adam Green, *Selling the Race: Culture, Community, and Black Chicago, 1940–1955* (Chicago: University of Chicago Press, 2007), 12.

47. James A. Porter, *Modern Negro Art* (New York: Dryden Press, 1943), 142. Quoted in Lowery Stokes Sims, "Elizabeth Catlett: A Life in Art and Politics," in *Elizabeth Catlett Sculpture*, 13.

48. Lawrence Jackson, *Ralph Ellison: Emergence of Genius* (Athens: University of Georgia, 2002), 164–65.

49. Sims, "Elizabeth Catlett," 13.

50. Ibid.

51. Ibid.

52. Ibid.

53. Catlett interview by Herzog.

54. Samella Lewis, *African American Art and Artists* (Berkeley: University of California Press, 1990). In 1941 when Catlett was head of the art department at Dillard, one of her students was Samella Lewis, who also studied with Catlett at Hampton Institute and went on to become a renowned art historian, artist, curator, and educator. In 2001, Lewis authored the first Catlett monograph, titled *The Art of Elizabeth Catlett*.

55. Quoted in Jean Florman's "Her Vision Her Way," DocsRush, accessed March 2, 2016, http://www.docsrush.net/1700688/her-way-university-of-iowa.html.

56. Elizabeth Catlett, interview by Gerry Hadden on National Public Radio (NPR), January 18, 2003.

Chapter Three

1. Fanny M. McConnell to President Bluford, July 18, 1936, box 12, folder 4, Ralph Ellison Papers, Library of Congress (hereafter cited as Ellison Papers). I refer to Fanny by her first name to avoid confusion throughout the chapter. The biographical note that introduces the Ellison Papers provides the dates of her marriages. She was married to Rodney Higgins from 1936 to 1937, and she was married to Ligon Buford from 1939 to 1945. She married Ralph Ellison in 1946 and they remained married until his death in 1994. Although she was technically still married to Rodney Higgins when she wrote to President Bluford, she signed the letter "Fanny M. McConnell."

2. Fanny McConnell to Mabel R. Hastings, 13 August 1936, box 12, folder 5, Ellison Papers.

3. "Former Fisk University Student Is Honored with Degree at Iowa U," *Nashville World*, June 19, 1936.

4. Dean Kay wrote to President Jessup explaining the logic necessitating the name change. He argued, "The Department of Speech has so effectively developed the dramatic aspects of the Department that it seems but proper to give this phase of the work . . . more distinct recognition than it now has. Moreover, for administrative and budgetary reasons it would seem to be of advantage to differentiate the dramatic phases from the other phases of the Department. I, therefore, recommend that the name of the Department of Speech be changed to Department of Speech and Dramatic Art." Quoted in H. Clay Harshbarger, *Some Highlights of the Department of Speech and Dramatic Art* (Iowa City: University of Iowa, 1976), 16.

5. Ibid., 25. The university began taking bids for the construction of the new theater on October 9, 1934.

6. Ibid., 13, quoting Glenn Merry to H. C. H., 2 December 1975.

7. Hallie Flanagan to E. C. Mabie, 28 August 1935, series 4, box 4, folder Purple Mask, Theatre Arts Records, University of Iowa Libraries, Iowa City, Iowa (hereafter cited as TA Records).

8. Hallie Flanagan to E. C. Mabie, 15 September 1935, series 4, box 4, folder Purple Mask, TA Records.

9. "WPA Productions Scheduled," series 4, box 4, folder Purple Mask, TA Records.

10. In response to one of Flanagan's missives regarding FTP success in New York, Mabie responded with a threat: "I am beginning to doubt whether we are going to succeed in avoiding political control of federal theatre projects. I am glad you are getting some things accomplished in New York. Out here evidence is accumulating that we are going to lose. State organizations seem to be interested only in perpetuating a financial racket on a colossal scale designed to return Mr. Roosevelt and the democratic party. They have lost sight of even the relief objectives. However I am going to continue to insist that money be sent to States in which I know destitute people are in need. If it doesn't get there within a reasonable time I shall resign and give that to the press as the reason." E. C. Mabie to Hallie Flanagan, 20 November 1935, series 4, box 4, TA Records.

11. Harry Allen to E. C. Mabie, 12 December 1935, series 4, box 4, folder Iowa, Mabie, TA Records.

12. E. C. Mabie to Hallie Flanagan, 26 December 1935, series 4, box 4, folder Iowa, Mabie, TA Records.

13. Harry Allen to Hallie Flanagan, 11 January 1936, series 6, box 2, folder Negro Theatre Proj Plan, TA Records.

14. Harry Allen to E. C. Mabie, 11 January 1936, series 6, box 2, folder Negro Theatre Proj Plan, TA Records.

15. E. C. Mabie to Hallie Flanagan, 6 January 1936, series 4, box 4, folder Iowa, Mabie, TA Records.

16. "Mabie Tells Theater Plans: New Plays Interpreting Mid-West Life," *Press Citizen*, 20 August 1934, clipping in series 1, box 6, Summer Session 1934, TA Records.

17. Unidentified document quoting Mabie in Box 11, folder Green, Paul 1933–1934, Edward C. Mabie Papers, University of Iowa Libraries, Iowa City, Iowa (hereafter cited as Mabie Papers).

18. Maibaum went on to find great success as a longtime writer for James Bond movies. As his career took off first in New York and then in Hollywood, Maibaum's letters to Mabie sound a familiar strain of regret that he cannot return to the Midwest to capture an essential authenticity. In one missive sent as Mabie's health declined, Maibaum asserts, "I often think of you and the great start you gave me . . . the fundamentals you knocked into my head . . . and the premium you placed on vitality and practical rather than theoretic theatre. . . . You made it possible for me to write and to learn and I shall never forget it." Richard Maibaum to E. C. Mabie, 14 September 1950, box 11, folder Maibaum, Richard, 1931–1954, Mabie Papers.

19. Typescript page, Scrapbook Summer Session 1936, TA Records.

20. Richard Maibaum to E. C. Mabie, 11 December 1934, box 12, folder Maibaum, 1933–1955, Mabie Papers.

21. E. C. Mabie to Richard Maibaum, 13 December 1934, box 12, folder Maibaum, 1933–1955, Mabie Papers.

22. E. C. Mabie to Richard Maibaum, 13 January 1934, box 12, folder Maibaum, 1933–1955, Mabie Papers.

23. "Broadway to See Play Based on Iowa Farmers' Uprisings: Author Tells Its Background," *Des Moines Register*, June 30, 1935, clipping in series 1, box 6, Summer Session 1936, TA Records.

24. E. C. Mabie to Clark Barrett, 18 April 1933, box 11, folder Clark, Barrett 1931–1952, Mabie Papers.

25. E. C. Mabie to Langston Hughes, 10 January 1935, box MsL H85, folder 893ma, Mabie Papers.

26. Langston Hughes to E. C. Mabie, 24 January 1935, box MsL H85, folder 893ma, Mabie Papers.

27. "Building a House for Iowa's Art," *Daily Iowan*, March 28, 1934, clipping in series 1, box 6, Summer Session 1934, TA Records.

28. Fanny McConnell to Judge Hueston, 18 July 1936, box 12, folder 4, Ellison Papers.

29. Fanny McConnell to John Sengstacke, 28 December 1939, box 7, folder 8, Ellison Papers.

30. Fanny McConnell to Mrs. A. L. Anderson, 2 June 1933, box 12, folder 4, Ellison Papers.

31. Fanny Buford to Ligon Buford, 16 January 1942, box 12, folder 4, Ellison Papers.

32. Fanny McConnell to her mother, Willie Mae Jordan, 21 September 1932, box 2, folder 1, Ellison Papers.

33. Fanny McConnell, registration cards, 1934–1935, box 12, folder 10, Ellison Papers.

34. Fanny McConnell, "Bird in Hand (First Performance)," typescript, box 13, folder 2, Ellison Papers.

35. "The University of Iowa by Richard Maibaum," *Des Moines Register*, August 1935, clipping in series 1, box 6, Summer Session 1935, TA Records.

36. "Noah and his Ark to Ride Waves Again on University of Iowa Stage Next Thursday," newspaper clipping in series 1, box 6, Scrapbook 1933–1935, TA Records.

37. Fanny McConnell Buford, complete work record, 1942, box 13, folder 8, Ellison Papers.

38. Susan Glaspell to E. C. Mabie, 18 November 1936, box 11, folder Famous Authors 1923–1954, Mabie Papers.

39. Negro People's Theatre Constitution, article 1, box 6, folder 9, Ellison Papers.

40. Typescript page, Scrapbook Summer Session 1936, TA Records.

41. E. C. Mabie to Samuel Selden, 21 July 1953, box 11, folder E. P. Conkle, 1936–1954, Mabie Papers.

42. Fanny McConnell to Langston Hughes, 4 April 1938, box 6, folder 9, Ellison Papers.

43. Hallie Flanagan to E. C. Mabie, 1 September 1937, box 2, folder Federal Theater Project-Mrs. Hallie Flanagan 1936–1937, Mabie Papers.

44. Melissa Barton, "'Speaking a Mutual Language': The Negro People's Theatre in Chicago," *TDR: The Drama Review* 54, no. 3 (Fall 2010): 54.

45. Ibid., 55.

46. Fanny McConnell to Negro People's Theatre members, 8 September 1938, box 7, folder 2, Ellison Papers.

47. Ibid.

48. Fanny McConnell to Negro People's Theatre members, 20 March 1938, box 7, folder 2, Ellison Papers.

49. Ibid.

50. Albert Sutan to Fanny McConnell, 6 December 1938, box 6, folder 13, Ellison Papers.

51. Thomas Pawley, "Experimental Theatre Seminar; Or the Basic Training of Tennessee Williams: A Memoir," *Iowa Review* 19, no. 1 (1989): 65.

52. Thomas Pawley, telephone conversation with Lena M. Hill, August 6, 2014.

53. H. Clay Harshbarger, *Some Highlights of the Department of Speech and Dramatic Art* (Iowa City: University of Iowa Press, 1976), 24.

54. Pawley, "Experimental Theatre Seminar," 69, 67.

55. Ibid., 68. Pawley includes a complete list of the sketches along with brief descriptions.

56. Thomas Pawley, "Three Original One Act Plays of Negro Life," (MA Thesis, University of Iowa), 1939.

57. Ibid., 5.

58. Thomas Pawley, telephone conversation with Lena M. Hill, August 7, 2014.

59. Pawley, telephone conversation with L. Hill, August 6, 2014.

60. Ibid.

61. Ibid.

62. Barrett Clark to E. C. Mabie, December 1, 1952, box 11, folder Clark, Barrett 1931–1952, Mabie Papers.

63. Pawley, telephone conversation with L. Hill, August 7, 2014.

64. Ibid.

65. Creed of Purple Mask Society, series 9, box 1, folder Purple Mask, TA Records.

66. Pawley, telephone conversation with L. Hill, August 7, 2014.

67. Ted Shine, for instance, explained his decision to forgo a career writing for the stage and television as a direct result of how much he enjoyed "teaching and working with young people." Shine explained that he "had a genuine interest in the students" so that his "first obligation was to them." Quoted in Whitney LeBlanc, "An Interview with Ted Shine," *Studies in American Drama, 1946–Present* 8, no. 1 (1993): 38.

68. The majority of the information in this paragraph is found in the preface to *The Black Teacher and the Dramatic Arts: A Dialogue, Bibliography, and Anthology*, ed. William R. Reardon and Thomas D. Pawley (Westport, CT: Negro University Press, 1970), xi–xvi.

69. Rampersad, *Ralph Ellison*, 82–83.

70. Ralph Ellison, review of *Big White Fog* by Theodore Ward, *New Masses*, November 12, 1940.

71. For a broader discussion of Ralph and Fanny Ellison's interest in the stage and visual art, see Lena Hill's "Performing Political Responsibility: Ralph and Fanny Ellison's Appeal to Visual Arts," *American Studies* 54, no. 3 (2015): 83–100.

72. Ellison responded negatively to numerous inquiries requesting the right to translate his novel into a play, movie, and even a comic. See box 153, folder 4, and box 154, folder 7, Ellison Papers.

Chapter Four

1. Nipson's tenure at the Iowa Writers' Workshop preceded Harper's by about fifteen years. Although Walker never attended the University of Iowa with either Nipson or Harper, her two separate terms at the workshop closely bracketed each of theirs. She first graduated in 1940, six years before Nipson entered the program. Harper enrolled at the University of Iowa in January 1961, and after the spring semester, probably sometime in May, he returned to Los Angeles to work as a lifeguard. Walker spent the summer of 1961 in Iowa City talking to Paul Engle and taking classes with Verlin Cassell. This was as close as the two came to meeting since by the time Walker came back in fall of 1962, Harper was already teaching at Pasadena Community College.

2. Mark McGurl, *The Program Era: Postwar Fiction and the Rise of Creative Writing*

(Cambridge, MA: Harvard University Press, 2009). McGurl grounds his examination of higher education in creative writing programs, but his research raises the kinds of questions that have led thinkers such as Christopher Newfield to scrutinize the modern college and university. For examples of Newfield's theses, see *Ivy and Industry: Business and the Making of the American University* (Durham, NC: Duke University Press, 2003) and *Unmaking the Public University: The Forty Year Assault on the Middle Class* (Cambridge, MA: Harvard University Press, 2008).

3. For Glass's and Bennett's views of the Iowa Writers' Workshop, see Loren Glass, "Middle Man: Paul Engle and the Iowa Writers Workshop," *Minnesota Review* 71–72 (2009): 256–68; Eric Bennett, "How Iowa Flattened Literature," *Chronicle of Higher Education*, February 10, 2014.

4. Miranda Hickman and John McIntyre offer a good history of New Criticism in *Rereading the New Criticism* (Columbus: Ohio State University Press, 2009). While this philosophy certainly influenced instruction at the Iowa Writers' Workshop, it was not adopted exclusively.

5. Walter Sullivan, interview by Stephen Wilbers, transcript, February 2, 1976, Record of the Iowa Writers' Workshop, series 11, box 2, folder 4, University Archives, Department of Special Collections, University of Iowa Libraries, Iowa City, Iowa (hereafter cited as IWW Record).

6. Herbert Nipson to Jean W. Cash, 30 June 1995, Jean Cash Papers, Special Collections, Georgia College and State University, Milledgeville (hereafter cited as Cash Papers). For expansive accounts of the housing situation for Iowa's black students circa the 1940s, see Richard Breaux's "Maintaining a Home for Girls: The Iowa Federation of Colored Women's Clubs at the University of Iowa, 1919–1950," *Journal of African American History* 87 (Spring 2002): 236–55 and "Facing Hostility, Finding Housing: African American Students at the University of Iowa, 1920s–1950s," *Iowa Heritage Illustrated* (Spring 2002): 14–15.

7. Earl Caldwell, "Chapter 3: Leaving the Nest," in *The Caldwell Journals* (Oakland, CA: Maynard Institute for Journalism Education, 1999), http://www.localcommunities .org/servlet/lc_procserv/dbpage=cge&gid=00091000000967482594843765&pg=00 112000000970362712951024.

8. Ibid.

9. Whereas civil rights era narratives often associated poverty with dysfunction, Nipson grew up at a different moment. He observes, "It was no crime to be poor during the Depression." Because there was no stigma surrounding his situation, his outlook and his actions remained hopeful. "Backstage," *Ebony*, July 1973, 21.

10. Ibid.

11. Ibid.

12. Among Nipson's classmates, two examples dramatize the writer's suspension between journalistic work and postgraduate fine arts training. Flannery O'Connor received a scholarship to the Iowa School of Journalism, but she "crossed over" to do "shum storrowies." James B. Hall to Jean Wylder, n.d., IWW Record, series 12, box 1, folder 3. Notwithstanding such crossover, she "really expected to get a degree in journalism" Jean

Wylder, "Flannery O'Connor: A Reminiscence and Some Letters," *North American Review* 255, no. 1 (Spring 1970): 59. James Sunwall, who studied poetry and fiction, also relates that in spring 1950, he was "working on a newspaper in New Orleans" when Paul Engle, the visiting poet at LSU, lured him with descriptions of the Iowa Writers' Workshop (James Sunwall to Jean Wylder, 11 January 1973, IWW Record, series 12, box 1, folder 3).

13. Adeshina Emmanuel, "Former Ebony Magazine Executive Editor," *Chicago Sun-Times*, December 24, 2011.

14. Stephen Clark, "Oral History Interview with Earl Caldwell," 2004, http://knightpoliticalreporting.syr.edu/wp-content/uploads/2012/05/earl_caldwell_oral_essay.pdf.

15. Regarding black access to white Leftist journals, see Rachel Rubin and James Smethhurst, "Ann Petry's 'New Mirror,'" in *Revising the Blueprint: Ann Petry and the Literary Left*, ed. Alex Lubin, 15–34 (Jackson: University Press of Mississippi, 2007), 19.

16. Emmanuel, "Former Ebony Editor."

17. Paul Engle, "How Creative Writing Is Taught at University of Iowa Workshop," *Des Moines Sunday Register*, December 28, 1947.

18. Hall to Jean Wylder, IWW Record.

19. Wylder, "Flannery O' Connor," 62.

20. Gene Brzenk to Jean Wylder, 26 December 1972, IWW Record, series 12, box 1, folder 3.

21. Herb Nipson to Jean Cash, September 1993, Cash Papers.

22. Hank Messick to Stephen Wilbers, 21 July 1976, IWW Record, series 11, box 2, folder 4.

23. Nipson to Cash, 30 June 1995, Cash Papers. Advancing a hypothesis regarding O'Connor's privileged position, Hank Messick opines, "I still think one reason for [O'Connor's] success was her stories confirmed the prejudices many so-called intellectuals in New York felt about the south. Had her southern characters been a bit more optimistic, she would not have been so successful. That doesn't mean I don't consider her a great writer. She was. But her subject matter wouldn't go over so well today in this age of Jimmy Carter when a more balanced picture of the south is emerging." Messick to Wilbers, 21 July 1976, IWW Record.

24. In a pair of December 1947 articles about the Iowa Writers' Workshop, the only writer Engle mentions by name is "Miss Flannery O'Connor of Georgia" who won a $750 fellowship from Rinehart & Co. Engle, "How Creative Writing Is Taught."

25. Joseph Langland to Jean Wylder, 5 June 1973, IWW Record, series 12, box 1, folder 3.

26. Steve Orlen to Stephen Wilbers, n.d., IWW Record, series 11, box 2, folder 3.

27. Nipson's membership in Sigma Delti Chi, an organization that "discouraged black membership," is newsworthy in itself. Since his sponsors at Penn State "neglected to tell the national office that" the pledge they were nominating was black, Nipson "may have been the first black member" of the group "Backstage," *Ebony*, July 1973, 21.

28. Engle, "How Creative Writing Is Taught."

29. A sampling of Nipson's photo credits for the *Daily Iowan* includes pictures on pages 1, 3, 5, and 6 in the June 23, 1948, issue and on page 4 of the April 2, 1949, issue.

30. "Backstage," *Ebony*, July 1976, 20.

31. Hall to Wylder, IWW Record.

32. Herbert Nipson, "'The Handball Court' and Other Stories" (MFA thesis, University of Iowa, 1958), 66.

33. Michael Harper to Stephen Wilbers, 17 August 1976, IWW Record, series 11, box 2, folder 2.

34. *The Only One*, a 2012 exhibit sponsored by the Johnson County Historical Society and the African American Museum of Iowa.

35. Keith D. Leonard, "Modern American Poetry: Michael Harper's Life and Career," in *The Oxford Companion to African American Literature*, de. William L. Andrews, Frances Foster Smith, and Trudier Harris (New York: Oxford University Press, 1997), http://www.english.illinois.edu/maps/poets/g_l/harper/life.htm. As late as 2009, Harper still counted the fact that "you couldn't rent an apartment" as one of the arch ironies of his time in the "'Athens of the Midwest,' Iowa City, Iowa." Michael Harper, "Interview with John Hoppenthaler," December 2009, *Connotation Press* 4, no. 7 (March 2016), http://www.connotationpress.com/a-poetry-congeries-with-john-hoppenthaler/2009/december-2009/233-michael-s-harper-poetry.

36. John Gilgun to Jean Wylder, 29 December 1972, IWW Record, series 12, box 1, folder 4.

37. Harry Barba, "Correspondence with Jean Wylder," 31 July 1974, IWW Record, series 12, box 1, folder 5. Barba offers his impressions in "A Connecticut Yankee's View of Iowa — Both Eyes Open," a unpublished piece that he composed in 1962 as a rejoinder to Philip Roth's *Esquire* article "Iowa, A Very Far Country Indeed" (1962).

38. Michael Harper, "Every Shut-Eye Ain't Asleep," in *A Community of Writers: Paul Engle and the Iowa Writers' Workshop*, ed. Robert Dana (Iowa City: University of Iowa Press, 1999), 80.

39. Harper to Wilbers, IWW Record, series 11, box 2, folder 2.

40. M. Harper, "Every Shut-Eye Ain't Asleep," 80.

41. Ibid., 82.

42. Ibid., 83.

43. Harper to Wilbers, IWW Record.

44. Ibid.

45. Harper, "Every Shut-Eye Ain't Asleep," 83.

46. Lamenting the workshop's inability to help him discover a jazz aesthetic, Harper states that he could not infuse his work with the "genius" of Billie Holiday and Harry Sweets Edison when he had "no models closeby except white Englishmen and white ex--G.I.s" Harper, "Interview With John Hoppenthaler."

47. Lewis Turco to Jean Wylder, 5 February 1973, IWW Record, series 12, box 1, folder 5.

48. Norman Peterson to Stephen Wilbers, 30 April 1976, IWW Record, series 11, box 2, folder 4.

49. Harper, "Every Shut-Eye Ain't Asleep," 87.

50. Ibid., 87.

51. Describing his interactions with Jones, Levine stated, "I came to Iowa in Sept. of 1953. The first person I met there was Calvin Jones." He continues, "My best friend was

a man in Social Work, a tall, husky Black guy named Larry Burke. Coming from Detroit & having just finished a long period of heavy work in factories, etc, I felt rather diffident with many of the workshop people, who struck me as artsy, remote. . . . I got to know Cal Jones fairly well; we used to eat in the same diner in the morning, and I played basketball with him and his buddies and Larry Burke." Philip Levine to Stephen Wilbers, 5 February 1976, IWW Record, series 11, box 2, folder 3. Jones is a legend in Iowa football, and one of his more memorable quotes concerned his recruitment. Asked why he had switched his allegiance from Ohio State to Iowa at the eleventh hour, he quipped, "I'll tell you why I came out here. They treated my [sic] like a white man, and I like it here. I'm going to stay." "Gridiron Glory: 100+ Years of Iowa Football," http://www.iowalum.com/magazine /football_history/1952.html.

52. Harper, "Every Shut-Eye Ain't Asleep," 81.

53. Ibid., 85.

54. Ibid.

55. In 2009, Harper gave a more detailed account of Jackson's impact on his budding artistic attitude: "We [Jackson and I] spent hours discussing 'The African Continuum,' 'Bantu Philosophy,' The Golden Stool of Akan Philosophy . . . Amos Tutuola's *The Palm-Wine Drunkard*, and most importantly *Things Fall Apart* by Chinua Achebe." Harper, "Interview with John Hoppenthaler."

56. Regarding Ellison, the black arts movement, and 1960s literature, see the introduction to *The Ethics of Swagger* by Michael DeRell Hill (Columbus: Ohio State University Press, 2013).

57. Harper, "Every Shut-Eye Ain't Asleep," 85.

58. M. Hill, *Ethics of Swagger*, 19.

59. For more on the New Breeds, see Larry Neal, "The Black Arts Movement," in *The Columbia Guide to Contemporary African American Literature*, ed. Daryl Dickson-Carr (New York: Columbia University Press, 2005); William R. Nash, "Black Arts Movement," in *The Oxford Encyclopedia of American Literature*, ed. Jay Parini (Oxford: Oxford University Press, 2003).

60. Michael Harper, "Blues and Laughter," (MFA thesis, University of Iowa, 1963), 5.

61. Ibid., 6.

62. Ibid., 22.

63. Harper to Wilbers," IWW Record.

64. Harper, "Every Shut-Eye Ain't Asleep," 86.

65. Ibid., 87.

66. Describing how institutions such as Penn, Oxford, and Iowa affected his artistic outlook, Wideman stated that he believed that he "had to prove something about black speech . . . and about black culture." He thought that he needed "a quote from T.S. Eliot" or "a Joycean allusion" to "authenticate" and "buttress" black expressions. Quoted in Bonnie TuSmith, *Conversations with John Edgar Wideman* (Jackson: University Press of Mississippi, 1998), 51.

67. Glass, "Middle Man."

68. Quoted in "Michael S. Harper," Poetry Foundation, accessed April 20, 2016, http://www.poetryfoundation.org/bio/michael-s-harper.

69. Harper, "Every Shut-Eye Ain't Asleep," 86.

70. Harper to Stephen Wilbers, IWW Record.

71. Engle makes this remark in his 1961 preface to *Midlands*, an anthology of writing by attendees of the Iowa Writers' Workshop. It is quoted in Robert Dana, preface to *Community of Writers*, vii.

72. Margaret Walker, *Margaret Walker: For My People*, California Newsreel, 1998.

73. Eugene Redmond associates Walker's poetry with stoicism in the article, "The Black American Epic: Its Roots, Its Writers," *Black Scholar* 2, no. 5 (January 1971): 15–22. Charles Rowell returns to this idea in "Poetry, History, and Humanism: An Interview with Margaret Walker," *Black World* 25, no. 2 (1973): 4–17.

74. Olga Opfell to Stephen Wilbers, 12 March 1976, IWW Record, series 11, box 2, folder 3.

75. Margaret Walker to Paul Engle, 21 March 1973, IWW Record, series 11, box 2, folder 1.

76. Ibid.

77. Walker, *Margaret Walker: For My People*.

78. Margaret Walker, "For My People: A Volume of Verse" (MFA thesis, University of Iowa, 1940), 11.

79. Ibid., 14.

80. Ibid., 24.

81. Ibid.

82. Ibid., 20.

83. Wallace Stegner, a student in the "Iowa writing program" before it was systematized, remembers that as early as 1930–1932, Stephen Vincent Benét was among the "occasional visitors" who presented. See Wallace Stegner to John Leggett, 13 March 1973, IWW Record, series 11, box 2, folder 4. Stephen Wilbers confirms Stegner's observation in *The Iowa Writers Workshop: Origins, Emergence, and Growth*, (Iowa City: University of Iowa Press, 1980), 26, 47.

84. Wilbers, *Iowa Writers Workshop*, 51.

85. Margaret Walker Journals, Journal 17, p. 8, Margaret Walker Center, Jackson State University, http://margaretwalker.jsums.edu/cdm/compoundobject/collection/uy/id/2640/rec/16.

86. Ibid., p. 19.

87. Ibid., p. 20.

88. Margaret Walker, "How I Wrote Jubilee," in *How I Wrote Jubilee and Other Essays* (New York: Feminist Press, 1990), 59.

89. Ibid., 53.

90. Hubbard, *New Dawns*, 22.

Chapter Five

1. "A Complex of Diamonds Called Pearl," UI *Spectator*, Fall 1999, 2; "UI Briefs: New Softball Complex to Be Named Pearl Field," *Iowa City Press Citizen*, July 16, 1999; "New Softball Complex to Be Named Pearl Field," *Daily Iowan*, July 16, 1999.

2. University of Iowa, "New Softball Field Is Nearly Complete, to Be Named Pearl Field," news release, July 15, 1999.

3. Letter from the associate director of Women's Intercollegiate Athletics–UI Foundation to Richard M. Breaux, 29 September 1999; UI news release.

4. Ibid.

5. Richard Breaux to Mark Jennings, senior director of development for Intercollegiate Athletics, 27, September 1999; David R. McMahon, "Remembering Black and Gold: African Americans, Sports Memory, and University of Iowa," in *Sport and Memory in North America*, ed. Stephen G. Wieting (Portland, OR: Frank Cass, 2001), 69, 95.

6. Philip G. Hubbard, *My Iowa Journey: The Life Story of the University of Iowa's First African American Professor* (Iowa City: University of Iowa Press, 1999); Hubbard, *New Dawns*; David R. McMahon, "Pride to All: African Americans and Sports in Iowa," in *Outside In: African American History in Iowa, 1838–2000*, ed. Bill Silag, Susan Koch-Bridgeford, and Hal Chase (Des Moines: SHSI, 2001), 470–85; McMahon, "Remembering Black and Gold," 63–98. A recent addition that also treats African Americans athletes as one-dimensional is an online review of Neal Rosendaal, "African Americans in Hawkeye Sports, 1895–1961," accessed September 22, 2013, http://nealrozendaal.com/2013/02/23/african-americans-in-hawkeye-sports-1895–1961/.

7. Ralph Ellison, *Invisible Man* (New York: Vintage International, 1990), 7–8.

8. John Hoberman, *Darwin's Athletes: How Sport Has Damaged Black America and Preserved the Myth of Race* (Boston: Houghton Mifflin, 1997); Eleanor Metheny, "Some Differences in the Bodily Proportions between American Negro and White Male College Students as Related to Athletic Performance," *Research Quarterly* 10 (December 1939): 41–53; David K. Wiggins, "Prized Performers, but Frequently Overlooked Students: The Involvement of Black Athletes in Intercollegiate Sports on Predominantly White University Campuses, 1890–1972," *Research Quarterly for Exercise and Sport* 62, no. 2 (June 1991): 164–77; David K. Wiggins, "Great Speed, but Little Stamina: The Historical Debate over Black Athletic Superiority," in *Glory Bound: Black Athletes in a White America* (Syracuse, NY: Syracuse University Press, 1997), 178–79.

9. William C. Rhoden, *Forty Million Dollar Slaves: The Rise, Fall, and Redemption of Black Athletes* (New York: Crown, 2006), 2–4.

10. Ellison, *Invisible Man*, 3.

11. Rhoden, *Forty Million Dollar Slaves*, 3.

12. W. E. B. DuBois, "The Year in Negro Education," *Crisis* (1930): 262–63; W. E. B. DuBois, "The Year in Negro Education, 1931," *Crisis* (1931): 262; Gabriel Victor Cools, "A Study of the Negro in Three Iowa Communities" (master's thesis, University of Iowa, 1918); Herbert Crawford Jenkins, "The Negro Student at the University of Iowa: A Sociological Study" (master's thesis, University of Iowa, 1933). The racial reality at UI continued to be contradictory. By the 1950s, future Hawkeye football and wrestling star Donald Tucker remembered that Iowa played African American players Calvin Jones, Frank Gilliam, Eddie Vincent, John Burroughs, and Mike Hagler in the same game and they were not being stacked in the same position, but on the "field at the same time" (Donald W. Tucker, *The Two-Edged Sword* [Indianapolis: Dog Ear Publishing, 2010], 36). This combined with Iowa being the alma mater of Cook County justice Frederick "Duke" Slater virtually guaranteed Tucker would apply to Iowa.

13. Jenkins, "Negro at University of Iowa," 21.

14. Sister Mary Constance Murray, "Term Paper, History 16:166," 6, University of Iowa Archives.

15. Estes later injured himself while playing basketball on a Des Moines playground during summer vacation. Estes tripped backward over another player and was paralyzed from the waist down, thus ending his Iowa football career. Although unable to play as a patient at the University of Iowa hospital, Estes attended the Iowa–Purdue game in 1948; "John Estes Leaves Hospital," *Daily Iowan*, February 23, 1949; Leola Bergmann, "Negro Students in Town Area, Second Semester 1946–47," Leola Bergmann Papers, State Historical Society of Iowa, Iowa City.

16. "Negro Couple Says Iowa Citians Prejudiced," *Daily Iowan*, August 13, 1955.

17. J. H. Mosby, "Southern Atmosphere," *Daily Iowan*, March 29, 1955.

18. Edwin Demoney and Dennis Robinson, "Race Relations," *Daily Iowan*, March 29, 1955.

19. William Edwin Taylor to James Weldon Johnson, 2 November 1921, series C, part 12, reel 10, frame 0598, NAACP Papers, microfilm, University of Iowa Law Library; James Weldon Johnson to William Edwin Taylor, 10 November 1921, series C, part 12, reel 10, frame 600, NAACP Papers, microfilm; James Weldon Johnson to L. M. Brown, 12 November 1921, series C, part 12, reel 10, frame 0604, NAACP Papers, microfilm; James Weldon Johnson to Mrs. Thetha E. Graham, 12 November 1921, series C, part 12, reel 10, frame 0606, NAACP Papers, microfilm; L. Black to R. Hurley, 5 April 1950, series B, part 19, reel 25, frame 0128, NAACP Papers, microfilm. In 1950, there were fifty-seven student members of the NAACP at UI; Howard Wolf to NAACP, 14 June 1955, series C, part 19, reel 26, frame 0723, NAACP Papers, microfilm; Herbert L. Wright to Howard Wolf, 15 July 1955, series C, part 19, reel 26, frame 0617, NAACP Papers, microfilm.

20. "Racial Problems in Housing Told," *Daily Iowan*, 7 December 1960.

21. Ibid.

22. Richard M. Breaux, "To the Uplift and Protection of Young Womanhood: African American Women at Iowa's Private Colleges and the University of Iowa, 1878–1928," *History of Education Quarterly* 50, no. 2 (May 2010): 176.

23. "Champion Hurdler Sued for Divorce," *San Antonio Light*, November 16, 1927; "Mrs. Seashore Gets Divorce; Brookins Sued," *Davenport Democrat and Leader*, November 16, 1927; "Relieve Charles Brookins of Old Gold Staff Duty," *Mason City Globe Gazette*, November 5, 1930.

24. Richard M. Breaux, "Women of 942 Iowa Avenue and other African American Women at the University of Iowa before 1947," unpublished manuscript in author's possession.

25. Sherman Howard quoted in Aaron Cohen, *The Forgotten Four: The Integration of Pro Football*, produced and directed by Johnson McKelvy (New York: EPIX–Ross Greenburg Productions, 2014), DVD.

26. See Don Tucker's testimonial, "The Two-Edged Sword," in this volume, following this chapter.

27. For a firsthand account of black professional gatherings connected to sporting

events in Iowa City, see Lois Eichaker's testimonial, "Iowa Was One More Step toward My Future," in this volume.

28. The soccer squad was UI's most racially diverse in history at the time with two Chinese, one East Indian, and an African American on the team. Off the field White wrote for the campus literary magazine, served as a correspondent to his fraternity's national magazine, hosted a campus radio program, and belonged to a host of campus groups including the racially liberal YMCA and Cosmopolitan Club. "The Year in Negro Education," *Crisis* (August 1930): 265; *Hawkeye* yearbook (1930), 300: *Hawkeye* yearbook (1929), 296.

29. See Richard M. Breaux, "We Must Fight Racial Prejudice Even More Vigorously in the North: Black Higher Education in America's Heartland" (PhD diss., University of Iowa, 2003), 285–86; McMahon, "Remembering Black and Gold"; Archie A. Alexander to Leola Nielson Bergmann, 24 November 1947, in Correspondence and Notes of Leola Bergmann, folder 2, SHSI(IC). For comment by Highland Park College officials, see W. E. B. DuBois, *The College-Bred Negro American: Proceedings of the 15th Annual Conference for the Study of the Negro Problems* (Atlanta: Atlanta University, 1910), 29–33; "Highland Park College Closed Against Negro," *Bystander*, 11 September 1908.

30. Raymond A. Smith, "He Opened Holes Like Mountain Tunnels," *Palimpsest* 66 (1985): 99. Also see Charles E. Wynes, "'Alexander the Great,' Bridge Builder," *Palimpsest* 66 (1985): 78–86. Ironically, President George MacLean would not let other schools discriminate against Iowa's black players during games in Iowa City, but he compromised by not playing black players in away games if the opponent protested. Archie Alexander was the player at the center of this debate. See W. N. Romidy to George McLean [*sic*], 21 November 1910, box 26, folder 4, George MacLean Papers, University of Iowa Archives, Iowa City (hereafter cited as MacLean Papers); George MacLean to W. N. Romidy, 28 November 1910, box 26, folder 4, MacLean Papers; A. Ross Hill to MacLean, 30 November 1910, box 25, folder 1, MacLean Papers; George MacLean to A. Ross Hill, 7 December 1910, box 25, folder 1, MacLean Papers; Stow Persons, *The University of Iowa in the Twentieth Century* (Iowa City: University of Iowa Press, 1990), 40.

31. Archie Alexander's experiences prompt impassioned, yet inaccurate accounts. For example, Arthur R. Ashe, Jr. incorrectly argues that UI simply refused to play Missouri, and he misidentifies Archie Alexander. See Ashe, *Hard Road to Glory: A History of the African American Athlete*, vol. 1, *1619–1918* (New York: Amistad Press, 1988), 94.

32. "Men Who Participated," *Hawkeye* yearbook (1911), npn; "Men Who Participated," *Hawkeye* yearbook (1912), 243; Wynes, "Alexander the Great'" 79; Smith, "He Opened Holes," 87–100.

33. *Hawkeye* yearbook (1913), 186.

34. "Jim Crow Sentiment Costly," *Davenport Times*, November 19, 1910; Romidy to McLean [*sic*], 21 November 1910; MacLean to Romidy, 28 November 1910; A. R. Hill to MacLean, 30 November 1910; MacLean to A. R. Hill, 7 December 1910; Persons, *University of Iowa in Twentieth Century* 40.

35. Jenkins, "Negro Student at University of Iowa," 32; "Capital City Bars Negro Grid Stars," *Bystander*, November 4, 1932. Wallace and Dickerson were members of Alpha

Theta chapter of Alpha Phi Alpha at UI, "Alpha Theta Stages Charity Football Game," *Sphinx*, December 1931, 31–32.

36. Historian Richard Kluger argues that Washington was dominated by racist protective housing covenants and deeply internalized racism despite the presence of Howard University. Washington was one of the cities named in the original *Brown v. Board of Education* suit before the district changed its policy to avoid the perception of the US Supreme Court's bias. Richard Kluger, *Simple Justice: The History of Brown v. Board of Education and Black America's Struggle for Equality* (New York: Vintage, 1977), 115–16.

37. Elmer A. Carter, "The Negro in College Athletics," *Opportunity*, July 1933, 209.

38. "Grid Ace Gets Two Jim Crow Doses," *Washington Afro-American*, October 15, 1938; Thomas Aiello, *The Kings of Casino Park: Black Baseball in the Lost Season of 1932* (Tuscaloosa: University of Alabama Press, 2011), 146; Jenkins, "Negro Student at University of Iowa," 32; "Capital City Bars Negro Grid Stars."

39. "Iowans Head to Two Towns for Big Game," *Minneapolis Spokesman*, November 6, 1936; "Bell, Reed, Ozzie Simmons, Harris, and D. Simmons," *Minneapolis Spokesman*, November 6, 1936."Don Simmons Is Capable Reserve End," *Minneapolis Spokesman*, October 9, 1936.

40. *Crisis*, November 1934, cover and 329.

41. "Iowans Head to Two Towns"; "Pan-Hellenic-Home Coming Committees," *Minneapolis Spokesman*, November 6, 1936.

42. "Hawkeyes Fail to Stop Gophers," *Twin-City Herald*, November 14, 1936.

43. Roy Wilkins, "Negro Stars on Big Grid Teams," *Crisis*, December 1936, 362–63.

44. Bob Hogan, "Homer Harris Elected to Lead Hawkeyes on the Field Next Year," *Daily Iowan*, December 8, 1936; Homer Harris, telephone interview with Richard Breaux, February 9, 2002.

45. "Brookins Breaks World's 220 Hurdle Record," *Daily Iowan*, May 6, 1923; "Brookins to Lead Iowa's Track Team," May 23, 1923; "Charles Brookins Sets National A.A.U. Record," *Daily Iowan*, July 5, 1925.

46. Skinner grew up hearing stories of fellow black Omaha native Ledrue C. Galloway, who played for the Hawkeye football team in the 1920s and was a member of Kappa Alpha Psi; see William L. Crump and C. Rodger Wilson, *The Story of Kappa Alpha Psi*, 2nd ed. (Philadelphia: Kappa Alpha Psi Fraternity, 1972), 76. Skinner also pledged Kappa Alpha Psi at UI and earned his BA and MA from Iowa. He went on to become the first African American principal and assistant superintendent of schools in Omaha.

47. "Oskaloosa Negro to Head Harriers," *Iowa City Press Citizen*, November 10, 1936; "Varsity Track," *Hawkeye* yearbook (1938), 300, 302, 303, 310.

48. "Charles Brookins, Assistant Coach," *Hawkeye* yearbook (1929), 236, *Hawkeye* yearbook (1930), 298, *Hawkeye* yearbook (1931), 299; Eugene Mallory preceded Nelson by seven years. Mallory ran on the freshman cross-country team in 1929 and on the varsity cross-country team in 1930. See "Freshman Cross Country," *Hawkeye* yearbook (1930), 298; "Varsity Cross Country," *Hawkeye* yearbook (1931), 298.

49. "Simon Roberts First Negro to Win Mat Title," *Iowa Bystander*, April 4, 1957.

50. Arthur R. Ashe Jr., *Hard Road to Glory: A History of the African American Athlete,*

vol. 2, *1919–1945* (New York: Amistad Press, 1988), 72; "Boxing," *Hawkeye* yearbook (1932), 300; "Boxing," *Hawkeye* yearbook (1934), 256.

51. "Sweet Revenge," *Indiana University Arbutus* yearbook (1945), 181.

52. "Hawks Fall to Miami in Finale, 14–6," *Daily Iowan*, November 25, 1950; Samuel G. Freedman, *Breaking the Line: The Season in Black College Football That Transformed the Sport and Changed the Course of Civil Rights* (New York: Simon and Schuster, 2013), 215.

53. "Cites Prejudice at Kansas City," *Daily Iowan*, March 25, 1955; Arlo Jacobson, "O'Connor Terms Discrimination 'Unfortunate'," *Daily Iowan*, March 25, 1955; George E. Bolden, "Cites Prejudice at Kansas City," *Daily Iowan*, March 25, 1955. By 1957, UI had five African American players on the men's varsity basketball team: Bobby Washington, Nolden Gentry, Americus John-Lewis, Clarence Wordlaw, and Thomas Payne.

54. Roberts quoted in Mark Palmer, "InterMat Rewind: Simon Roberts," InterMat Wrestling, June 14, 2007, accessed March 22, 2016, https://intermatwrestle.com/articles/2813. Other African American wrestlers at UI, such as Don Tucker and Wilbur Devine, would follow in Roberts's footsteps.

55. *Hawkeye* yearbook (1925), 273; Hubbard, *New Dawns*, 26; University of South California *Daily Trojan*, November 17, 1930; *Hawkeye* yearbook (1926), 242, 257, 275, 339; *Hawkeye* yearbook (1930), 298; *Hawkeye* yearbook (1931), 299. Brookins was fired in 1930 when in a public divorce it was revealed that he was cheating on his wife. One year later he was charged with bigamy for being married to two other women; see "Brookins' Wife Files an Action for Divorce," *Milwaukee Journal*, November 16, 1927, "Granted Divorce," *St. Petersburg Times*, December 2, 1927; "Brookins' Case Is Continued," *Milwaukee Journal*, January 2, 1931. While it fails to note that Brookins was African American and to name the particpants in the scandal, a book by Mike Finn and Chad Leistikow does mention Brookins's firing for getting "married, divorced, and married again." See Finn and Leistikow, *Hawkeye Legends, Lists and Lore: The Athletic History of the Iowa Hawkeyes* (Champaign, IL: Sports Publishing, 1998), 52.

56. All of the following from National Archives and Records Administration (NARA), Washington, DC: Passport Applications, January 2, 1906–March 31, 1925, ARC Identifier 583830 / MLR Number A1 534, NARA Series M1490, roll 2522; Thirteenth Census of the United States, Oskaloosa Ward 2, Mahaska, Iowa, roll T624_412, p. 3A; Enumeration District 0074, FHL microfilm 1374425, Fourteenth Census of the United States, Oskaloosa Ward 3, Mahaska, Iowa (1920), roll T625_501, p. 14A; Enumeration District 81, image 278.

57. Neither John C. Gerber nor Philip Hubbard ever raised this question in any of their books; however, Neal Rosendaal does in "African Americans in Hawkeye Sports, 1895–1961." Gerber doesn't mention the race of any of UI's early Olympians. John C. Gerber, *A Pictorial History of The University of Iowa* (Iowa City: University of Iowa Press, 1988), 126.

58. Finn and Leistikow, *Hawkeye Legends, Lists and Lore*, 39, 47, 52; McMahon, "Remembering Black and Gold," 68; Rosendaal, "African Americans in Hawkeye Sports, 1895–1961."

59. Wiggins, "Prized Performers, but Frequently Overlooked Students."

60. *Daily Iowan*, February 6, 1957.

61. It took a massive campaign in 1967 to bring about fair and open housing policies to Louisville, Kentucky, a campaign which included Charles E. Kirby, Dr. Martin Luther King Jr., and Rev. Alfred D. King. Cassius Clay left a segregated Louisville to fight in the 1960 Olympic Games in Rome.

62. By the late 1950s and early 1960s, men's fencing and men's gymnastics teams included Orville Townsend (fencing) and Elvin Walker and James Liddell (gymnastics). Two black students also earlier made UI's gymnastics team, one in 1933 and one in 1936. Golf had been desegregated by George Roddy by 1929; "Golf," *Hawkeye* yearbook (1929), 289; "Golf," *Hawkeye* yearbook (1933), 255; *Hawkeye* yearbook (1933), 309. Roddy also won the "UGA, Negro amateur championships in Casa Loma, Wisconsin in 1930."

63. "Martin Luther King, Jr. Itinerary, October–November 1958," Martin Luther King Jr. Center for Nonviolent Social Change Digital Archive, accessed March 22, 2016, http://www.thekingcenter.org/archive/document/mlks-itinerary-october-november-1958; Martin Luther King Jr., "The Future of Integration," November 11, 1959, Martin Luther King Jr. Center for Nonviolent Social Change Digital Archive, accessed March 22, 2016, http://www.thekingcenter.org/archive/document/future-integration-1; "Ask Action on Bias in Frats," February 17, 1960, clippings located in the Federal Bureau of Investigation–Freedom of Information Act Collection #06–00, box 2, folder 1, University of Iowa Archives, Iowa City, IA; Walter Shotwell, "SUI Frat Racial Bars Are Argued," March 1, 1960, clipping in FBI-FOIA file #06–00, box 2, folder 1, UI Archives; Jerry Grossman, "Whatever Happened to SUI's Racial Equality Policy?" *Daily Iowan*, December 14, 1962; "SUI Losing Opportunity to Protest Segregation," *Daily Iowan*, December 14, 1962; "Negro Loses Court Fight in Clemson Case," *Chicago Daily Tribune*, December 22, 1962.

64. "Black Players Ask Support of All University Athletes," *Daily Iowan*, April 25, 1969; Connie Hughes, "University Is a Ghetto, Blacks Charge at Rally," *Daily Iowan*, April 25, 1969.

65. "Coming to SUI Duke Ellington and His Famous Orchestra in Concert, March 11," *Daily Iowan*, February 23, 1949; "Pearl Buck, 'Duke' Ellington on Union Program This Week," *Daily Iowan*, March 3, 1951; Duke Ellington Plays Here," *Daily Iowan*, March 14, 1953; "35th Annual Day of Dad Set at SUI," *Daily Iowan*, October 29, 1957; Ken Vail, *Duke's Diary: The Life of Duke Ellington, 1950–1974* (Lanham, MD: Scarecrow Press, 2002), 30, 3, 298.

66. Betty Jean Furgerson interview, n.d., posted on Iowa Public Television website as "Jazz in Iowa: Betty Jean (BJ) Furgerson's Memories," accessed March 22, 2016, http://www.iptv.org/jazz/bj_furgerson.cfm.

Testimonial Five

1. This testimonial is excerpted from Donald W. Tucker, *The Two-Edged Sword* (Indianapolis: Dog Ear Press, 2010).

Conclusion

1. For an extended look at the white savior film, see Matthew Hughey, *The White Savior Film: Content, Critics, and Consumption* (Philadelphia: Temple University Press, 2014).

2. David Sirota, "Oscar Loves a White Savior," *Salon*, February 21, 2013, http://www.salon.com/2013/02/21/oscar_loves_a_white_savior/.

3. Jones made this remark to the Big Ten commissioner who was investigating his decision to attend the University of Iowa notwithstanding his long ties to Ohio State. It is quoted in Stephen G. Wieting, *Sport and Memory in North America* (Portland, OR: Frank Cass, 2001), 82.

4. In this regard, McPherson follows in the footsteps of John Edgar Wideman. A Rhodes scholar who finished his term in 1965, Wideman attended the Iowa Writers' Workshop in 1966–1967 and completed his first novel, *A Glance Away* (1967), while he was in residence.

5. James A. McPherson to Ralph Ellison, 22 January 1970, box 57, folder 4, Ellison Papers.

6. James Alan McPherson, *Crabcakes* (New York: Simon and Schuster, 1998), 82.

7. James A. McPherson, "Introduction," *Ploughshares* 34, no. 2/3 (2008): 5.

8. James A. McPherson, "The Done Thing," *Ploughshares* 16, no. 2/3 (1990): 2.

9. Ibid., 3.

10. Ellison, *Collected Essays*, 379–80.

11. McPherson to Ellison, 22 January 1970.

12. James A. McPherson, "Pursuit of the Pnuema," *Daedalus*, Winter 2011, 184.

13. Ibid.

14. Ralph Ellison, *Shadow and Act* (New York: Vintage, 1964), 105–6.

15. Ellison, *Invisible Man*, 580.

16. McPherson to Ellison, 22 January 1970.

17. Ta-Nehisi Coates, "What Obama Means for . . . King's Legacy." *Washington Post*, November 8, 2008, http://www.washingtonpost.com/wp-dyn/content/article/2008/11/07/AR2008110702897.html.

18. Ta-Nehisi Coates, "Sarah Palin and White Privilege," *Atlantic*, September 16, 2008, http://www.theatlantic.com/entertainment/archive/2008/09/sarah-palin-and-white-privilege/5883/.

19. Stephen Bloom, "Observations from 20 Years of Iowa Life," *Atlantic*, December 9, 2011; Joe Blair, *By the Iowa Sea* (New York: Scribner, 2012); Marybeth Slonneger, *The Burg* (Iowa City: Hand Press, 2011); Eric Bennett, "How Iowa Flattened Literature," *Chronicle of Higher Education*, February 10, 2014.

20. Ellison, *Shadow and Act*, 105–6.

INDEX

Note: Page numbers in *italics* refer to illustrations

Abbe, George, 126
"Address to America" (Walker), 128
Aden, Alonzo J., 53, 63
advanced degrees. *See* graduate and professional education
African American Museum of Iowa, 118
agency, black, 176
Alexander, Archie, 147, 153, 155–56, 210n30
Alison's House (Glaspell), 88
Allen, Harry, 79–80
Allred, James V., 22
Alpha Kappa Alpha, 46, 153, 158
Alpha Phi Alpha: alumni visits with members of, 153; and Culberson, 149; and home games, 153, 158; housing offered by, 147, 148; meals offered by, 148; *Sphinx* publication of, 145; and White, 155
Alpha Tau Omega, 166
alumni of University of Iowa, 146, 153, 157
Ames, Jessie Daniel, 22
Anderson, Edison Holmes: breakdown suffered by, 28–29; faculty positions of, 43, 194n67; and funding for out-of-state education, 22, 27, 192n37; graduate education of, 28, 29, 30, 35, 192n40, 195n86
Anderson, Gloria Edwards, 28–29, 35
Anderson, Marian, 10, 40
Anderson, Thomas Jefferson "T. J.," 42
Armstrong, Louis, 166–67

Arnett, Betty Jean, 150
artists, Ellison's advice to, 9–10
arts departments: degrees awarded in, 196n2; and historically black colleges and universities, 7; interracial collaboration in, 9; and size of black student population, 2. *See also* specific departments
Ashford, James Timothy, 42–43
Associated American Artists (AAA), 59
athletic programs and black athletes, 141–67; and away games, 154, 155–58, 162–63, 210n30; baseball, 154; basketball, 154–55, 212n53; boxing, 161; and civil rights movement, 166; coaches of, 159–60, 161, 162, 163; *Crisis* coverage of, 157; and dining options, 148–50; expectations of black athletes, 144; and female companionship, 152–53; fencing, 213n62; football, 154, 155–60, 169–70, 171–72; freshmen sports, 142; golf team, 155, 213n62; gymnastics, 213n62; and Harper, 121, 124; and historically black colleges and universities, 7; and homecoming festivities, 153–54; and home games, 153, 210n30; and housing challenges, 145–48, 150–52; inconsistent treatment of athletes, 154, 162, 163; interracial collaboration in, 9; and invisibility of black athletes, 141–43, 144; Iowa–Minnesota game (1935), 158–59; and lodging during away games, 156, 162; and NCAA Men's Basketball Tournament (1955),

162–63; and number of black athletes on field, 154, 158, 169, 208n12; Olympic athletes, 138–39, 163–67, 213n61; progressive reputation of, 155, 156–57, 159, 161; recruitment of, 135–36; rifle club, 155; and scholastics, 137, 157, 165, 170–71; and size of black student population, 2; soccer team, 155, 210n28; and social opportunities, 158; swimming, 155; track and field, 154, 160–61, 164–65; and University of Missouri, 155, 210n31; Wheeler's experience in, 135–39; wrestling, 154–55, 161, 163, 172–73

Bach, Marcus, 88
Banks, Earl, 150
Barba, Harry, 118, 123
Barnes Foundation, 53
Barton, Melissa, 91
baseball, 154
basketball, 154–55, 212n53
Beebee: The Drama of Negro Lady Doctor (Lamb), 97
Belafonte, Harry, 4
Belk, George, 174
Bell, Horace, 158
Belle, Kenneth and Hulette, 103, 106
Benedict, H. Y., 23
Benét, Stephen Vincent, 128–29, 207n83
Bennett, Bernard, 162
Bennett, Eric, 107, 185
Berner, Bob, 120
Berry, Dora Martin, 14, 67–73
Berry, Henry, 143
Bethel AME Church of Iowa City, 46–47, 105
Big Ten schools, 124, 145, 155, 159
Big White Fog (Ward), 95, 101
Bird in the Hand (Housman), 87–88
Birthright (Maibaum), 88
Black, Hugo, 94
black arts movement, 132
Black Athletes Union, 166

black bourgeois taste, 108, 116, 133
The Black Teacher and the Dramatic Arts: A Dialogue, Bibliography, and Anthology (Pawley and Reardon), 99
Blair, Joe, 185
Bland, Leon, 150
Blattner, Helene, 75
"The Blonde Liberal" (Harper), 122
Bloom, Stephen, 184–85
"Blues and Laughter" (Harper), 122
Board of Education of Museum Extension Aid, 89
Boas, Franz, 31
Bob Pearl Softball Field, 141–42
Bontemps, Arna, 79, 127
Bourjaily, Vance, 1
boxing, 161
Bradley, Harold, 162
Bradshaw, Roy Eugene, 150
Breaux, Richard, 15, 121, 141–67, 183
Bremner, Barron, 163
Bresnahan, George, 2, 161
Bridgman, George B., 61
Briggs, Shirley, 196n2
Briggs, Wilson, 160
Brookins, Charles, 153, 161, 164, 212n55
Brooks, Gwendolyn, 129
Brown, Sterling, 127
Brown University, 108
Brown v. Board of Education, 25, 42, 211n36
Brzenk, Gene, 112, 120
Buford, Ligon, 87, 92, 199n1
The Burg (Slonneger), 185
Burke, Larry, 206n51
Burke, Selma, 63
Burns, Ben, 116
Burns, Jerry, 174
Burroughs, John, 169, 208n12
Butcher, James, 99
Buxton, Iowa, 7
By the Iowa Sea (Blair), 185

Cain, Carl "Sugar," 143, 162–63, 165

Caldwell, Earl, 109, 110

Caldwell, George Overall: advanced degree of, 19; as early graduate of music program, 31; as faculty at Rust College, 44; and Iowa's admission of black students, 18–19

Caldwell, Robert G., 174

Calloway, Cab, 10

Carnegie Institute of Technology, 52

Carpenter, C. E., 194n67

Cassill, Verlin, 130, 131, 132, 202n1

Catlett, Elizabeth, 13–14, 51–65; art history interests of, 59–60; committee of, 63–64; courses and grades of, 57; faculty positions of, 64, 194n67; family history of, 61; figures that influenced, 63; *For My People* (prints), 197n32; graduate education of, 51, 54, 55–60, 63–64; *Invisible Man* monument, 63, 64–65; and lithography, 59; living quarters of, 153; master's project of, 61; and Mexican art, 56–57; mother of, 61; *Negro Mother and Child*, 55, 62–63, 64; in official histories of UI, 175; scholarship established by, 197n32; sculptures of, 51, 55–56, 59, 60, 61, 62–63, 64, 197n32; *Stepping Out*, 197n32; success and status of, 8; thesis of, 61–62; undergraduate education of, 52–55; and Walker, 60, 197n32; and Wood, 11, 51, 55, 58, 59, 63–64

Chadwick, George W., 32

Charlot, Jean, 56–57

Chester, Illinois, 45–46

Civil Rights Act (1964), 10

civil rights movement: and determinative nature of race, 133; graduates' participation in, 8, 154; and Harper, 123; in Iowa City, 119; role of artistic/athletic performance in, 4, 144, 145, 158, 166; and segregated fraternities, 166; and Walker, 131; and white protestors, 123

Clapp, Philip Greeley: and academic pipeline, 13; and academic success of students, 39–40; and Anderson's graduate education, 29, 30, 195n86; on "color problem," 36–37; control of music department, 30; correspondence with students, 41; death of, 42; director duties assumed by, 30; and education of future HBCU faculty, 39; and Fuller, 17–18, 31, 32, 33, 34, 35; and gratitude of students, 40–41; influence of, 8; and Iowa's admission of black students, 19; legacy of, 41–42; and Mabie, 77; progressive reputation of, 2, 30; and racial climate in music department, 37–38, 39–40; "Of Science and Skulls," 30; and Southall, 195n92; on talent, 31

Clark, Alexander G., 7, 189n4

Clark, Barrett, 97

class-based discrimination, 46

Clay, Cassius, 165, 213n61

Clemson University, 166

Coates, Ta-Nehisi, 184

Cochran, J. P., 69

Coffee, J. C., 161–62

College Inn, 148

Coltrane, John, 122

Commack, Don, 162

Committee for State Aid for Negroes in Austin, Texas, 27

A Community of Writers: Paul Engle and the Iowa Writers' Workshop (Dana), 124

Congress of Racial Equality (CORE), 152

Conkle, E. P., 84, 94

Converse, Frederick Shepherd, 32

Cools, G. Victor, 148

Corbin, Delmar, 162

Coulette, Henri, 119

Crabcakes (McPherson), 178–79

Crawford, Robin, 142–43

Cretzmeyer, Francis, 2, 135–36, 138, 161

Crisis, 126, 145, 157

Crispus Attucks (Pawley), 96

Cross, George Lynn, 23–24
Crump, James W., 147
Culberson, Carl and Frances, 146
Culberson, Richard "Dick," 149
Cullen, Countee, 79, 125
Currier Five, 103–4
Currier Hall, 68, 104, 105, 150

Daily Iowan, 85, 113–14, 141, 162
Dallas Negro Chamber of Commerce, 21
Dana, Robert, 124
Davenport, Iowa, 7
Davenport Times, 156
Davis, Frank Greene, 34, 194n67
Davis, Frank Marshall, 121, 127
Davis, McKinley "Deacon," 143, 162
"The Deer Hunt" (Nipson), 115
"Delta" (Walker), 128
Delta Sigma Theta, 153
democratic pluralism, 15, 108, 132, 177, 180, 181–82
Dent, Albert Walter, 17–18, 36, 38
department of art, 51–65, 196n2. See also Catlett, Elizabeth
department of fine arts, 33, 76
department of graphic and plastic arts, 55
department of music: academic pipeline of, 7, 13, 19, 20, 35, 43–44; and academic success of students, 39–40; admission of black students, 18–19; advanced degrees earned by blacks in, 19; and Clapp's recommendation of Fuller, 17–18; and "color problem," 36–37; fine arts credits in, 33; first black student to attend, 31; and funding for out-of-state education, 26–27; and future faculty of HBCUs, 20, 39, 42; leadership of, 42–43 (see also Clapp, Philip Greeley); master's and doctoral theses produced in, 40; number of black students in, 36–37; racial climate in, 37–38, 39–40;

and radio programs, 33; and Rita Benton Library, 48; undergraduate faculty of, 20
department of speech and dramatic arts, 75–102; academic pipeline of, 99; and artistic philosophy of Mabie, 77, 82, 101; atmosphere of, 90; and black themes, 82, 94; building for, 11, 76, 81, 199n5; and doctorate of fine arts, 90; and drama societies, 98–99; and experimental theater, 14, 81–85; and Fanny Ellison, 88–89; founding of, 76; graduate students of, 77; and historically black colleges and universities, 77, 93, 99–100; influence of graduates from, 78; and interracial romances, 98; and Lamb's expulsion, 97–98; leadership of (see Mabie, Edward C.); and LeBlanc, 98; legacy of, 99, 102; name change of, 76, 199n4; and Pawley, 93–101; and playwrights, 94; and regionalism, 11, 14, 77, 81–83
desegregation/integration: and Brown v. Board of Education, 25, 42, 211n36; of dormitories, 103–4, 150, 152; and funding for out-of-state education, 23, 26–27; of graduate programs, 19, 22–23; narrative of, 133; ongoing process of, at UI, 9; and progressivism of UI, 2, 12; and theater department, 85; at University of Mississippi, 189n6; and white rescuers/redeemers, 177
Des Moines, Iowa, 7
Des Moines Register, 83
Dickerson, Voris, 156, 157, 210n35
Dillard University, 99
Distant Drums (Totheroh), 88
Dixson, Audrey, 69
Dodson, Owen, 100
Don't You Want to Be Free? (Hughes), 90, 91, 92, 95
Dooley, T. P., 34, 194n67
Douglas, Aaron, 54

Downs, Allen, 196n2
DuBois, W. E. B., 126, 127, 147, 159
Dungy, Madgetta Thornton, 35–36
Dunjee, Roscoe, 24

Ebony, 12, 108, 109, 113, 116, 117, 132
Edwards, Kathleen, 13–14, 51–65
Eichaker, Lois, 14, 103–6, 179
Eliot, T. S., 11, 132
Elizabeth Catlett Mora Scholarship,
    197n32
Ellington, Duke, 137, 166–67
Elliott collection of African art in the
    Museum of Art, 48
Ellison, Fanny, 3, 85–93; and Buford, 87,
    92; and drama scene of Iowa, 8; and
    Federal Theater Project (FTP), 89,
    91; graduation of, 75–76; job search of,
    75–76; marriages of, 199n1; memories
    of discrimination at UI, 1, 189n2; and
    Negro People's Theatre, 89–92; on
    theater and cultural identity, 101; and
    theater department, 88–89; and UI's
    role in racial drama of America, 4;
    undergraduate education of, 75–76,
    85–89; and Walker, 127
Ellison, Ralph, 3; on African American
    focused theater, 101; Catlett's memorial
    honoring, 63, 64–65; on democracy,
    182–83; and Eliot, 11; and Harper,
    122; and Hughes, 101; on invisibility
    of blacks, 143; and Iowa Writers' Work-
    shop, 1, 178, 189n2; and Langston Uni-
    versity, 35; marriage of, 199n1 (*see also*
    Ellison, Fanny); on maturity, 180; and
    McPherson, 178, 180, 181; and Neal,
    132; segregation metaphor of, 5–6; and
    UI's role in racial drama of America,
    4; "A Very Stern Discipline," 9–10; and
    Ward, 101; on white paternalism, 180;
    "The World and the Jug," 5–6, 183. See
    also *Invisible Man*
employment of black Americans, 36

Engle, Paul: favoritism exercised by, 112,
    204n24; and Harper, 118–20; influence
    of, on students, 8; prestige brought to
    UI by, 108; on process of writing, 113;
    and progressive reputation of UI, 2; re-
    cruiting efforts of, 204n12; on seminar
    system of Workshop, 111; on success
    stories, 125; and Walker, 126, 127–28,
    129, 132, 202n1
Estes, John M., 150, 209n15
Estes, Simon, 175
Euclid Club, 147
Evasheski, Forrest, 169, 172
extracurricular activities, 105

Farmer, Lee, 148
Federal Theater Project (FTP), 78–81, 89,
    91, 199n10
Felton, Norman, 94
feminism, black, 132
fencing, 213n62
Ferguson, Estella and Steve, 137, 148, 159
Finch, Gastro Lee, 138, 139
Fine Arts Summer Session, 33
Finney, Otis, 150
Fisher, Ada Lois Sipuel, 24, 25, 26, 27, 40,
    42
Fisher, Julie, 69
Fisk University, 86–87
Flanagan, Hallie, 78–80, 91, 199n10
Fleming, Willie, 172
Fletcher, Winona Lee, 99
Foerster, Norman, 108
football, 154, 155–160, 169–70, 171–72
For My People (Walker), 125
"For My People" poem (Walker), 128,
    197n32
"For My People" thesis (Walker), 128, 132
Ford, Nick Aaron, 127
Fountain of the Four Seasons (Petersen),
    54
Franklin, Jimmie Lewis, 20–21
Freedom in My Soul (Pawley), 94, 95

Freedom Riders, 123
Freels, Eugene, 150
Friar, Kimon, 127
Fuller, Meta Warrick, 63
Fuller, Oscar Anderson: ability to negoti-
    ate racial climate, 37–38; and academic
    pipeline, 8, 43; advanced degrees of, 19,
    33, 34; and Anderson, 28; background
    of, 31–32; and Clapp, 17–18, 31, 32, 33,
    34, 35; as early graduate of music pro-
    gram, 20, 31; faculty positions of, 33, 43,
    194n67; and funding for out-of-state
    education, 21, 22, 27, 192n37; graduate
    education of, 32–33, 34, 192n40, 193n58,
    194n61; and Iowa's admission of black
    students, 18–19; on ranking instruc-
    tors, 190n9; reputation of, 40; "The
    Teaching of Music in the Leading
    Negro Colleges," 33–34
Fuller, Oscar, Sr., 31–32, 40
funding for out-of-state education: and
    desegregation, 23, 26–27; impact of, on
    graduate school attendance, 34; legis-
    lation behind, 20–22, 191n18, 191n22;
    and Pawley, 96; proponents of, 23; in
    response to need for black profession-
    als, 191n10
Furgerson, Lee B., 154, 167
Furgerson, Lily, 167

Gaines, Lloyd, 23, 191n23
Gaines v. Canada, 23, 24, 34
Gallaway, Marian, 95, 99
Galloway, Ledrue C., 211n46
Gantt, Harvey B., 166
Gayden, Fern, 127
Geddes, Virgil, 88
Gentry, Nolden, 173, 212n53
George H. Scanlon Foundation, 141
George Washington University, 156, 157
Gerber, John, 108
Gibbons, Mary, 62
Gibson, Althea, 10

Gilgun, John, 118
Gillette, Arnold, 98
Gillette, JoEllen, 98
Gilliam, Frank, 169, 208n12
Gilpin Players, 101
Girls' Home, 148
Glaspell, Susan, 88, 89, 91
Glass, Alana, 194n67
Glass, Loren, 107, 123
Goins, Eddie, 44, 48
golf team, 155, 213n62
Gordon, Ed, 164–65
graduate and professional education:
    and admission of black students at
    UI, 18–19; in department of speech
    and dramatic arts, 77; desegregation
    of, 19, 22–23, 42; and Ellison's Invisible
    Man, 93; galvanizing effect of, 34;
    importance of advanced degrees, 20;
    increases in numbers of advanced de-
    grees, 34; lack of, in HBCUs, 6; limits
    placed on number of black students
    accepted in, 37; satisfaction of students
    with, 36; surge in number of advanced
    degrees, 34, 36–37, 194n65; and
    teaching commitment of graduates, 8;
    in theater department, 90, 93. See also
    funding for out-of-state education
Graham, Maryemma, 128
Grange, Edward "Red," 158
"great man" theory of history, 186
Greek organizations: Crisis coverage of,
    157; establishment of black fraternal
    organizations, 147, 157; and home
    games, 153; housing offered by, 147,
    148; and Iowa–Minnesota game (1935),
    158; meals offered by, 148; and oppor-
    tunities to socialize, 153–54; racial
    discrimination in, 151; role of, in social
    network, 68; segregation of, 166. See
    also specific fraternities and sororities,
    including Kappa Alpha Psi and Alpha
    Phi Alpha

Greeley, Horace, 32
Green, Adam, 63
Green, Paul, 81–82, 84
Green Pastures (Connelly), 84
Greensboro sit-ins, 9
gymnastics, 213n62

Hagler, Mike, 169, 208n12
Hall, James, 111–12, 113, 114, 120
Hallstoos, Brian, 7, 13, 17–44
Hamburg Inn #1, 148
Hamilton, Richard T., 21–22
Hancher, Virgil, 148–49
"The Handball Court" (Nipson), 115
"'The Handball Court' and Other Stories" (Nipson), 115
Hanley, Dick, 157
Hansberry, Lorraine, 77
The Happy Merger (Bach), 88
Harlem Negro Unit of the Federal Theater Project, 79, 89, 91
Harlem Renaissance, 52, 77, 125
Harlem Suitcase Theatre, 90
Harper, Earl Enyeart, 42
Harper, Harry D., 154
Harper, Lillie, 154
Harper, Michael, 14, 107–8, 117–24; and athletes of Iowa, 121, 124; "The Blonde Liberal," 122; "Blues and Laughter," 122; as cultural ambassador, 109; and Ellison, 122; friendships of, 120–21, 206n55; instructors of, 119–20; and Iowa Writers' Workshop, 119–24, 133, 202n1; and Jackson, 121, 206n55; and jazz aesthetic, 122, 205n46; lodging challenges of, 118–19; as marginalized, 121; and McPherson, 184; "Phoenix or All the Things You Are," 122; post-Workshop career of, 132; "The Primal Chair," 122
Harris, Earl Preston, 44
Harris, Herbert, 27, 44
Harris, Homer, 148, 154, 158, 159–60

Harris, Tricka, 70
Hawkeye yearbooks, 143, 155–56, 164
Hawkins, Connie, 124, 173
Hawkins, Yusef, 179
Heeschen, Carl, 196n2
Herring, Clyde, 158
Herring, James V., 52
Hester, Roy and Wilda, 146
Hicks, Leon, 11, 48
Higher Education Act (1965), 7
Highland Park College, 155
Hightower, Lowetta, 69
Hill, A. Ross, 155
Hill, Isaac G., 143
Hill, Lena, 1–15, 75–102
Hill, Michael, 14, 107–33, 175–86
Hillcrest residence hall, 150
Hinton, Al, 121
historians of University of Iowa, 142–43
historically black colleges and universities (HBCUs): and academic pipeline, 7, 8, 13, 19, 44, 51, 99; accreditation pursuits of, 6, 9, 20, 39, 190n9; and Clapp, 39; educational backgrounds of faculty in, 195n76; education of future faculty of, 9, 20, 42; lack of graduate programs in, 6; and Morrill Act of 1890, 6; state of drama instruction in, 99–101; and theater program of Iowa, 77, 93, 99–100; and Walker, 130
Holbrook, Frank K., 154, 155
homecoming festivities, 153–54
Horne, Lena, 10
housing for black students and faculty: for athletes, 145–48, 165; and civil rights organizations, 151–52; and Congress of Racial Equality (CORE), 152; difficulty of securing, 35; and Harper, 118–19; for in-state/out-of-state students, 137; in Iowa City, 109, 146, 150–51, 165; for married couples, 109, 150–51; and Nipson, 109; and referral/greeting service for new students, 146;

and segregation/desegregation of the
dormitories, 42, 60, 103–4, 150, 152;
segregation in room assignments, 150;
and Wheeler, 137
Houston, Charles, 22, 23, 26
"How Iowa Flattened Literature" (Bennett), 185
Howard, Joseph, 162
Howard, Sherman, 153
Howard, Sidney, 88
Howard University, 52–53, 99, 100, 104,
211n36
Howe, Irving, 5–6
Howell, Miriam, 97
Hubbard, Philip G.: on benign neglect
of black students, 176; boarding space
offered by, 146; on Brookins, 164;
and bureaucracy of university, 179;
on degrees of HBCU faculty, 195n76;
on discriminatory practices, 4–5; on
racial tolerance, 38; on supportive
department heads, 41–42; on UI graduates as faculty in HBCUs, 8
Hughes, Langston: *Don't You Want to Be
Free?* 90, 91, 92, 95; and Ellison, 101; and
Fanny Ellison, 90–91; and Mabie's pursuit of new material, 84–85; "Mother
and Child," 85; *Mulatto*, 77, 85, 101; success and status of, 77, 95; and Walker,
125, 127; *The Ways of White Folks*, 85
Hughey, Matthew, 176
Hurston, Zora Neale, 79, 111

Illinois Writers' Project (IWP), 126
Inada, Lawson, 120
"Indivisible Man" (McPherson), 178
Institute of Black Repertory Theatre, 100
integration. *See* desegregation/
integration
Inter-Fraternity Council, 151
interracial collaboration, 9, 123–24
interracial romances, 38–39, 98, 137,
152–53, 176–77

Invisible Man (Ellison): and advanced
degree recipients at UI, 93; and Armstrong's "Black and Blue," 167; on invisibility of blacks, 15, 143; and requests
for rights, 101, 202n72; stage adaptation
of, 1, 101–2, 185
Invisible Man monument, 63, 64–65
"Iowa and *Invisible Man*: Making Blackness Visible" residency, 1, 185
Iowa Black Alumni Association (IBAA),
72, 106
Iowa *Bystander*, 145, 147, 157
Iowa City, Iowa: and Anderson family,
35; Berry's experience in, 68; and civil
rights movement, 119; democratic
pluralism in, 180; dining challenges
in, 148–49; Harper's experience with,
118; housing challenges in, 109, 146,
150–51, 165; and integration, 12; in the
late fifties and early sixties, 118; and
McPherson, 15, 180–81; Penny's expe-
rience in, 46–47; racial discrimination
and segregation in, 35–36, 60, 78, 97,
119, 145, 149, 151; and Walker, 130
Iowa City Chamber of Commerce, 151
Iowa City Press Citizen, 141
Iowa Federation of Colored Women's
Clubs, 146, 148
Iowa Memorial Union, 54, 56, 60, 148,
150, 166
Iowa School of Journalism Hall of Fame,
117
Iowa State College (later Iowa State
University), 34, 54
Iowa Supreme Court, 7
Iowa Women's Archives, 106
Iowa Writers' Workshop, 107–33;
cultivation of writers in, 120; cultural
insensitivity in, 127–28; and Ellison,
1, 178, 189n2; faculty of, 119–20, 126,
127–28, 129–30, 131, 133; favoritism in,
112–13, 204nn23–24; first black student
to attend, 125; founding of, 124; and

informal criticism sessions, 113; lack of recognition for writers, 117, 132; leadership of, 108 (*see also* Engle, Paul); limitations on number of black students accepted in, 14; and McPherson, 133, 177–78; network of, 119, 129; and New Criticism, 108, 203n4; productive tension of, 127; role in writers' success, 125; seminar system of, 111; and *workshop* term, 123. *See also* Harper, Michael; Nipson, Herbert; Walker, Margaret
Isherwood, Christopher, 119
"I Want to Write" (Walker), 126

Jackson, Mahalia, 4
Jackson, Oliver, 121
Jackson State University, 108, 130–31
James, Henry, 132
Janson, Horst W., 56, 63
Jarrett, Gene, 115
jazz musicians and music, 137, 166–67, 205n46
Jedgement Day (Pawley), 94–95
Jenkins, Herbert, 148
Jeter, Bob, 172
Jim Crow era: and academic pipeline, 7; and Anderson's mental health, 29; and athletics at UI, 142, 144, 154, 155–58, 162–63; Berry's experience in, 68; and civil rights activism, 8; courts' dismantling of, 26; and funding for out-of-state education, 23; in Iowa City, 78, 145, 149; and light-skinned blacks, 142, 164. *See also* segregation
John-Lewis, Americus, 212n53
Johnson, Clifton H., 61
Johnson, Fenton, 127
Johnson, James Weldon, 86–87, 125, 151–52
Johnson, John H., 116
Johnson, Lulu Merle, 149
Johnson, Lyndon B., 9
Johnson County Historical Society, 118

Johnson C. Smith University, 99
Jones, Calvin: death of, 170; and Harper, 124; and Levine, 121, 205n51; and number of black athletes on field, 169, 208n12; in official histories of UI, 175; and Slater, 154; treatment of, 176, 206n51; and Tucker, 169
Jones, Charles "Deacon," 161, 165, 173
Jones, Loïs Mailou, 52, 59
Jones, Phil, 181–82
journalism, 110–11, 113–14, 203n12
"The Joy Forever" (Nipson), 115
Joyce, James, 132
Jubilee (Walker), 125, 132
Julius Rosenwald Fellowship, 57
Justice, Don, 119–20

Kappa Alpha Psi: alumni visits with members of, 153; baseball team members in, 143; *Crisis* coverage of, 157; and Harris, 159; and home games, 153, 158; housing offered by, 147, 148; *Journal* of, 145; meals offered by, 148
Keeton, Werdner Page, 25
Kentucky State University, 99
King, Alfred D., 213n61
King, Martin Luther, Jr., 4, 49, 166, 213n61
Kinsey, Joni, 55
Kirby, Charles E., 213n61
Kluger, Richard, 211n36
Koos, Lynn, 118
Krause, Herb, 126
"Ku Klux" (Pawley), 94
Ku Klux Klan, 151

Lamb, Arthur, 8, 97–98, 194n67
Langland, Joseph, 113, 120, 127, 130
Langston University: and Anderson, 28; and Ellison, 35; and Fisher, 24; graduates of, 44; law program of, 24; and Southall, 43; and state allocations, 39; UI alumni's ties with, 43

Lasansky, Mauricio, 11, 48
Lavergne, Gary, 23, 26
law program, first black student admitted
    to, 2, 133, 189n4
LeBlanc, Whitney, 98, 99
Lechay, James, 48
lectures, distinguished, 49
Lemme, Helen and Allyn, 118, 136–37,
    146, 166, 167
LeMoyne College, Tennessee, 7
Levealle, M., 194n67
Levine, Philip, 121, 205n51
Lewis, Edmonia, 63
Lewis, Samella, 198n54
Lewis, Sean, 185
Liddell, James, 213n62
light-skinned blacks, 142, 164
Lincoln University, 23, 43, 96, 99
lithography, 59
Little Rock Nine, 9
*Lloyd Gaines v. S. W. Canada and the
    University of Missouri*, 6
Locke, Alain, 52
lodging. *See* housing for black students
    and faculty
Longman, Lester, 55, 58, 63–64
"Look Down the Long Dark Barrel"
    (Nipson), 115
Louis, Joe, 10
Louisville, Kentucky, 213n61
Ludins, Eugene, 48
Lytle, Andrew, 112

Mabie, Edward C.: and advanced de-
    grees, 90, 93; artistic philosophy of, 11,
    77, 85, 101; and black themes, 82; and
    Clapp, 77; as department head, 76–77;
    and experimental theater, 14, 81–85;
    and Fanny Ellison, 89; and Federal
    Theater Project (FTP), 78–81, 89,
    199n10; interdisciplinary approach of,
    90; and Lamb's expulsion, 98; legacy
    of, 93; and Maibaum, 88, 200n18; and

material for black actors, 84–85, 91;
    and Pawley, 94–96; and playwrights,
    94; and progressive reputation of UI,
    2; racial attitudes of, 77–78, 79; region-
    alism emphasis of, 11, 14, 77, 81–83; and
    theater building, 76, 81
Macbeth (Shakespeare), 79
MacLean, George, 155, 156, 210n30
Maibaum, Richard, 82–84, 88, 90, 95,
    200n18
Maid-Rite, 148
Mallory, Eugene, 161, 211n48
marginalized students, 121, 144
Margold, Nathan, 23
married students at UI, 109, 150–51
Marshall, Thurgood, 23
Martin, Dora, 143
Maryland, 7, 191n22
maturity, 180
Mayberry (Lewis), 185
McCarthy, Joe, 105
McCray, Francis, 56
McCuskey, David, 172
McElroen, Christopher, 1, 102
McGurl, Mark, 107, 202n2
McKay, Claude, 125
McLaurin, George W., 24–27, 29, 40, 42
McLaurin v. Oklahoma State Regents, 25,
    26
McMahon, David R., 142, 143
McNeely, Lois Towles, 22, 27, 40, 44
McPherson, James Alan, 15, 133, 177–85
Mechler, Zula Mae, 153
Mells, Herbert Franklin, 22, 35, 40–41, 43
Meredith, James, 189n6
Merry, Glenn, 76
Messiah (Pawley), 96–97
Messick, Hank, 112, 204n23
Miller, Barbara, 72
Minneapolis Spokesman, 145, 157, 158
Minor Teachers College, 53
Miss State University of Iowa contest,
    68–72

Mississippi, 20

Missouri, 7

Missouri ex rel Gaines v. Canada, 189n5

Modern Negro Art (Porter), 52, 63

monuments in Washington, D.C., 53

Moore sisters, 69

Morgan, Stacy, 54

Morgan State College, 99

Morrill Act of 1890, 6

Mosley, Eugene, 173

"Mother and Child" (Hughes), 85

Mozee, Tallie, 44

Muck, Karl, 30

Mud on the Hoofs (Geddes), 88

Mudge, Mary, 112

Mulatto (Hughes), 77, 85, 101

Muscatine, Iowa, 45–46

Museum of Art, University of Iowa, 48

Nashville World, 75–76

National Association for the Advancement of Colored People (NAACP):
and athletics of Iowa, 157; and *Crisis*,
126, 145, 157; and desegregation, 19,
22–23, 25; and funding for out-of-
state education, 22, 26; and housing
challenges in Iowa City, 151–52; Legal
Defense and Educational Fund, 2, 4

National Theatre Conference, 78

National Urban League, 157

NCAA Men's Basketball Tournament
(1955), 162–63

Neal, Larry, 132

Negro Agricultural and Technical Col-
lege of North Carolina (later North
Carolina Agriculture and Technical
State University), 33

Negro Forum, 149, 152

Negro Mother and Child (Catlett), 55,
62–63, 64

Negro People's Theatre (NPT), 89–92

Negro Theatre (Harlem Negro Unit of
the Federal Theater Project), 79, 89, 91

neighboring, 179

Nelson, Don, 173

Nelson, Robert "Bob," 160–61

New Criticism, 108, 203n4

New Deal programs, 53, 54

New York City's Art Students League, 61

Nipson, Herbert, 14, 107–8, 109–17; background of, 109–10, 203n9; as cultural
ambassador, 109; "The Deer Hunt,"
115; determination of, 111; doctoral
studies of, 114, 116; and *Ebony*, 12, 108,
109, 113, 116, 117, 132; on favoritism,
112–13; "'The Handball Court' and
Other Stories," 115; and housing at UI,
109; and Iowa Writers' Workshop, 110,
111–13, 115–17, 133, 202n1; and journalism, 110–11, 113–14, 116, 204n29; "The
Joy Forever," 115; "Look Down the
Long Dark Barrel," 115; and O'Connor,
112–13; in official histories of UI, 175;
peers of, 120; post-Workshop career of,
132; "The Return," 115; and Sigma Delti
Chi, 204n27; writings of, 115–16

Noah (Obey), 88–89

North Carolina Agricultural and Technical College, 75, 77

North Texas Teachers College (later University of North Texas), 192nn36–37

Obama, Barack, 15, 184, 185

Obey, Andre, 88–89

"Observations from 20 Years of Iowa
Life" (Bloom), 184–85

O'Connor, Flannery, 112, 113, 203n12,
204nn23–24

"Of Science and Skulls" (Clapp), 30

Okerbloom, Charles, 56

Oklahoma: and desegregation of
advanced degree programs, 19; and
funding for out-of-state education, 21,
23, 26; pipeline between UI and, 7, 13,
20; segregation laws challenged in,
24

Olympic athletes, 138–39, 163–67, 213n61
Omega Psi Phi, 158
Opfell, Olga, 126
Opportunity, 145, 157
Orange Bowl Stadium, 162
Orozco, José, 56–57
out-of-state education. *See* funding for out-of-state education
Owens, Jesse, 165

Panhellenic Council, 151
Parks, Suzan-Lori, 101
Patterson, Zella J. Black, 21
Pawley, Thomas: and academic pipeline, 8; *The Black Teacher and the Dramatic Arts: A Dialogue, Bibliography, and Anthology* (Pawley and Reardon), 99; doctoral studies of, 96–97; on experience at Iowa, 98; faculty position of, 194n67; and funding for out-of-state education, 96; and Lamb's expulsion, 98; master's studies of, 93–96; and Purple Mask Society, 98–99; state of drama instruction in HBCUs, 99–101; on theater building, 11; thesis of, 94–95
Payne, Thomas, 212n53
Pearl, Robert L., 141–42
Pearson et al. v. Murray, 6, 23, 191n22
Peniston, Eugene and Nellie, 150–51
Penn State, 111, 117
Penny, Dianna, 13, 45–50, 175, 179
performing arts departments, 7–8. *See also* department of music; department of speech and dramatic arts
Perry, Dayton, 124
Perry, Rufus P., 34, 194n67
Petersen, Christian, 54–55
Petersen, Jewel, 196n2
Phi Beta Kappa, 155
"Phoenix or All the Things You Are" (Harper), 122
Pi Kappa Alpha, 166
pipeline, academic: and historically black colleges and universities (HBCUs), 7, 8, 13, 19, 44, 51, 99; and Jim Crow south, 7; to music department, 7, 13, 19, 20, 35, 43–44; and network of black alumni, 20, 51; to theater department, 99; from UI to HBCUs, 8, 43–44
Plessy v. Ferguson, 25
pluralistic democracy, 15, 108, 132, 177, 180, 181–82
Poitier, Sidney, 4
police officers, 173
Popular Photography, 114
Porter, James A., 52, 53, 61, 63
Potter's Field (Green), 84
Prairie View College (later Prairie View A&M State University): educational backgrounds of faculty, 34, 194nn66–67; and Fuller, 33; graduates of, 44; and graduates of UI theater program, 99; and Pawley, 96; relationship with UI music department, 43; and state allocations, 39; UI alumni's ties with, 43
Prather, Mai Olive, 42–43
Prestage, Jewel, 10, 124, 184
Price, Florence, 32
"The Primal Chair" (Harper), 122
Princess Café, 148
professors and instructors of University of Iowa: first tenured black American professor, 4–5; students' relationships with, 10–11, 12. *See also* Clapp, Philip Greeley; Engle, Paul; Mabie, Edward C.; and other specific instructors
The Program Era: Postwar Fiction and the Rise of Creative Writing (McGurl), 107
Prophet, Nancy Elizabeth, 63
Public Works of Art Projects (PWAP), 53, 54
Purple Mask Society, 98–99
"Pursuit of the Pneuma" (McPherson), 181, 184

Quadrangle residence hall, 150

racism and racial discrimination: Berry's
    experience with, 68, 72; black athletes'
    experience with, 143–44; dismantling
    of institutional, 145; and Fanny Elli-
    son, 1, 189n2; Fuller's ability to defuse,
    38; in Greek organizations, 151; in Iowa
    City, 151; prior to 1947, 145; as related to
    number of black students, 194n75; in
    restaurants and lunchrooms, 148–49;
    in Washington, D.C., 211n36; Wheeler
    on, 137
radio programs, 33
A Raisin in the Sun (Hansberry), 77
Randak, Leigh Ann, 118
Randall, A. M., 194n67
Reardon, William, 99–101
recreational opportunities, 47
Reich's Café, 148
residences. See housing for black students
    and faculty
restaurants and lunchrooms, 148–49
Rethinking Social Realism: African
    American Art and Literature, 1930–1953
    (Morgan), 54
"The Return" (Nipson), 115
Rhoden, William C., 144
Rice, Elmer, 79
Rich, Donald Cayton, 62
rifle club, 155
Riley, Mike, 162
Rita Benton Library of the School of
    Music, 48
Roberts, Simon, 161, 163, 173
Robeson, Paul, 10, 40
Robinson, Eddie, 175
Robinson, Jackie, 10
Rockefeller Foundation, 81
Roddy, George, 213n62
Roethke, Theodore, 111
Romidy, W. N., 156
Roosevelt, Franklin D., 78, 199n10
Rose Bowl, 70, 171–72
Roth, Philip, 119

Roughshod Up the Mountain (Lamb),
    97–98
Rubenstein, Arthur, 40
Russell, Bill, 163
Rust College, Mississippi, 7
Rutsala, Vern, 120

Sadler, Sammye Mae, 153
Saunders, Amera, 137
Savage, Augusta, 63
Savoy Café, 148
Scanlon family, 141–42
Scarlet Mask Society, 98–99
School of Fine Arts, 76
School of Journalism, 110, 114, 116, 117
Schramm, Wilbur, 108, 124
Searcey, Etta J., 152–53
Seashore, Carl, 2
segregation: and Anderson's mental
    health, 28–29; and Brown v. Board of
    Education, 25, 42, 211n36; and deter-
    minative nature of race, 133; education
    bills as means to maintain, 22, 23;
    Ellison's jug metaphor for, 6; in grad-
    uate and professional programs, 19; of
    Greek organizations, 166; Hallstoos's
    chronicling of, 13; humiliation engen-
    dered by, 25, 40; in Iowa City, 35–36,
    60, 97, 119; and music department, 40;
    and "separate but equal" education,
    22–23, 25–26; on UI campus, 35–36, 42,
    60. See also Jim Crow era
"separate but equal" education, 22–23,
    25–26
Shakespeare, William, 79
Shattuck, Theobald K., 127
Shaw University, 99
Shine, Ted, 99, 202n67
Short, Hayward, 146
Sigma Chi, 166
Sigma Delta Chi, 204n27
Sigma Nu, 166
Simmons, Don, 147, 148, 154, 158, 159

Simmons, Ozzie, 147, 148, 154, 157–58,
    159, 160
Sioux City, Iowa, 7
*Sipuel v. Board of Regents of the University
    of Oklahoma*, 24, 25, 189n5
Sirota, David, 176
skin colors of black students in Jim Crow
    era, 142, 164
Skinner, Eugene, 148, 160, 211n46
Slater, Frederick "Duke," 152–53, 157,
    208n12
slavery, 7, 126, 131
Slonneger, Marybeth, 185
Smith, A. Maceo, 26
Smith, Lamar, 160
Smith, Raymond A., Jr., 155
Smith, Roland, 149
Smith, William Oscar, 38–39, 44
Smith's Café, 148–49
Smokey (Pawley), 94, 95
soccer team, 155, 210n28
Solem, Ossie, 147, 159–60
"Sorrow Home" (Walker), 128
"A Soul Goes Marching" (Maibaum),
    82–83
South Side Writers Group in Chicago,
    126, 127
Southall, Geneva, 10
Southall, Mitchell, 26–27, 43, 44, 192n32,
    195n92
Spectator, 141
Spencer (dorm director), 137
Spencer, Gerri, 70
sports. *See* athletic programs and black
    athletes
Stark, Herald, 29, 42, 48
State Association of Colored Teachers, 21
State University of Iowa, 2, 12, 36, 51. *See
    also* University of Iowa (UI)
St. Christopher (Charlot), 56
Stegner, Wallace, 130, 207n83
Stepping Out (Catlett), 197n32
stereotypes, 144

Still, William Grant, 32
Stinson, Harry E., 54, 63, 64, 196n2
St. Louis Woman (Cullen and Bontemps),
    79
stoicism, black, 126
Student Council for University of Iowa,
    152
Sulek, J. W., 29
Sunwall, James, 204n12
Swanson, Chuck, 1
Sweatt, Heman Marion, 25, 26, 42
Sweatt v. Painter, 25, 26, 189n5
swim team, 155

Talcott, John Albert, 32
Tate, Bettye and Junious, 136, 137, 146,
    166, 167
Tau Ipsilon Tsest, 147
Taylor, Edwin, 151
"The Teaching of Music in the Leading
    Negro Colleges" (Fuller), 33–34
Tennessee, 7
Texas: advanced degree programs in, 19;
    and funding for out-of-state education,
    21–22, 23, 26, 27, 34, 191n18; pipeline
    between UI and, 7, 13, 20
Texas State Inter-Racial Commission,
    21
Texas State University, 27
Thatcher, Harry, 33
theater department. *See* department of
    speech and dramatic arts
Titus, John Kenneth, 143
Tomasini, Wallace, 49
Totheroh, Dan, 88
Townsend, Orville, 213n62
track and field, 154, 160–61, 164–65
The Tree (Maibaum), 82, 88, 95
Trent, Vivian, 148
Tucker, Don, 15, 153, 169–74, 208n12
Tunnell, Emlen, 124, 150, 154
Turco, Lewis, 120
Turner, Nat, 96–97

Turner, Robert, 150
Turner, Thomas, 42

Unger, Leonard, 127
United States Office of Education, Disadvantaged Youth Branch, 100
University Chorus, 48
University of Iowa (UI): advanced degrees of (*see* graduate and professional education); attitude toward mid-twentieth-century black students, 175; creative writing program of (*see* Iowa Writers' Workshop); first black law student at, 2, 133, 189n4; first black student admitted to, 2; first black student to graduate from, 7; housing options at (*see* housing for black students and faculty); modernization of, 5; and out-of-state students (*see* pipeline, academic); progressive reputation of, 2, 4, 20, 155, 156–57, 161, 176; social opportunities at (*see* Greek organizations); sports at (*see* athletic programs and black athletes). *See also* specific departments
University of Iowa Alumni Association Board of Directors, 106
University of Iowa Gymnastics Media Guide (2013—2014), 117
University of Maryland Law School, 23
University of Minnesota, 158–59
University of Mississippi, 189n6
University of Missouri, 2, 155, 210n31
University of Missouri Law School, 23
University of Oklahoma, 2, 20–21, 23, 24–25
University of Oklahoma Law School, 24, 25
University of Texas, 22, 23
University of Texas Law School, 25
University of Washington, 159
U.S. Supreme Court, 19, 23–27, 42

"A Very Stern Discipline" (Ellison), 9–10
Vincent, Eddie, 169, 208n12
Vinson, Fred M., 26
Virginia, 7
Vivian's Chicken Shake, 148
Voxman, Himie, 41–42

Wabash Young Men's Christian Association (YMCA) camp, 89
Walk Together Children (Wilson), 79
Walker, Elvin, 213n62
Walker, Jim "Iron Man," 148, 150, 153
Walker, Margaret, 14, 107–8, 124–32; "Address to America," 128; background of, 125–26; and Catlett, 60, 197n32; and civil rights movement, 131; confidence of, 126–27; as cultural ambassador, 109; "Delta," 128; doctoral studies of, 124, 130; and Engle, 126, 127–28, 129, 132; exposure to veteran authors, 126–27; fellowships of, 131; *For My People*, 125; "For My People" (poem), 128, 197n32; "For My People" (thesis), 128, 132; and Iowa Writers' Workshop, 126–32, 133, 202n1; "I Want to Write," 126; Jackson State position of, 130–31; *Jubilee*, 125, 132; in official histories of UI, 175; personal difficulties of, 129; post-Workshop career of, 132; recognition of, 129; "Sorrow Home," 128; stylistic evolution of, 125; success and status of, 8; thesis of, 128–29; undergraduate education of, 125, 129
Wallace, Wilbur "Windy," 156, 157, 210n35
Waller, Thomas "Fats," 167
Ward, Theodore, 95, 101
Washington, Bobby, 173, 212n53
Washington, D.C., 53, 156, 211n36
Washington, James, 12
Washington, Richard, 150
Washington University, 155–56
Waterloo, Iowa, 7

The Ways of White Folks (Hughes), 85
Wells, James Lesesne, 52
West Virginia, 7
Whalum, Wendell, 48
Wheeler, Theodore "Ted," 14–15, 135–39;
    on dating, 176–77; misidentified as
    first distance runner, 161; in official
    histories of UI, 175; as Olympic athlete,
    165
Whetstone's Pharmacy, 149
White, Louis B., 155, 210n28
white rescuers/redeemers, 176, 177
Wideman, John Edgar, 123, 206n66,
    214n4
Wilbers, Stephen, 124, 129
Wilkins, Roy, 159
Williams, Annie Laurie, 97
Williams, Joe, 124
Williams, Tom "Tennessee," 94
Williams, Wirt, 119
Williams-Furgerson, Lily, 154
Williamson, Mac Q., 24
Wilson, August, 101
Wilson, Frank, 79
Woman with Cradle (Charlot), 56
women enrolled at University of Iowa,
    152–53. *See also* specific women,

including Catlett, Elizabeth; Ellison,
    Fanny; and Walker, Margaret
Women's Intercollegiate Athletics, 141
Wood, Audrey, 97–98
Wood, Grant: and Catlett, 11, 51, 55, 58, 59,
    63–64; and Longman, 55, 58, 64; and
    progressive reputation of UI, 2; and
    Public Works of Art Projects (PWAP),
    54
Woodruff, Hale, 54, 63
Wordlaw, Clarence, 212n53
Works Progress Administration (WPA),
    78
"The World and the Jug" (Ellison), 5–6,
    183
World War II, 37, 42
wrestling, 154–55, 161, 163, 172–73
Wright, Richard, 111, 125, 127
Wright, Robert, 150
W.S.U.I. radio station, 33
Wylder, Jean, 112

Yale Younger Poets prize, 128
Yellow Jack (Howard), 88
Young, Marguerite, 126

Zorach, William, 63